APPLIED MODELING

ENCYCLOPAEDIA

MILITARY VEHICLES VOLUME

Squadron Signal
Euro Modelismo

MILITARY VEHICLES VOLUME

PART 1 MILITARY VEHICLES

PART 2 AIRBRUSH KITS AND MILITARY VEHICLES

PART 3 DETAILING WITH PHOTO-ETCHED PARTS

PART 4 MODERN VEHICLES

PART 5 RESIN KITS

Original Title *Modelismo Aplicado, Vehículos Militares*

This is the first volume of the *Applied Modeling Encyclopaedia*, a collection of books assembled by Rodrigo Hernández Cabos.
Collaborators: Carlos de Diego Vaquerizo, Miguel Jimenez Martín, José A. Velázquez Encinas, Agustín Lagartos, Cristobal Vergara Durán, J. David Hernández Chacón.
Drawings and colour views by Julio C. Cabos Gómez, Carlos de Diego Vaquerizo, Angel Luis Gónzlaez.
Photographs by: Salvador Gómez Mico and Rodrigo Hernández Cabos.
The publisher wishes to thank the manufacturers: *Casa Galan*, *Revell*, *Pemar Model*, *Bizak*, *Soldat* and *Miniaturas Andrea*.

The English version has been translated and published by ACCION PRESS, S.A.
Translator: Andrés Pérez Fernández.
Edited by Ian Parsons

ISBN 0-89747-496-1

squadron/signal publications

1115 CROWLEY DRIVE
CARROLLTON
TEXAS 75011-5010
US

Layout and Composition: *Accion Press S.A.*, and *Kommad Publicidad S.L.*, English version made by *Accion Press S.A.*

Printed on September 2005 by *IBERGRAPHI 2002, S.L.L.*, in Spain.(UE).

Foreword

The dream of a self-propelled, highly armored fighting vehicle has been the pursuit of mankind throughout recorded history. Leonardo da Vinci, a visionary, designed a machine back in the 16th century that closely resembled our modern conception of such a device. However, it wasn't until the 20th century that the dream became a reality. The British were the first to put them into action under the name of 'tanks'. This was to confuse any spies and to make them believe that these large unwieldy 'containers' were to be used for storing liquids. From 1917 until the present day, this infernal machine has accomplished its unholy function of killing, spearheading the domination of armies across the globe. These terrible attributes have always held a certain attraction over many people, model makers included. The capacity to move over any terrain imbues them with an aesthetic quality. If we then add all the technology inherent in these vehicles, we get a clearer picture of their hypnotic attraction.

Armored Military Vehicles

If there is one thing to remember about any model kit, it is the capacity to 'customize' them to achieve any number of different specifications. This is because no two vehicles are exactly the same after they have been on the front line for any length of time. It is also because of the variety of elements that any crew will gather in order to make their life on the front as easy as possible. Many degrees of wear and battering will often bear witness to the tough and often short life that the vehicles will undergo. In addition, there are also other factors, including any additional protection fitted by the crew, different combinations of camouflage schemes and weathering. It is all these factors that fire the

Panzer III model H, with original Gunze Sangyo chassis, (also available from Revell) scratch built from a resin KMR kit with Africa Korps camouflage scheme.

A 1/35 Azimut kit in resin of a German Bussing-4500A truck, Russian Front.

Sdkfz-263, popular open cockpit, eight wheel version with a 75mm gun, 1/35 Tamiya kit and conversion set from KMR.

Popular mid-run 'Tiger' built by Agustin Lagartos, just like the kits on the previous page.

enthusiasm and imagination of the model maker. And, if this isn't enough, armored vehicles are eminently suitable for including in dioramas, where they can become part of the most dramatic and/or amusing scenes. It is also fair to say that these vehicles are often quite ugly, as many model makers will attest once they get to see their particular vehicle up close in a museum.

What can be done to make a vehicle more attractive? After all, just about any kit can be neatly assembled and painted as if for a parade or as an exhibit. However, we can also give it a very weathered appearance, which allows the vehicle itself to announce its location.

The model maker can choose to portray any period in a vehicle's life, ranging from a

M1-A1 Abrams 'Desert Storm', 1/35 Academy Minicraft kit.

1/35 Chieftain MK.5, with European camouflage, 1/35 both vehicles built by Cristobal Vergara Duran.

new machine to a complete wreck. Only expertise and the skilful use of the proper techniques, together with the knowledge of your own limitations, will dictate what can, or cannot be achieved.

We will attempt to show a number of machines exhibiting different degrees of wear, in order reveal the scope that can be achieved. While doing so, we will also show that our personal tastes tend toward the expressive, so expect a number of diverse figures and scenes. In addition, we tend to steer clear of 'showcase' vehicles, and usually try to express our own personal views of historic events.

The development of the different painting techniques is always reaching towards perfection, and we are witnessing some marked

A Renault R-40 captured by the German army, a combination resin and plastic 1/35 kit from Ironside.

Sdkf-234/2 Puma. Eight-wheel version 1/35 Italeri kit with photoetch parts. Vehicles built by Carlos de Diego Vaquerizo.

Shilka Version used in Afghanistan, 1/35 Italeri Dragon kit built by J. David Hérnandez Chacón..

Sdkfz 10/4 Pak 38 with a 50mm gun, 1/35 Gunze Sangyo kit built by Carlos de Diego Vaquerizo.

tendencies in the handling of such techniques. This is evident even in the underlying 'philosophy' concerning the use of different tools. Some top model makers are particularly sensitive about the heterogeneous application of paint, while others prefer softer tools, such as pastels, lightly applied.

In the following pages, we will review most of the options, so a choice can be made, from the plainest assembly possible, to the highest degree of detail, both of the paintwork and the actual details. We will cover scratch building and fine finishes, using a mixture of techniques, easily explained and making use of the most up to date means available to the model maker.

A totally destroyed Pz IV, Italeri kit and a Verlinden conversion kit, built by Miguel Jiménez Martín.

M-48 'Mine clearer' Israeli army. Mixed kit: Academy Minicraft built by José A. Velázquez Encinas.

Assembly Techniques: Introductory Ideas

Basically, all military vehicles have a similar assembly process. The beginner, on opening the box discovers a comprehensive instruction sheet, along with all the parts on a sprue. The first thing to do is to carefully remove each part from the sprue without damage. Under no circumstances should the parts be twisted off by hand. That is a sure way of damaging them. There are several ways to do it correctly. One way is to cut them off with a curved X Acto knife. A better method is to remove them with a pair of small scissors (well sharpened). However, the best way, is to use a set of sharp side cutters specifically designed for the job and available at most model shops.

Once the part has been removed from the sprue, there is usually still some unwanted plastic remaining. This can be carefully removed with an X Acto knife. Even if the master mold is very good and the plastic has been properly injected, often there is some 'flash' around the part. This can also be removed with a triangular X Acto knife, and then sanded down for a perfect finish.

GLUE

There is an enormous array of different glues on the market today. Because of this, many beginners use the incorrect type of glue for their kit. This quite often results in a temporary fix, so to speak, as after a little while the model begins to come apart. It is, therefore, most important to use the correct type of glue for each kit. An easy solution is to use the glue recommended by the kit manufacturer. Today, we are witnessing the growing popularity of cyanocrylate glue or 'super glue', as it will glue practically anything, including almost all types of plastic. Superglue also has the added attraction of requiring miniscule amounts to glue parts together adequately, and it usually comes in very convenient tubes with a nozzle to help you apply it correctly.

Only specific glues for plastic have to be employed.

HOW AND WHEN TO USE THE DIFFERENT TYPES OF GLUE?

Experience usually dictates what glue must be employed. However, as a rule of thumb, the following advice is given: Glues specifically formulated for polystyrene plastics usually contain a thinner that will slightly melt the plastic, along with some cement that will fill the gaps between the parts and make a solid joint. There are also some that just have the thinner component. Most of the polystyrene glues will have a very liquid texture. The more viscous polystyrene cements usually come in tubes, and are to be employed in a few specific cases only. On the other hand, superglue is very good for small parts, because very little of it is required, and it does not 'attack' the plastic. Many of the parts to be glued can be held in your hands

Cutting the parts with small scissors.

Precision side cutters, more expensive, but with better results.

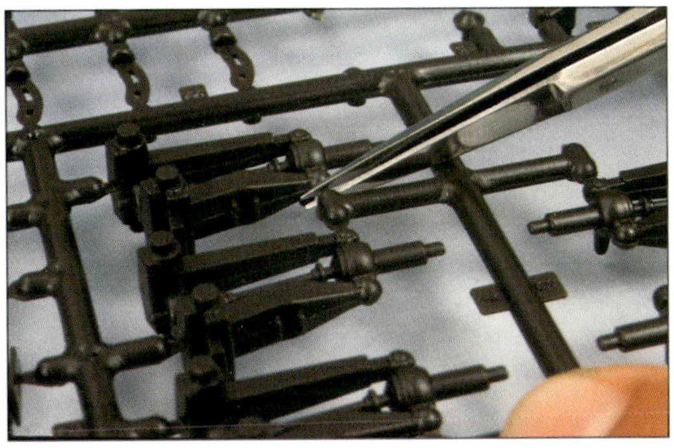

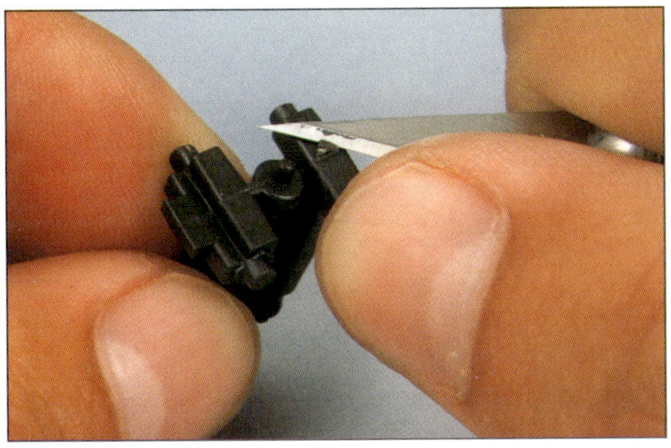

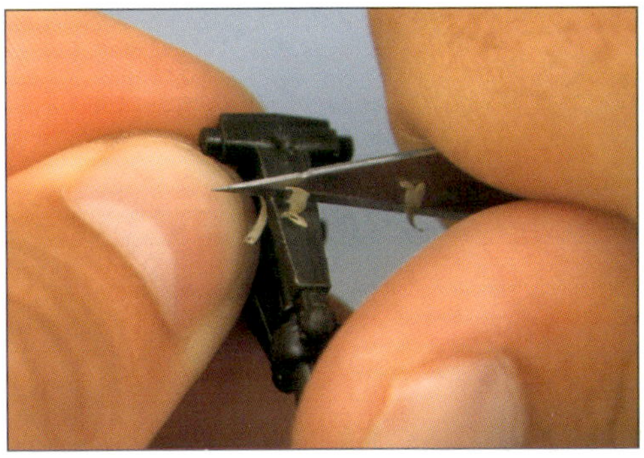

Removing residual plastic

Scraping residual plastic on the joints.

Glues commonly used with plastic kits.

The long tube helps with the glue dosage.

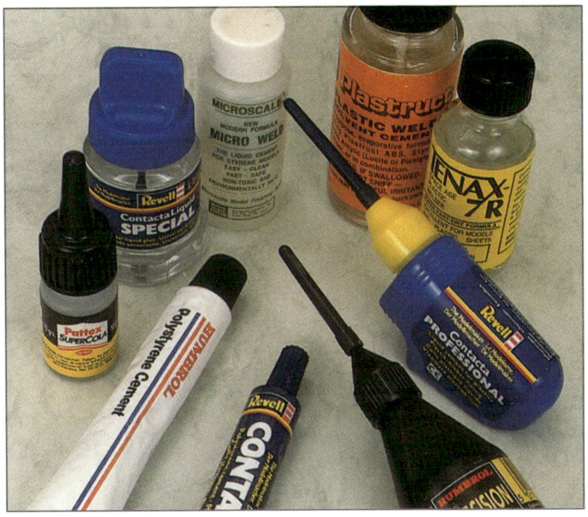

Liquid glue applied with a brush. It fills the gaps nicely, but takes longer to dry. It makes a strong bond, because it melts the parts together.

Sanding the parts.

Tweezers are convenient for handling and gluing small parts.

Parts not easily accessible should be positioned with tweezers.

during assembly. However, the smaller parts are best handled and glued using tweezers (this also applies to the 'hard to get at' parts).

SPECIFIC PROBLEMS

Sometimes, once the part has been assembled, you will detect small indentations or raised areas on a particular surface that should be perfectly flat. These are small irregularities in the molding process and can be remedied by filling and then sanding, or just by sanding.

Epoxy filler putty should be applied with a small spatula, similar to those used by dentists.

Another very common problem is a tank's gun barrel. It usually comes in two halves that are easily seen even when assembled properly. Very careful filling and sanding will improve its appearance, but leading model makers usually prefer to spend a little more money and obtain a 'turned' metal barrel replacement, that obviously looks much better.

PAINTING: INITIAL CONCEPTS

Even today, when the airbrush has acquired an incredible relevance in model making, there are still many vehicles that can be brush painted. Both the Allied and Axis forces often had hand painted camouflage schemes, having sharply defined, unfeathered edges. These schemes can be done very well with the brush. Looking through contemporary photographs, we came across a vehicle that fitted the bill, in this instance a PUMA. Many versions were built all utilizing the same chassis, and many of them were camouflaged with hand brushed schemes, complete with well defined, hand painted spots.

Oil based colors must be applied on top of the acrylics, never the reverse.

Once the two part kit has been assembled, it is best to wash it in warm soapy water and let it dry thoroughly. The base color is Tamiya's XF 60 or Vallejo's 881 applied with a medium (No. 4 or No. 6) brush. Stir the paint well, and then brush it out over the model to avoid any drips. Give the vehicle a good covering, applying the paint with regular strokes in the same direction. It is better to have a thin, homogeneous coat than a thick, irregular one. As a rule, two coats of paint will suffice. However, if you see some areas requiring more paint, don't hesitate to give them another coat.

As acrylic paint dries quickly, we can proceed with the second color, which is an olive green applied in irregular spots. If you chose to paint a slightly different scheme than the one on the box, it is always best to test it first on paper before painting the model. 975 Vallejo, or XF 58 Tamiya was the color chosen for the camouflage spots. First, outline the edges of the spots with a brush, and then fill them in with a No. 1 brush.

Once this has been done, we should have a well painted vehicle. The only thing wrong is that it will look like a toy. Now is the time to carry out a few procedures in order to improve its looks.

Spreading filler with a spatula.

Sand after drying for 24 hours.

Remove flash.

Fill the gaps with filler thinned with acetone.

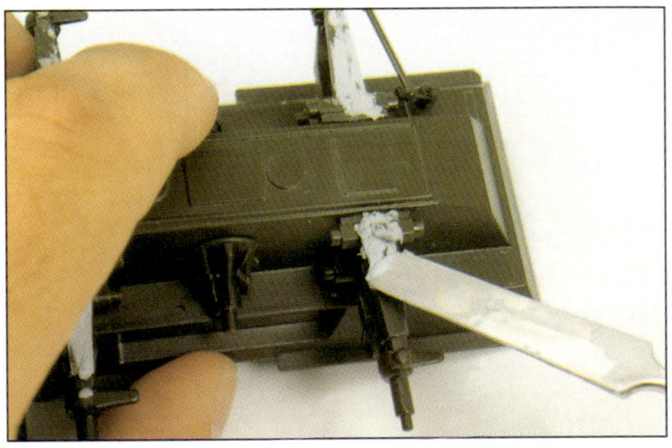

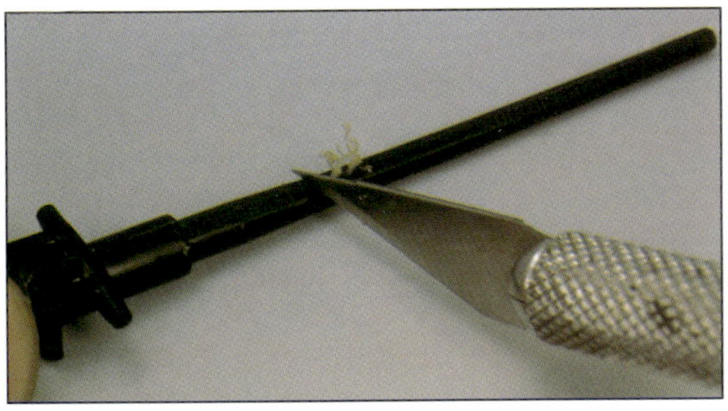

The interior of the vehicle is painted with Gunze Sangyo's H27.

Later, add some tea brown color to give it character, and then dry brush with a sand color.

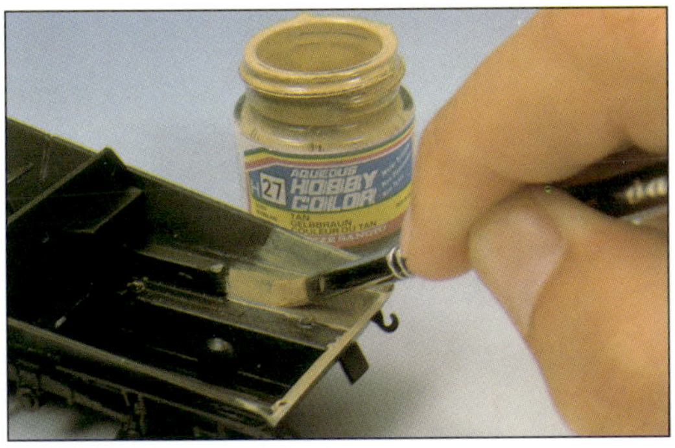

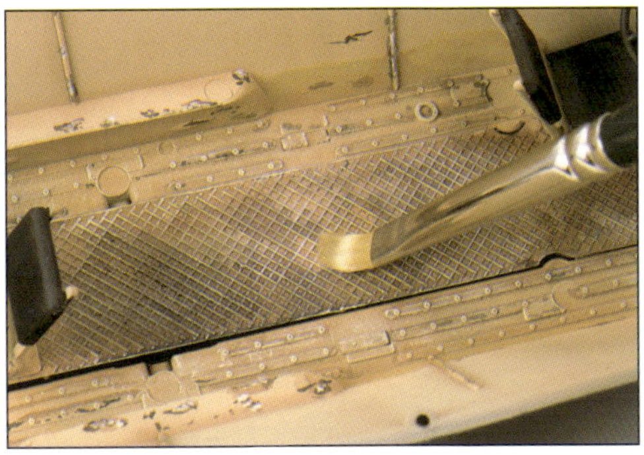

The camouflage spots are first outlined with a thin brush.

Then fill them in.

Two color scheme 881 and 975.).

The dirt on the lower areas is done with yellow ochre.

DIRT ON THE LOWER AREAS

Tanks are designed to operate in open country, and will inevitably get some wear, dirt, scratches, etc... And, it is the lower areas of a vehicle that will get the majority of the wear and dirt.

Conveying wear and dirt to the lower parts of the vehicle seems easy, but it is not. Some modelers may, at first, indiscriminately apply stroke upon stroke of paint in a hap hazard fashion. While dirt is certainly aesthetic, it does have to be carefully applied to make it appear realistic. Get ting dirt to look right can be a tiring combination of paint washes, blends, dry brushing, etc... These methods will be dealt with later.

We will begin with a burnt sienna oil wash, getting the paint into all cracks and joins. Next, use the brush to add light touches of yellow ochre sienna, sand and a little white. These will 'melt' onto the already wet surface and blend thoroughly with the other colors.

The exhausts can be painted with Vallejo 985 to convey rust then given a wash of 956 followed by a little dry brush ing with the same color.

PAINTING THE WHEELS

A beginner will usually paint tires with black or dark gray paint, and then dry brush with gray afterwards. However, to get the feel of real rubber, first apply a mixture of 950 and 874. Then give the tire a trans parent wash of burnt sienna. And, once dry, dry brush with some 882 and 977.

SPECIAL RETOUCHING

So far we've just painted the vehicle and weathered its lower areas. However, the vehicle doesn't yet look con vincingly realistic. This is all due to the undefined charac ter of its lines, the lack of contrast, and the monotony of the paint job. This can be easily remedied with the use of some simple techniques: First, apply a general wash of highly diluted burnt sienna. While applying the wash, it is important not to leave circular 'wash stains'. To avoid this, the wash must be applied quickly over the whole model so that it does not dry in parts before the job is fin ished. Also, try to get as much pigment into all the cracks and joints as possible. Once this has been complet ed, the appearance of the vehicle will have most certain ly improved. However, it still needs some highlights. These are applied using the dry brush technique, using a lighter shade of green, such as 975, on the green areas, and 881 over the sand areas. A really excellent finish can be achieved if Humbrol enamels are used: 80 with a little white, and 71 with more white on the lighter areas.

Never dry brush white over a dark color.

By now the kit would have lost its look of a toy, but there is still a small procedure we can carry out to make it look even better. We can make those little scratches and paint peels that are normally sported by any vehicle in heavy use. Use two colors for this: 972 and 956, and pro ceed as follows. Using a fine brush, use the lighter color for the larger area of the paint peel, and then outline and blend it with the darker color. Once all these small imper fections have been done, it is advisable to give the model a coat of matt varnish to elimi nate any residual shine.

The model is almost ready but there is still the final job. This is to apply the appropri ate insignia and numbering by using decals. This job will be dealt with in the next chapter.

We apply new colors such as burnt Sienna and white.

In order to unify and highlighten yellow green mixed to white is dry-brushed.

Silencers and exhaust pipes are painted a mix of black and dark earth.

The tires are painted using a mixture of black and dark earth.

Dry-brushing and retouching with desert yellow 977 and middlestone 882.

The grooves are given a wash of bunt umber oil paint.

Dry-brushing a mixture of military green and white.

Subtly painting peels and chips with dark brown and orange.

The whole set is given a coat of mat varnish.

Waiting for almost 12 hours until the varnish is dry and then posing the decals.

What & How

The Micro Set/Micro Sol decal application system

This is a particularly important area of model making, and is also where many model makers, as often as not, fear to tread. Decals, as a rule, usually come printed on a sheet and carry the numbers, insignia, etc... Decals, once immersed in water for a little while, become adhesive. At this point, the beginner will lift the decal off the backing sheet and place it on the model's surface. The result, as a rule, is pretty poor: The decal wasn't as transparent as it first appeared, it has an unnatural sheen and, worst of all, it doesn't look as though it has been painted onto the surface of the model. It all seems such a pity to spoil a good job right at the end! However, help is at hand, and the problem can be solved using the proper products and procedures.

It really is important to cut a motif sharply around its edges so that only that part of the decal remains that is required for the model. The best way to achieve this is with a steel rule and a new scalpel blade. Then the decal is immersed in water long enough to be able to slide off the decal and place it on the model. Before doing so, first apply some Micro Set liquid to the area. Once the decal is in position, flatten it out as much as possible with the brush to remove any trapped air.

Cutting decals with the help of a steel rule.

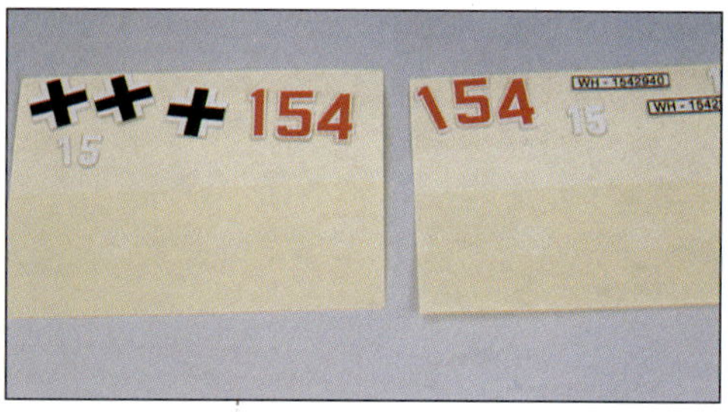

All decals are cut exactly to measure.

They are immersed one-by-one in clean water.

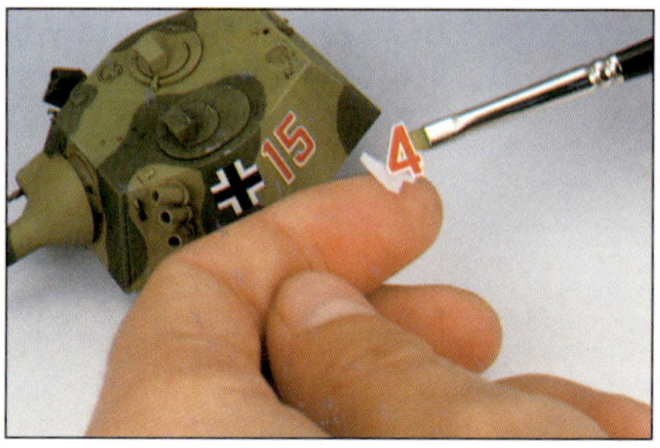

They are placed in the correct position. The area must first be moistened with Micro Set liquid.

The brush helps to position it correctly.

Micro Sol is applied over the decal.

Repeat the process using Micro Set for the cross.

Once in position, apply Micro Sol.

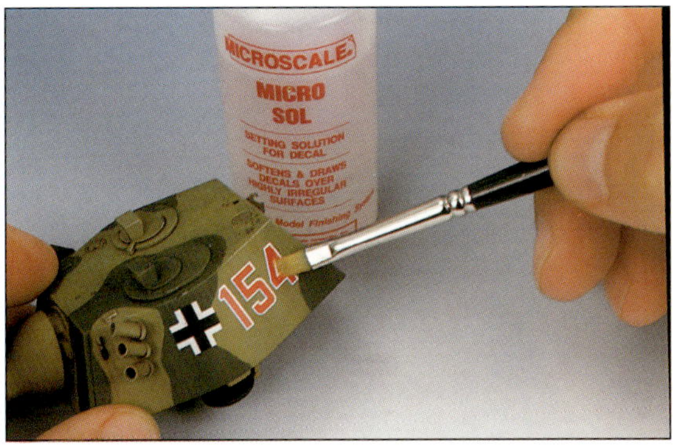

Now it is time to apply the Micro Sol liquid that will stretch the decal to the maximum allowing it to adapt perfectly to the model's surface. Even if the surface of the model is pretty uneven, Micro Sol will make it look perfect. That said, if the surface is too uneven, then even Micro Sol would be hard pressed to 'pull' the decal down perfectly. Now is the time to lay the model aside for a couple of hours to allow it to dry thoroughly. Once dry, apply matt varnish and, after allowing four hours drying

After a couple of hours, give the decal's surface a coat of matt varnish.

In order to give the decals a worn appearance, apply a coat of brown wash.

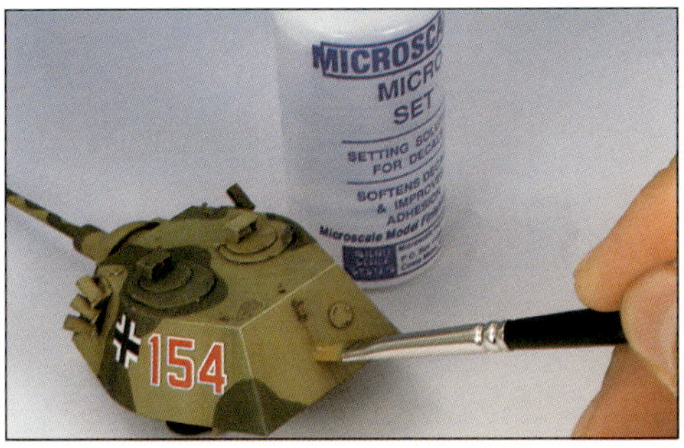

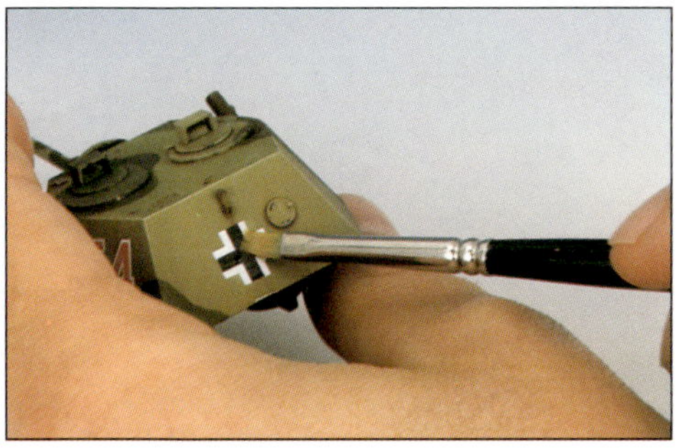

Some modelers prefer to apply a coat of gloss varnish to the surface where the decal will be positioned to give it better adaptation.

time, give the whole of the decaled area a wash of medium brown to assimilate them into the worn look of the remainder of the model. We can now say that the model is finished. If we have carefully followed each process and possessed a steady hand, the end product should look pretty good.

What & How

Paint washes, filters and transparent effects

These effects would appear, at first glance, to be identical, but they most definitely are not. A wash is the application of a highly diluted color onto an area, mainly into cracks and joints. It is done to accentuate the shadows and give them contrast. It could be said that it is an opposite technique to dry brushing, because the former darkens and the latter lightens, so that they become complementary techniques. As a rule, washes should not actually change the color of a model, unless the wash is a general, overall one that then becomes what is called a filter or transparency. It then has the same effect as a filter used in photography that alters the colors in a picture. Normally, filters darken the model because slightly darker colors are used as a filter. However, it is really up to the modeler as to what color to use for a given filter.

A wash process is made as follows: Place a very small amount of paint into a container and then add 85 90% thinner or water (depending on what type of paint you are using). This will give you a highly diluted color. Next, dip your brush into the mixture and apply it to the crevices of your model. Being very liquid, the paint should run freely into the crevices. If it doesn't, you can always wet the surface with either water or thinner in order to make the paint wash run freely. If the wash goes onto a wrong area, simply absorb it with a clean, dry brush.

Overall washes (filters or transparencies) are

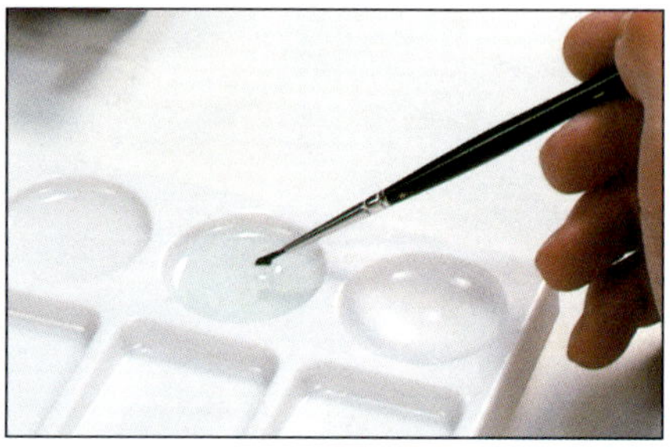

Washes and filters can be done with acrylics, but better results are obtained with enamels or oils.

Fill a container with enamel thinner.

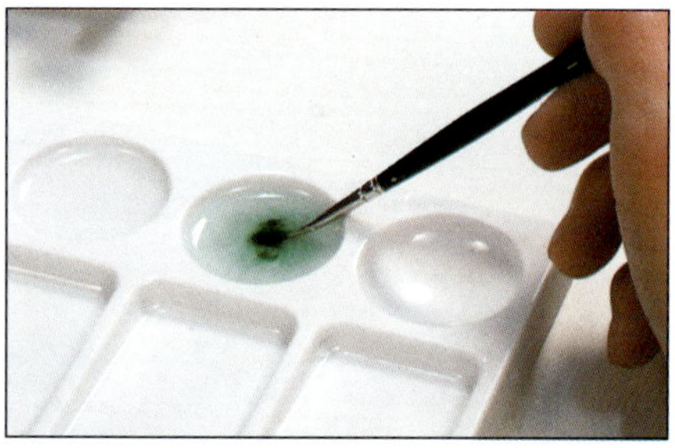

Add a small amount of green paint.

Stir carefully.

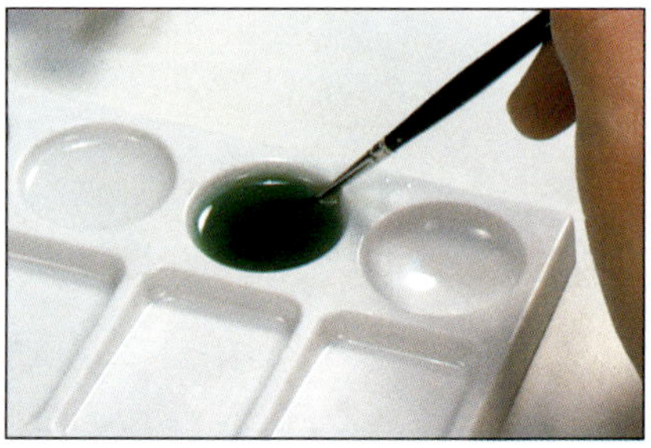

The color should be darker than the base color of the model. If, after applying some wash, there is no change in color, add a little black.

The mixture should now be dark enough to be noticeable on the model's surface.

Paint is applied to the crevices in sufficient quantity to make them stand out. Place more paint on those areas where shadows would naturally make the surface darker.

Sometimes, the wrong area may get paint on it. Clean it off with a clean, dry brush.

The process is repeated on the side parts, concentrating on the lower areas..

Once the process has been completed the details will stand out, while the remainder of the vehicle will largely remain as it was.

best made using a No. 4 or 5 brush. The color is prepared in the same way, but it is applied over the whole model. Washes can be done with acrylics. Fine pigment acrylics like the ones most suitable for use with an airbrush, are highly recommended. However, best results are always to be obtained with enamels and/or oils. That said, before applying an overall wash, always allow 24 hours to pass if the model has been painted with acrylics, or 48 hours in the case of enamels, otherwise you will run the risk of spoiling your paintjob. The original base color must equally be of the correct thickness because, if it is too thin, the wash can lift it. This applies equally if the base color has been applied too thick.

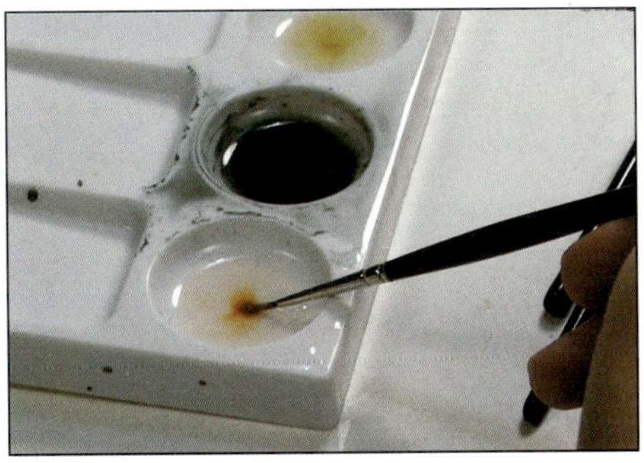

Repeat the process with brown which will make the green tones more intense..

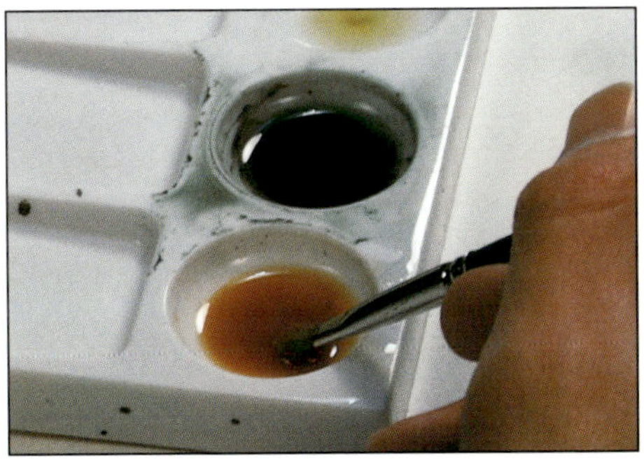

Black is unnecessary, because we're looking to achieve a slightly rusty or dusty effect.

An overall wash that slightly changes the underlying color should properly be called a filter or transparency.

Oils used for filters or transparencies.

There are thinners that have a mild turpentine smell.

Wet the brush with clean thinner.

Apply an overall wash with pure thinner.

Before the thinner dries, apply small touches of green, white and ochre.

Using the brush, 'melt' the colors into the liquid.

The filter, or transparency, alters the base color with different color shades.

The surface is ready for dry brushing.

Repeat the process on the other side.

The amount of pigment used dictates how much the base color will be affected.

The visibility of the brush strokes will depend on how much thinner is used..

The result adds chromatic richness to the base color.

What & How

Dry Brushing

Advances in model painting techniques can, in many ways, be attributed to the transposing of traditional painting techniques from a flat canvas to the three dimensional form. Dry brushing is a case in point, albeit a recent one, because up to a decade ago, its use was confined to two dimensional support, where it has been used since antiquity. Today, the concept would appear to be well known when, in fact, the opposite is the case. One becomes tired of hearing, more often than not, a supposed 'guru' say 'Dip your brush in the paint, let it dry, and then paint with it.' It is best not to look too closely at the results obtained by following these instructions to the letter. However, we do feel that using this technique properly has yet to yield its full potential while, at the same time, abusing it, as is quite often the case, will give a somewhat mediocre result. The technique itself is quite simple, and it can be done as follows: Using a flat No.4 or 6 brush, dip it into the chosen color. Then, rub the brush on a cloth until the bristles are just slightly stained and appear to be free of paint. This becomes apparent when we rub the brush in small circles on the model and tiny particles of pigment should be

The dry brushing technique used on this M-1 makes the details stand out, giving it both volume and neatness.

Begin with a lighter shade of green.

Dip a flat brush into the paint.

Excess paint is rubbed off onto a cloth.

The color particles remaining on the brush will be transported to the model.

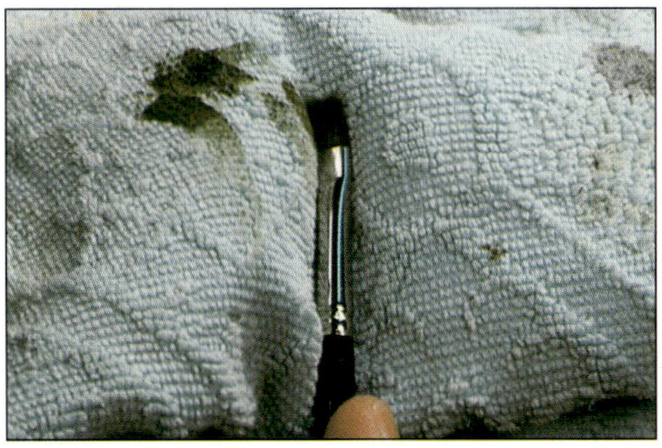

Next, choose an even lighter shade of green.

deposited on its surface. The secret for realising the best results is getting just that right degree of 'dryness'! If the paint isn't dry enough, it will completely cover the surface (or almost), while, if it is too dry, no paint will appear at all.
Here, we can see other errors such as using pure white. This should never be done, unless the base color is really light. It is also worth remembering that the difference between the base color and the dry brush color must never be excessive. Furthermore, it is always advisable to use two colors in succession, first a darker tone, and then a lighter one. Another very common mistake is when the vehicle has a camouflage scheme using several colors. The model maker, anxious to complete his model, uses just one color across the whole surface, thus ending up with a very poor result. Even if it may be tedious, it's really worth the effort to employ as many colors as on the vehicle.
The dry brush technique always looks better when using enamels over an acrylic base. Paint the base color in acrylics, allow six hours drying time, and then dry brush with enamels, or even diluted oil paint. While acrylics can be used, experience has shown us that enamels are better for the job.

This new color gives a greater range, but always try to avoid covering the previous color.

Adding ochre to the last color used will give a mixture for the highlights. Try to apply very little of it. In fact, basically, just along the edges that really need highlighting.

Try to move the brush in smooth circles, as though you were dusting the model. Keep on doing it until you get the desired effect.

A detail showing where the dry brushing technique has been used. Previously, only washes and filters had been applied.

Merkava kit painted with washes and the dry brush technique.

ton with two settings: A high one and a low one. Pressure is regulated by simply pulling this device up and moving the dial button to the left or right. When the manometer indicates the pressure required, the dial button is lowered again to the initial position. This is carried out once the air container is fully charged, otherwise it will not work. If your compressor has a different system, the instruction manual will tell you how to regulate it.
We should now be all set to go to work. The airbrush, via its hose, is connected to the compressor and we wait while the motor fills the air tank. Suddenly, the 'hissing' of escaping air can be heard. Have we bought a 'duff' piece of equipment? Generally speaking, no. Sometimes the parts have not seated perfectly and this is easily solved. All it takes is some 'plumbers tape'. Wrap it round the threads of the connector screw and replace it. In the majority of cases, this usually does the trick. So, once again, we are ready to paint.

17. Pressure regulation system where the dial is lifted before turning it right or left. (when replaced, this acts as a locking device)

18-19. Turn it either left or right to raise or lower the air pressure.

20. Once we have the correct pressure, return the dial button to its original position.

21. Hose connectors. In the center is the screw-on fixed connection, while on each side are the quick release types.

22. The smallest, and cheapest available compressors are the membrane types. They are quite adequate, but will not provide all the modeler's needs. One major drawback is the need to stop every forty minutes or so to allow it to cool down. On the high side of the price scale, we have the silent compressors, with a refrigerator-type motor, an air tank capable of holding 3 to 6 liters of compressed air, and an air intake of 50 to 60 liters per minute that is adequate for supplying two airbrushes simultaneously.

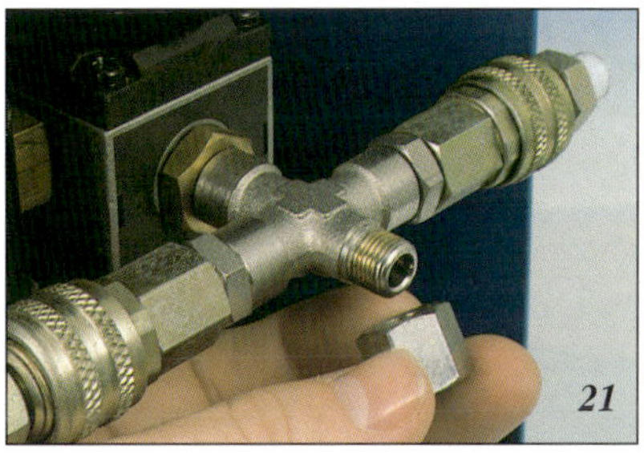

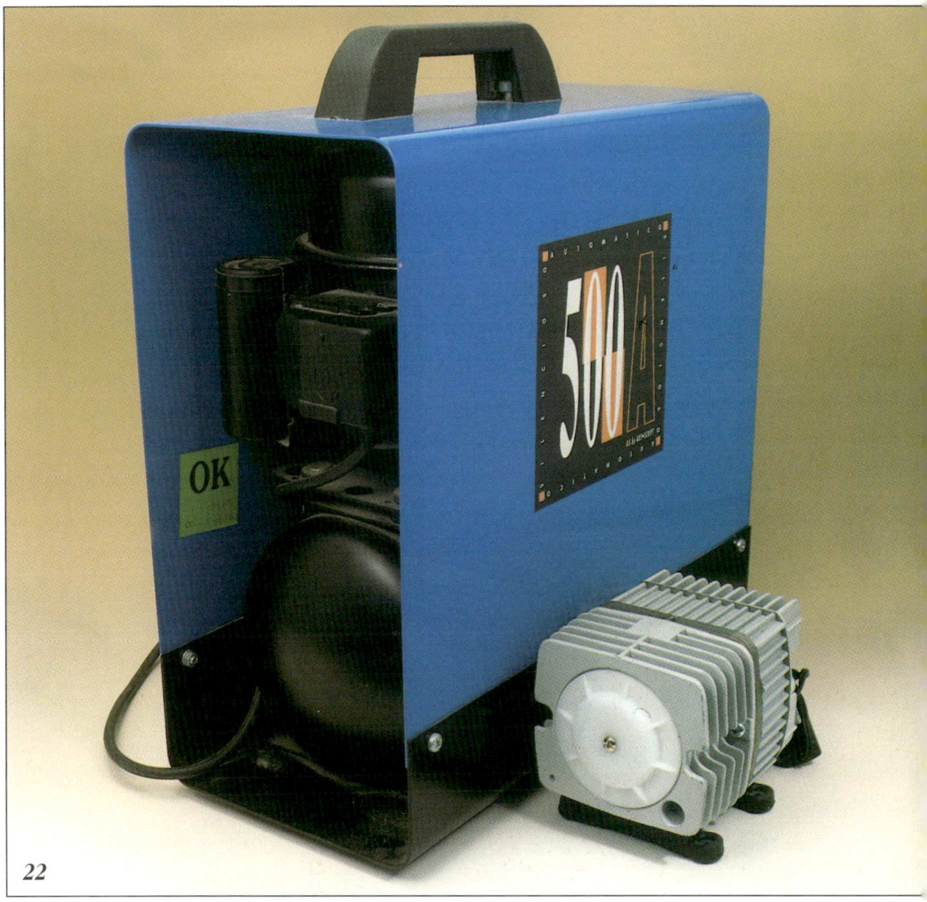

Vehicles and the Airbrush

The airbrush, or paint gun, began to be used on full-size vehicles at the beginning of the twentieth century, and especially during WWI. Its use was restricted to covering large flat surfaces. Its use on military vehicles for applying camouflage schemes was somewhat limited. This work was largely done by hand, although the Germans slowly began to use it for a few camouflage schemes. Some time would pass until the Spanish Civil War, where color combinations began to appear that would be further developed during WWII. The Republican Army in the Spanish Civil War positioned in the industrial areas, began to use the airbrush on the Spanish-made vehicles, the Russian T-26 and BA-6, and the French Schneiders. The Nationalist Army also used the airbrush on all captured vehicles and their own German Pz I's. However, these are exceptions to the rule, as the large majority of vehicles sported hand painted camouflage schemes.

WWII

The Thirties brought with it some in-depth studies of camouflage schemes. The French, British, Italian and Japanese all carried them but, nonetheless, most schemes still had rough hand-drawn edges. Later, the Germans once again carried out some experimentation, closely followed by the Americans.

At the beginning of WWII, Germany hardly bothered with the prewar schemes, continuing to use the monotonous Panzer gray that was only really of any use in urban warfare, when concealment in the shadow of buildings is possible. The more elaborate camouflage schemes were sported by French and British vehicles while, in the early years of the war, the Germans continued with their inefficient gray. Europe is full of small roads and closely-knit towns. The desert battles that took place are marked by the imaginative schemes used by the British vehicles displaying three colors with all gradations in between, which contrast markedly against the Italian vehicles that sport a mere one or two schemes. When the Germans arrived in the theatre they, too, only applied just two sand color tones over the gray base, or simply applied a crust of mud on top.

In 1941 and 1942, the Germans began adding sometimes green, sometimes sand color, over the ubiquitous gray. By this point in time, the Americans had fully entered the war, and bought along their corresponding studies on camouflage patterns and schemes. However, little of it was seen on the battlefield.

1943 marked the great change. Germany made an elaborate study based on three colors: Dark yellow sand, olive green, and red brick, combined in multiple schemes, all applied with the airbrush. These were, by far, the richest schemes seen during the course of the war. This decision would prove vital to Germany, because by May 1943, and the almost total loss of the Luftwaffe and the need to retreat once the initiative was lost, adequate camouflage was even more necessary.

Although, by this time, most armies were using the airbrush to some extent to paint their vehicles, the German army made it standard. Not all battlefronts had elaborate schemes. For example, vehicles in Russia had very limited means at their disposal, while vehicles closer to the German territories had access to all the infrastructures necessary for an adequate paintjob. Another exception was Operation Citadelle where the paintjobs were somewhat sloppy.

Since WWII, all camouflage schemes have been applied by airbrush, while the individual schemes are variations and adaptations of those developed during the war.

CONVEYING SCHEMES WITH YOUR AIRBRUSH

What the modern model maker attempts to do, is imitate the efforts made by the original worker when painting the original vehicle. He had a paint gun powered by a device that connected to the vehicle's engine and produced sufficient air pressure for painting. Sometimes, dedicated compressors were used for the job, along with standard masking for numerals and insignias, while, at other times, they were done by hand. What we model makers try to do is to follow these same steps taken by the original painters. First, like them, we apply a base color, which is then followed by the given camouflage pattern. Finally, we try to convey the wear and tear that a given vehicle will be subjected to during its lifetime. While the airbrush becomes a basic tool for all these steps, we will always have to use a brush as well.

In order to understand the process when doing a German camouflage scheme, we have used, as an example, a single vehicle that includes all possible variants, explaining each one in turn. This section concentrates on the German patterns. Later, however, we will consider other nationalities.

The following exercises were carried out with a double-action, gravity-fed airbrush. Each airbrush has its own little tricks and peculiarities and it is, therefore, advisable to take these into account when studying the following suggestions

BEFORE PAINTING

Many beginners have trouble with their first airbrush. Sometimes, the end result is not what they wanted or the airbrush refuses to work. Below are some of the more common causes:

- ❑ Paint is not thin enough, the mixture is too thick or has paint, or other particles, floating in it.
- ❑ Not enough paint for an airbrush. This could mean that the paint is too thick and cannot pass through the nozzle.
- ❑ The air pressure is too low, giving the paint uneven coverage and, in consequence, small dots appear.
- ❑ Dirty or obstructed airbrush. If your airbrush is even slightly dirty, you may get a faulty paint jet, or no paint coming out of the nozzle.
- ❑ Technical problems with the airline, nozzle or air regulation system.
- ❑ The most important thing you must remember is to maintain your airbrush and keep it scrupulously clean.

The moment you have finished spraying, clean your airbrush thoroughly. Also, when switching colors, thoroughly clean the airbrush after each one. This includes dismantling the nozzle. It is not good enough to merely spray some thinner through it.

BASE COLOR

This is what we call the very first coat that is sprayed onto the model. It is important that this coat is perfectly smooth. This smoothness is achieved by diluting the paint so that it adheres to the model's surface. If the paint is too thick, it becomes like dry dust, and won't adhere properly to the surface. The correct paint density must be similar to milk. If it is like water, it will not cover, while, if it is like yoghurt, it will be too thick and will obliterate all the fine detail.

Once you have the right density, you must spray paint from side to side, from left to right, or vice versa, never staying too long in one particular spot. Depending on the color choice, you may need to apply two or three coats in order to properly cover the surface. The spraying distance from airbrush to object should be approximately five centimeters, and never less than three in some circumstances. The airbrush trigger must be between a quarter and halfway open.

So, let us begin to paint. First, release air alone and then slowly pull the trigger back until we get a medium paint jet. It is best to try it out on a piece of paper first before going on to the model. This will also ensure that any paint spurt has been cleared from the airbrush. Once the model has been given a good covering of the base color, we can proceed to the camouflage scheme.

TYPES OF CAMOUFLAGE

These can be divided into two main groups: Those done by hand (feathered edges) and those done by first masking and then airbrushing to give sharp, well-defined edges. However, a feathered edge can also be achieved with an airbrush by simply lifting the mask away from the surface. This is how both are done...

A very important rule to remember when using an airbrush is: Begin by releasing only air and finish by doing the same. In simple terms, pull the trigger to release air before releasing the paint, then, at the end, close the paint release and allow only air through the nozzle.

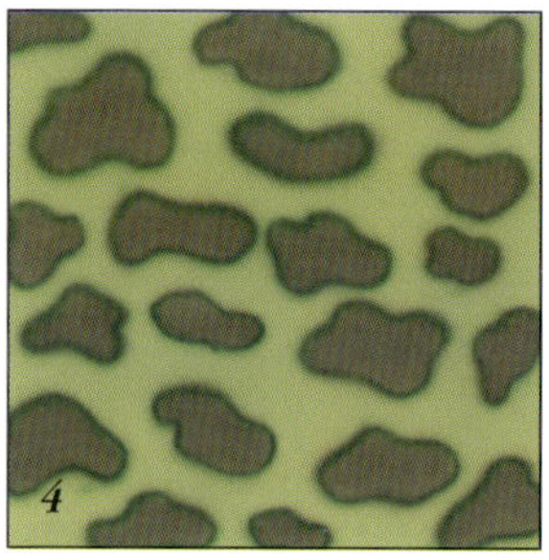

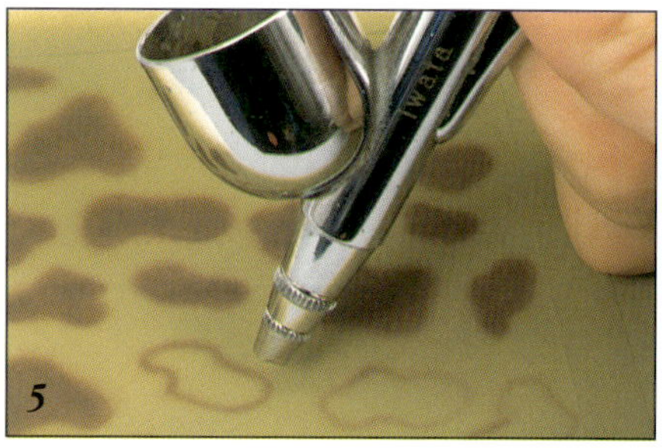

4. Different sizes of Leopard spots. They are the color of brick in the center, surrounded by a green edge. They are applied to AFVs like Panthers, Tigers, Hetzers and Bisons.

5. Begin by drawing the outline and then filling in each spot. Finish with a green outline.

6. They are precision outlined spots, so it is important to reduce the distance between airbrush and the model's surface.

1. First trigger position: No air or paint released.

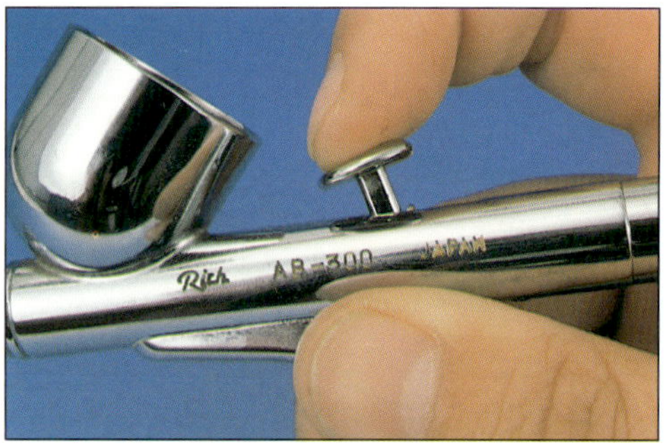

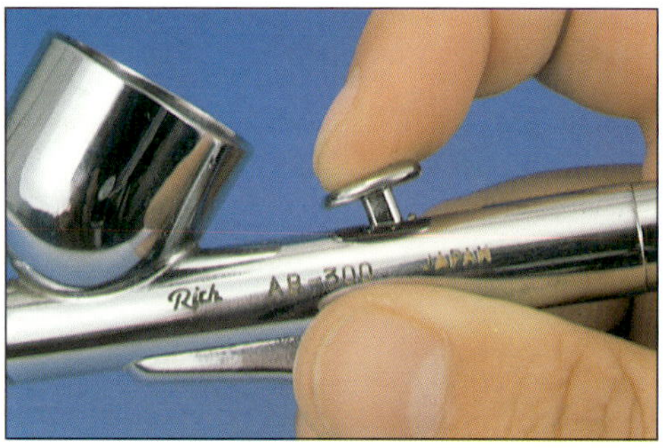

2. By pressing down the trigger air will begin to flow, the harder you press the more air comes out.

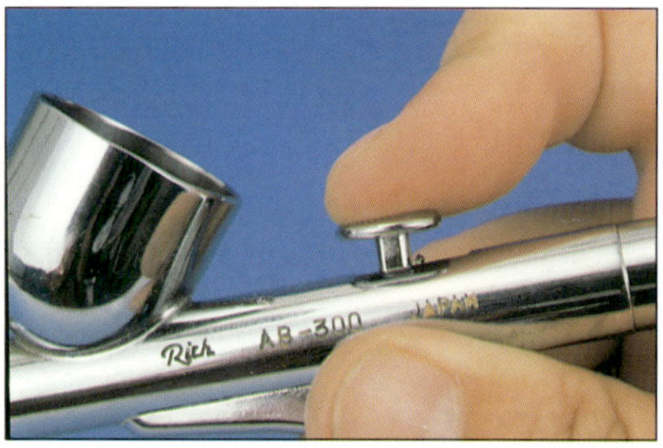

3. By pulling the back on the trigger, paint will be released, the further back you pull it, the greater the paint jet.

7. *Before applying your camouflage scheme, you must first apply a base color. Get the best results by airbrushing from left to right, making sure the paint is properly diluted.*

8. *When working on the camouflage spots, it is best to have a piece of paper close at hand on which to test before working on the model.)*

9. *Once the camouflage scheme is complete, give it a very light shade coat with the airbrush. For this, there must be minimum paint flow, so that the shading is thin enough for the right effect, and also thin enough so that it does not obliterate the camouflage spots.*

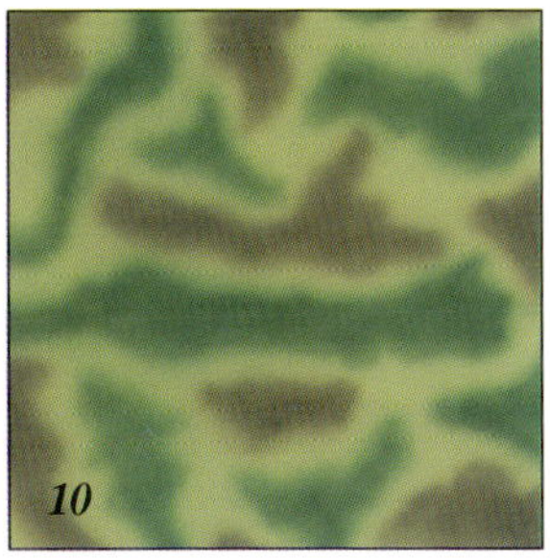

10. *Irregular spots over a sand color base. The most common camouflage scheme to be seen on almost all German vehicles.*

11. *This is also done by painting an outline first, and then filling in the center. Spray at a medium distance from the model, getting closer when necessary.*

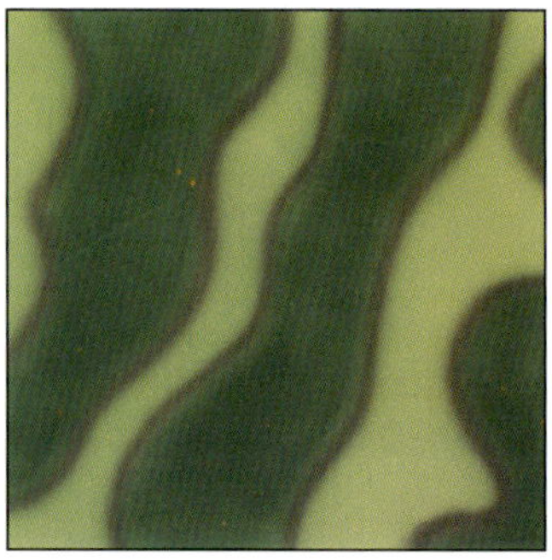

12. Irregular green bands with a brick red outline. This is a variant on the leopard skin scheme, but covering large areas. Usually, they are done vertically and can be applied to almost any vehicle.

13. When painting the green spots, spray from a medium distance from the surface, doing the outline first, and then filling it in. You will, however, have to move closer when spraying the brick red outline.

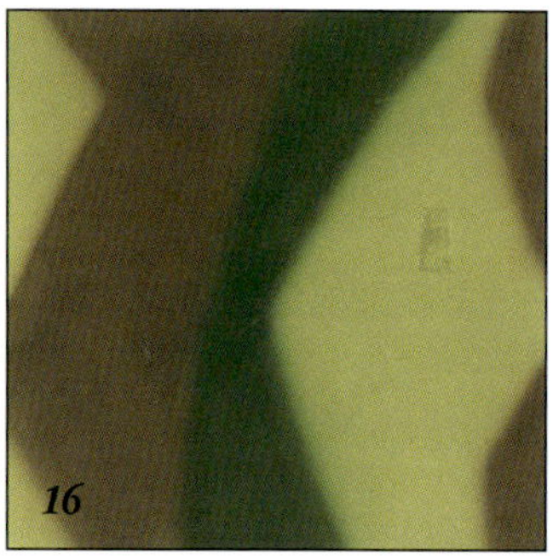

16. A common scheme made of geometrical straight and zigzag lines. It can be done with defined or feathered edges. It was very common on Panthers, but can also be seen on trucks and halftrack vehicles.

17. This scheme can be done with paper or cardboard masks that, if a feathered edge is wanted, are held slightly away from the vehicle's surface. If we want a well-defined edge, place the mask directly onto the model's surface.

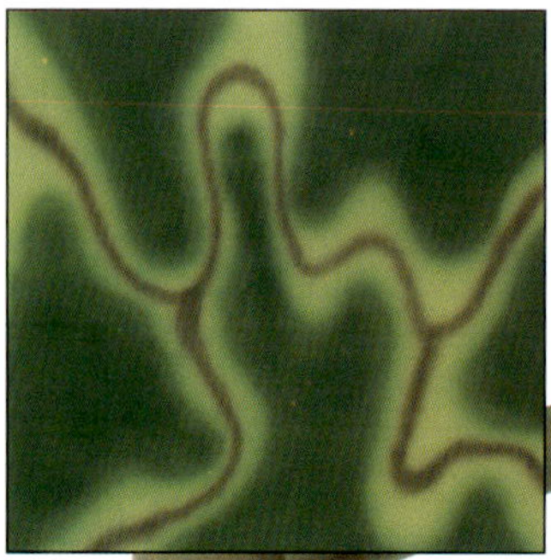

14. Irregular, large, green spots, with narrow 'streets' divided by a brick red line. It is quite a strange scheme used mainly on self propelled guns and transport vehicles.

15. The green spots are easy to do, but the brick red line is a little difficult to center and takes practice.

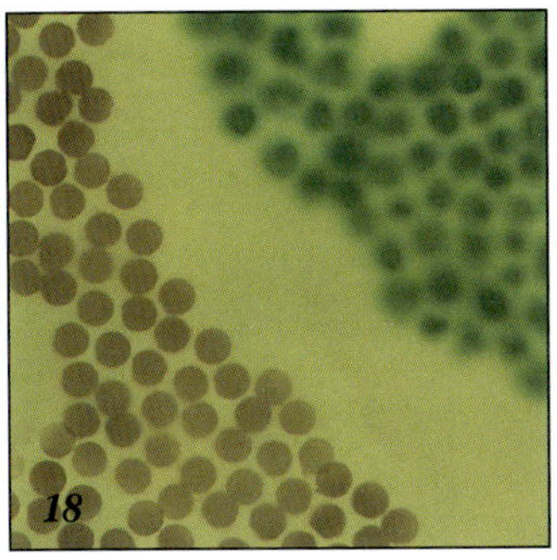

18. An interesting scheme with feathered or defined edges made using either a brush or an airbrush. These dots were seen on all types of German vehicles during the latter part of the war, 1944-45.

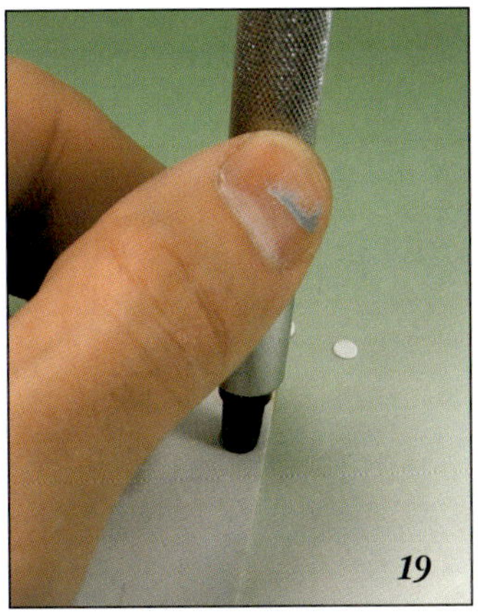

19. This scheme is done with a cardboard mask pierced with circular holes of the correct diameter.

20. They can also be done without masking. Do it by working closer to the surface of the model, although there is a risk of the size of the spots varying a little.

21. It is easier to work with a mask, and they can be used over and over again.

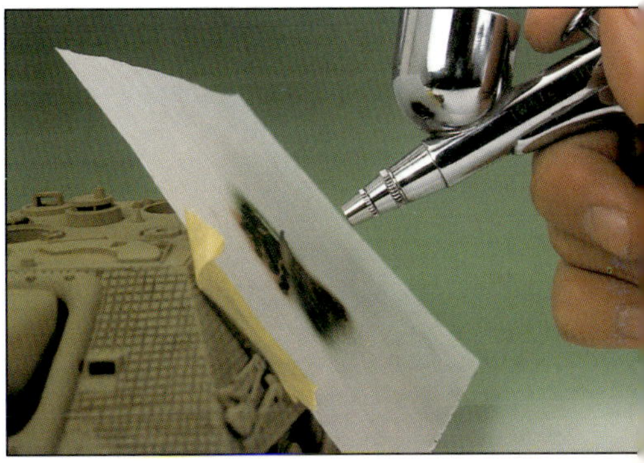

22. At a medium distance, we get well-defined dots.

23. If you choose to do them by hand, you have to maintain a steady air/paint flow and at a constant distance. If the airbrush has an adjusting screw, these factors are easily controlled.

25. The undulating green line requires practice in order to get a continuous, steady line and is done at a constant distance.

24. A curious scheme of undulating green lines and brick red spots. It was done on Panthers and halftrack vehicles.

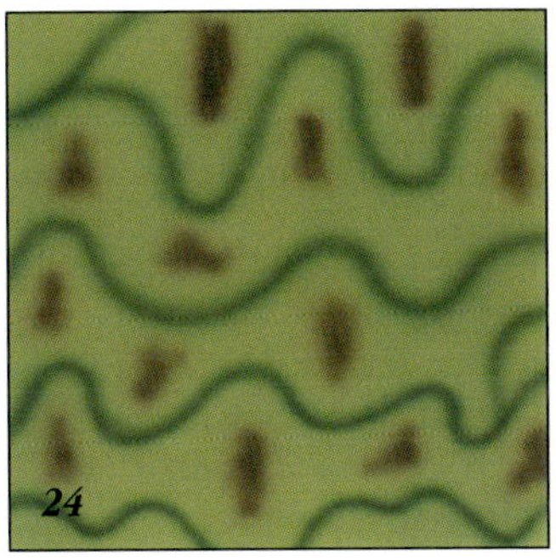

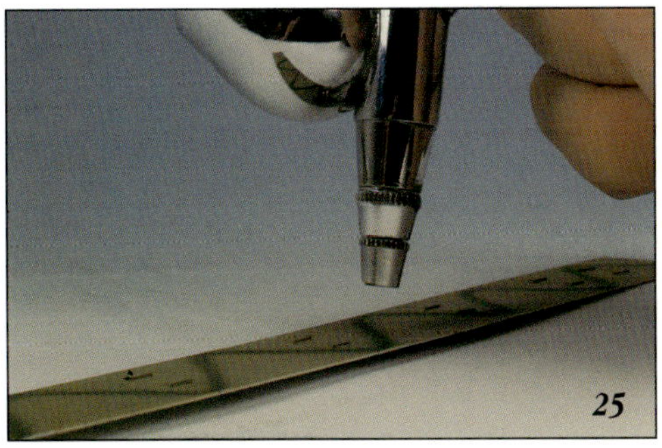

26. *Irregular spots with defined edges in either green or brick red. A very common scheme that appeared on just about all vehicles, done either by hand or with an paint gun.*

27. *It's done using pre-cut cardboard masks and moving them around the model. The spraying distance can be varied.*

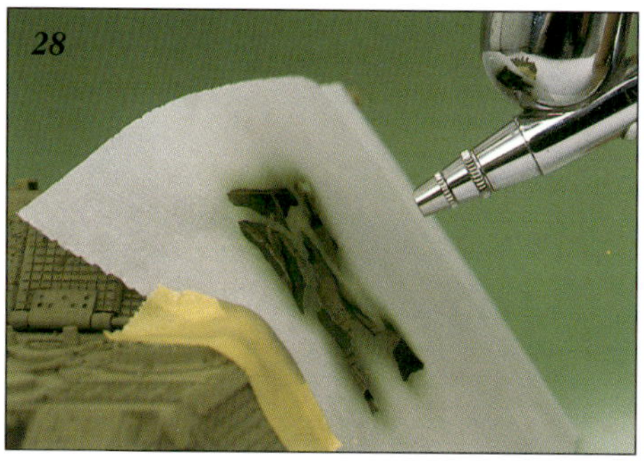

28. *All schemes done with masking may have feathered or defined edges, depending on the distance between the mask and the model's surface.*

29. *Small, irregular brick red and green spots. They were found on assault guns, halftrack troop transports or reconnaissance vehicles, such as the Puma or the Sdkfz-232.*

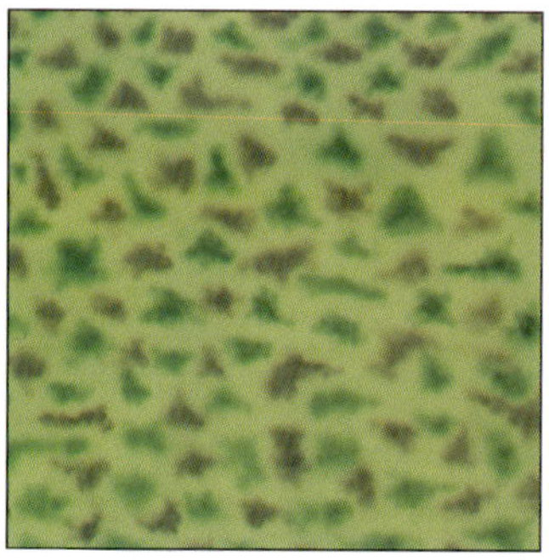

30. *An accurate airbrush is required for this scheme, as we need to get rather close to the surface of the model. Take care to have the correct air pressure, too low a pressure will result in disastrous 'spider legs' effect.*

31. Connected, irregular green lines over the base color, mixed with brick red. It was found on some Ferdinands (the ones at Kursk), on some trucks and halftrack transports.

32. As it is to be done by hand, it may first require some practice on paper, and the lines must be regular.

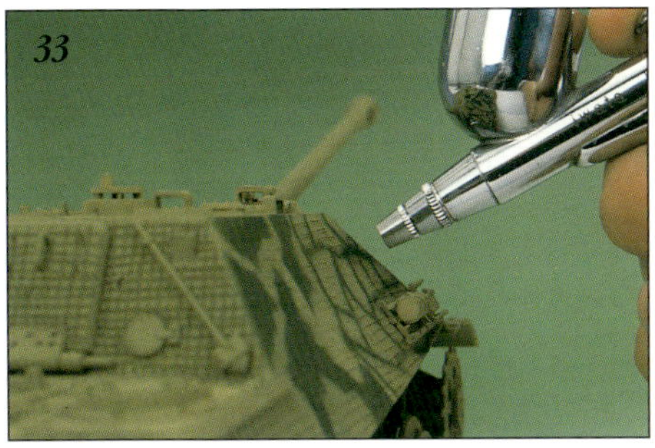

33. You have to get rather close to the surface of the model, and use a medium air/paint jet. However, it all depends on how thick you want to make the lines.

34. When working over the joins, etc., you must be careful as the air may 'curve out' with the result that the lines will cease to be homogenous. This can be avoided by maintaining a steady painting motion at right angles to the model.

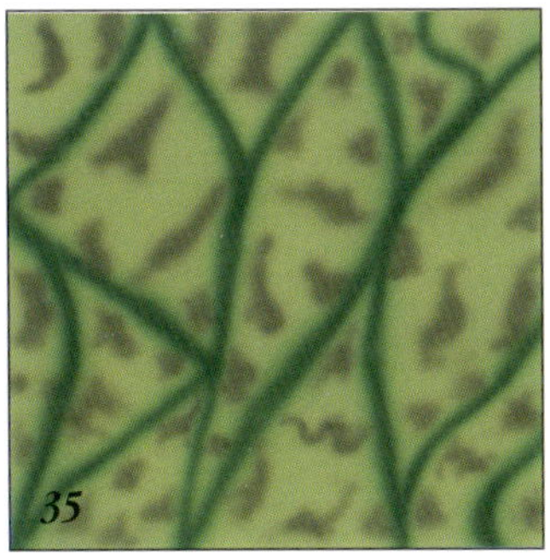

35. Connected, irregular green lines with small, irregular brick red spots inside. This scheme was done on halftrack vehicles, heavy tanks such as the Royal Tiger, and some assault guns. It is achieved by combining the techniques of the previous two schemes.

36. The strangest, and most peculiar hand painted scheme. It was used on assault guns (There is a remarkable example at Kursk, and that also includes small spots, and also a Panther which used both sand color and green.

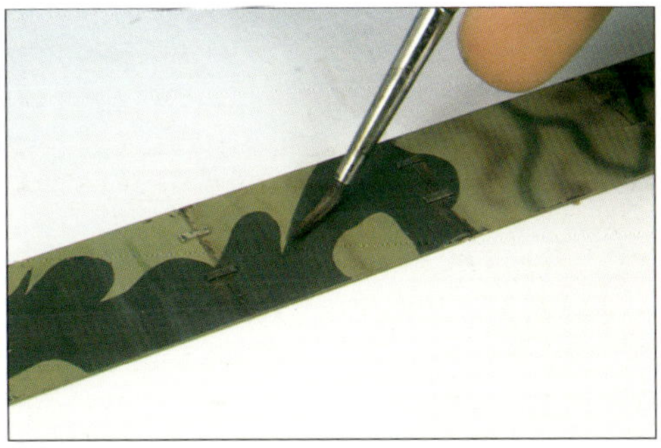

37. It is done entirely by hand. It is advisable to practice this awkward scheme on paper first.

What & How

Airbrush, Cleaning and Care

When you first hold an airbrush in your hands it may look like some sort of magic device, full of mystery that only you can unravel. Is it some little miracle-maker that can be compared to a magic wand? Once you start to use it, stand by for some heartache. You will have some accidents that, at one time or another, may result in the virtual destruction of the airbrush itself. It is time to face facts...most modelers have made fatal mistakes with their most precious of tools.

It may have been the improper use of acetone that was used to clean hardened paint residue. That lesson taught us that acetone could be lethal on the joints of the airbrush, making a useless, gooey mass of the rubber seals.

On another occasion we spilt it around the trigger, which affected all the delicate mechanisms within...

A painfully common occurrence is when the nozzle breaks, leaving part of the screw inside, making it virtually impossible to extract the remains of the broken screw. This is a particularly common accident with the cheaper airbrushes because the part is made from chromed tin. High quality airbrush nozzles are made from a platinum alloy, so if this piece breaks, it's going to cost a lot to replace. Although a platinum part is pretty strong, if you have to loosen it with the small spanner it may also end up being broken as well. The trick is to screw it down firmly...but not too tight.

Basically, however, most problems emanate from 'lazy cleaning sessions', when you don't clean your airbrush as well as you know you should or 'I'll leave it until tomorrow'... or even longer... When you finally get round to cleaning it, you find that the paint has become an unyielding cement that has definitely ruined your airbrush. It is, therefore, crucial never to leave the cleaning for later but to do it the moment you have finished the airbrush session. If you do, in most instances you'll only have to clean the nozzle and needle.

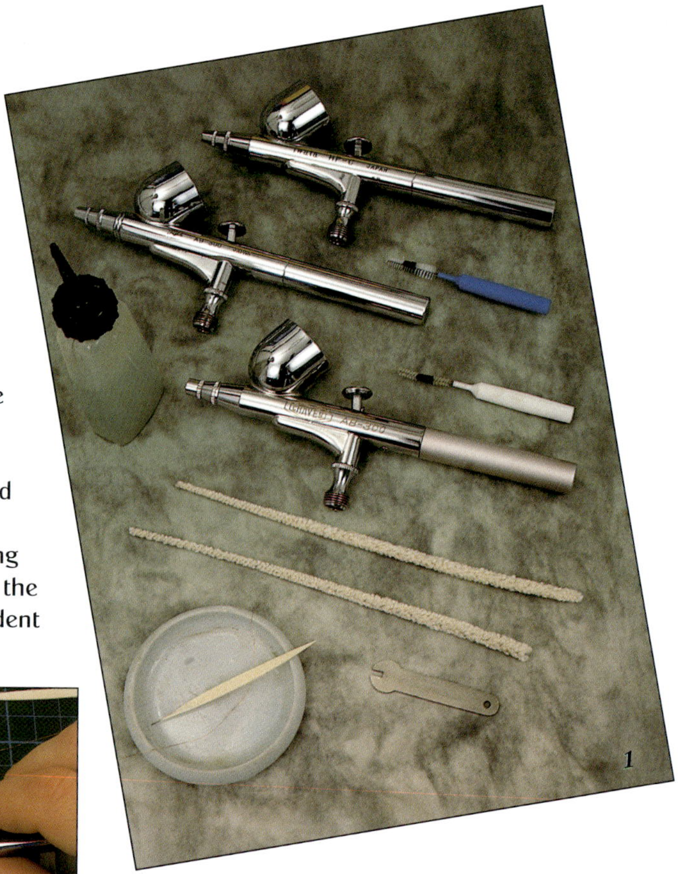

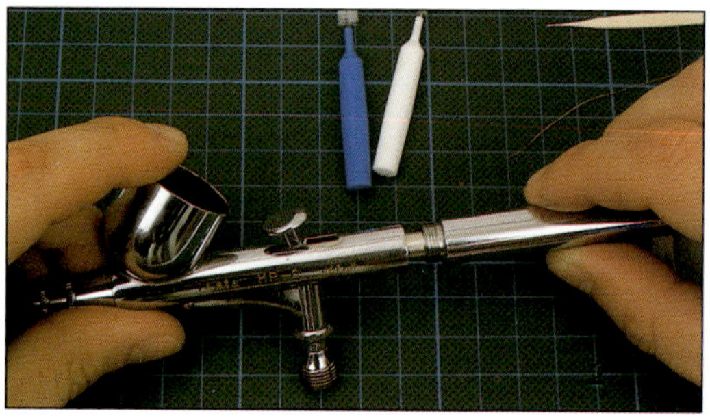

1. The same type of airbrush kit by different manufacturers. The differences lie in the quality of materials employed.

2. Unscrew the rear of the handle.

3. Undo the needle mount so you can free the needle.

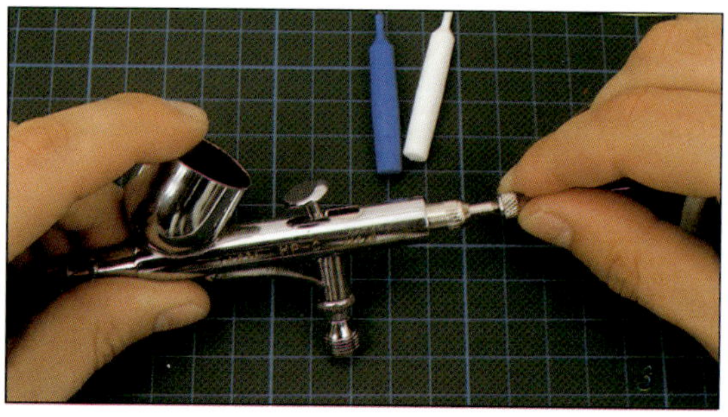

4. Pull the needle back. Make sure you keep the needle straight, as a bent needle will cause problems.

5. Loosen the needle's cover, also known as the crown.

6. Manually loosen manually the nozzle cover.

7. Unscrew the nozzle with the special tool (key) provided with the airbrush.

8. Carefully remove it by hand.

9. To clean each part, submerge them in the correct thinner; use a china, not plastic, bowl.

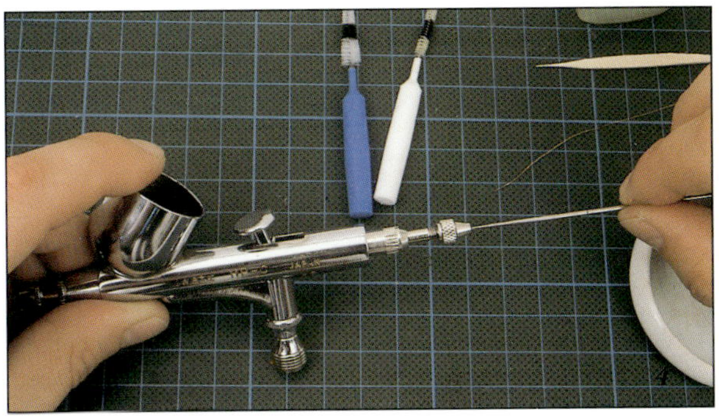

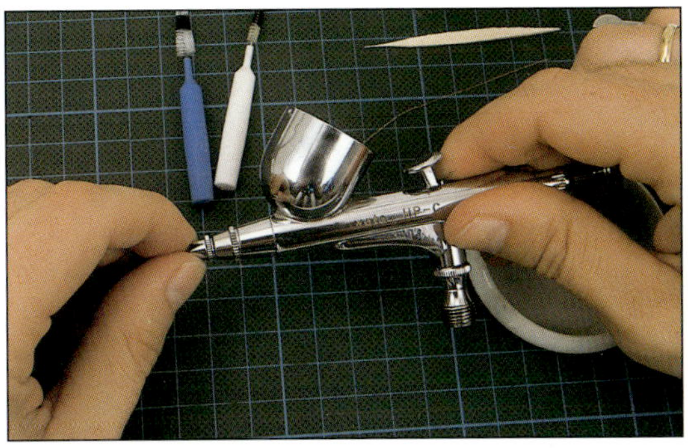

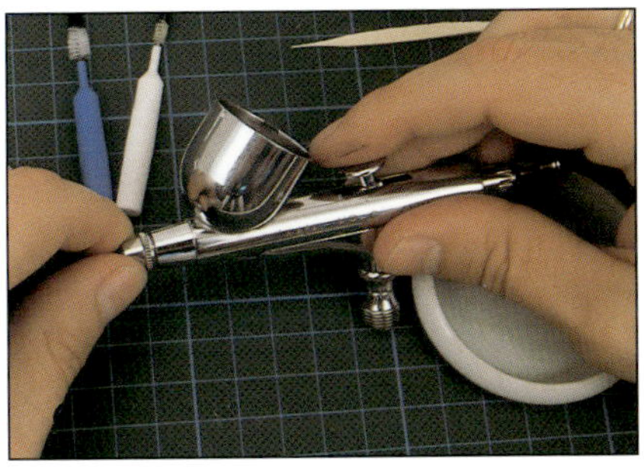

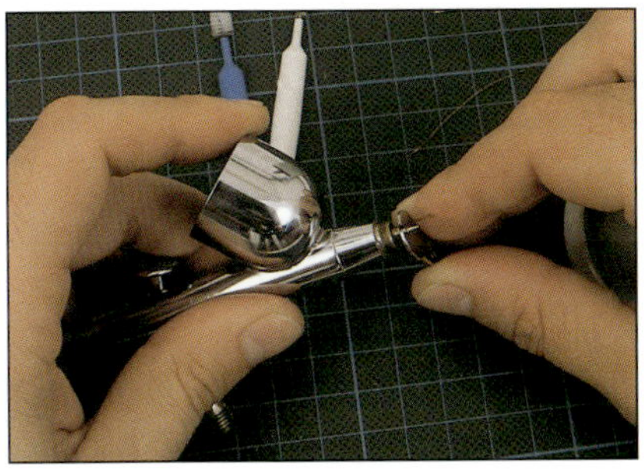

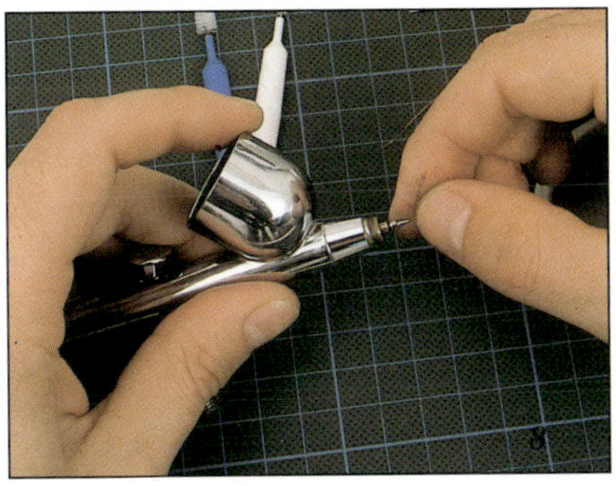

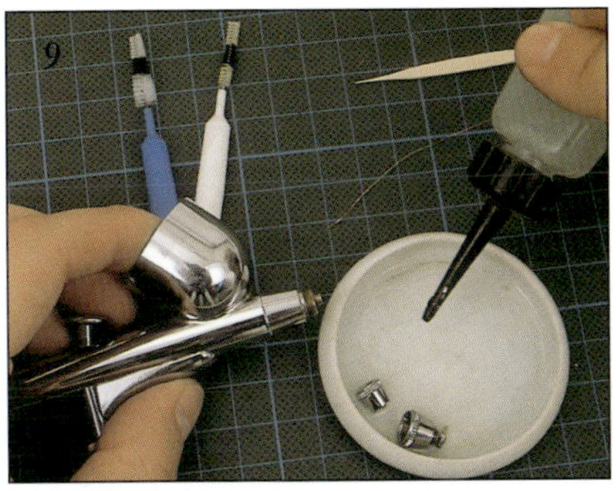

10. Cleaning the paint container with absorbent paper soaked in the correct thinner.

11. If you need to thoroughly clean the paint container, make an impregnated cotton ball and use tweezers.

12. The tweezers will help you get to those awkward places.

13. Cleaning the paint feed duct with a special toothbrush.

14. Get the dental brush inside and twist it around.

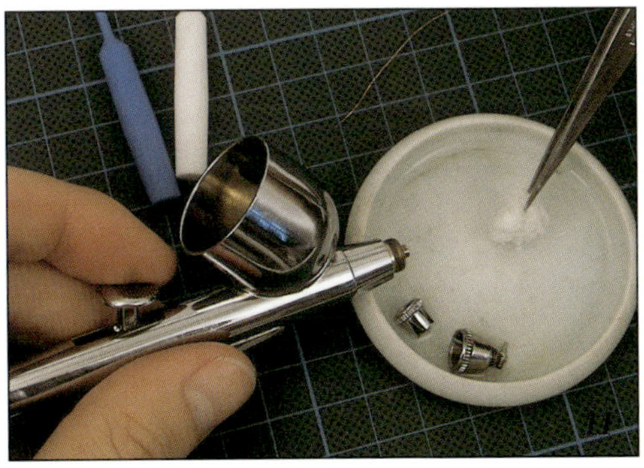

15. *Look for the other end of the brush from the paint container end.*

16-17. *Here can be seen how much residue has been removed. Re-introduce the brush from the other end.*

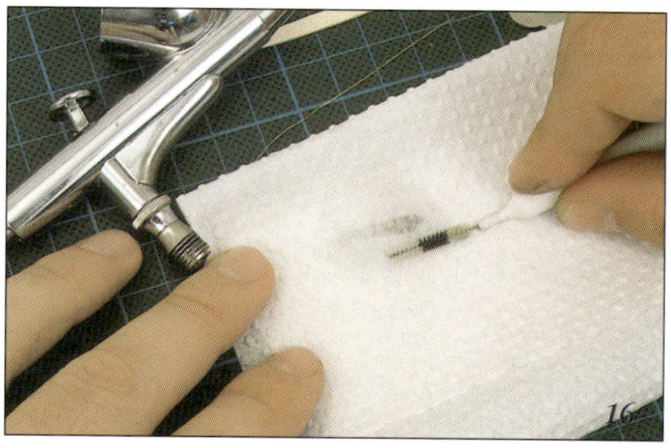

18. *As before, look for the tip from the other end.*

19. *The nozzle can be cleaned using the tip of a toothpick..*

20. *Roll the nozzle in your fingers to ensure that the toothpick cleans the inside properly.*

21. *Further cleaning can be done by inserting a piece of fine copper wire.*

22. *A magnifying glass will help to see any dirt remains.*

23. *For a really thorough cleaning, you will have to remove the needle's mount.*

24. *Remove the main part by hand.*

25. *Next, it is the turn of the rear spring.*

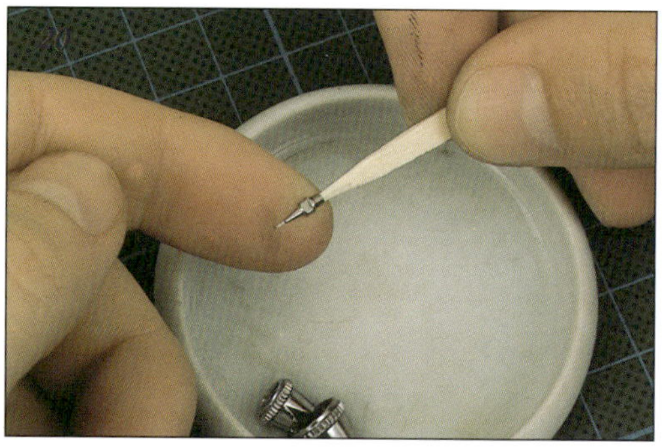

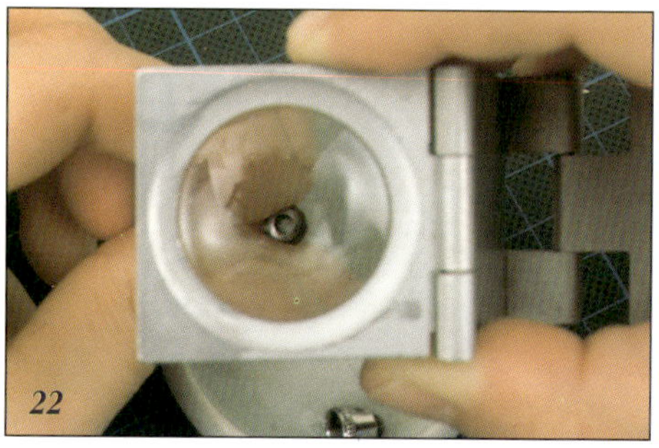

26. Finally, remove the needle's mount.

27. The trigger comes out easily, simply turn it and pull it upwards.

28. The stopper is removed with tweezers.

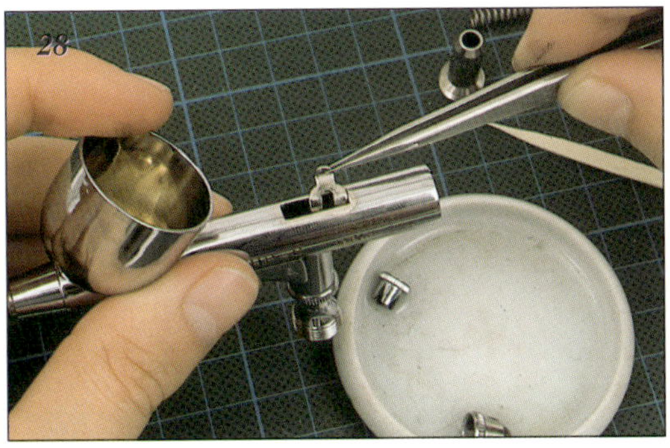

29. Small thinner-soaked brush.

30. Introduce it and try to reach the reservoir.

31. Dirt collects in this area. Now, reassemble the parts.

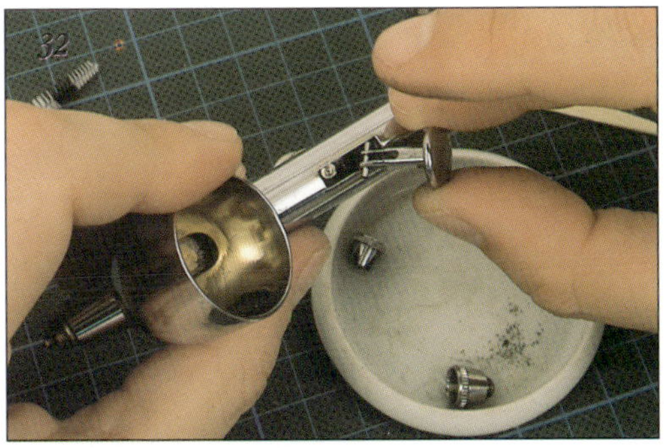

32. Replacing the trigger.

33. Check to see that the trigger moves smoothly.

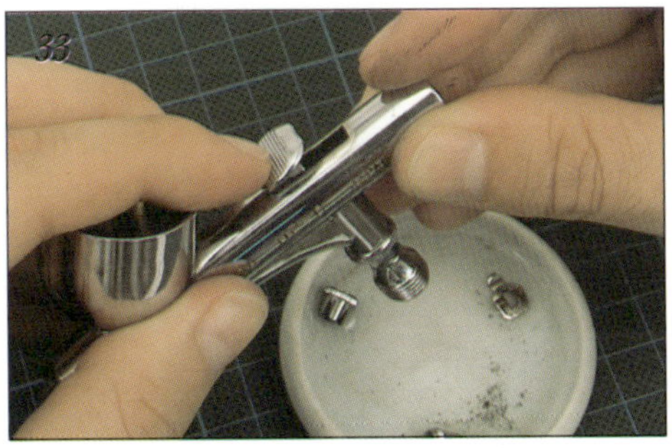

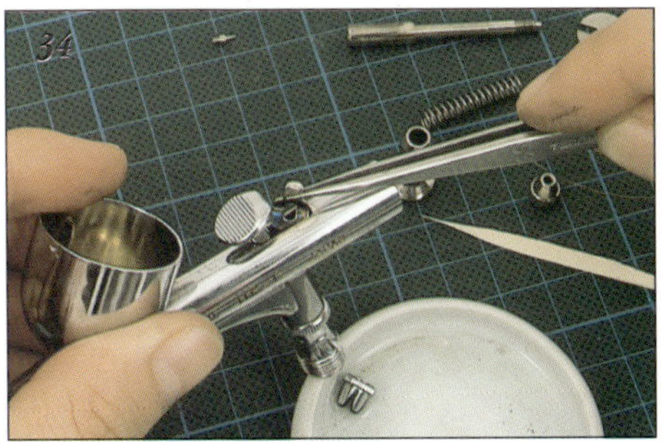

34. Replace the trigger's stop. It only has one position, so if the trigger doesn't move, change its position.

35. The correct position.

36. Replacing the needle's mount.

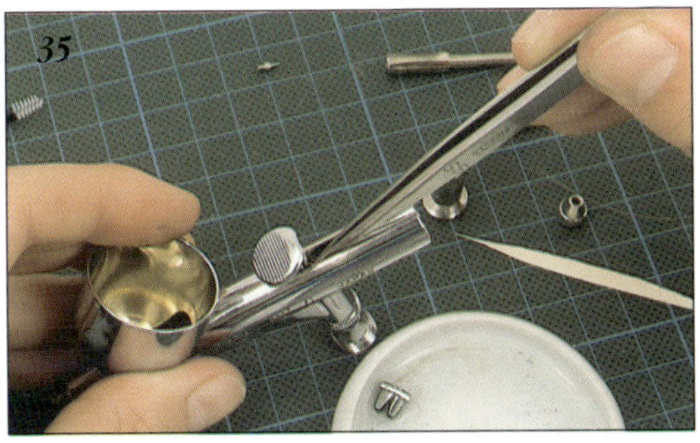

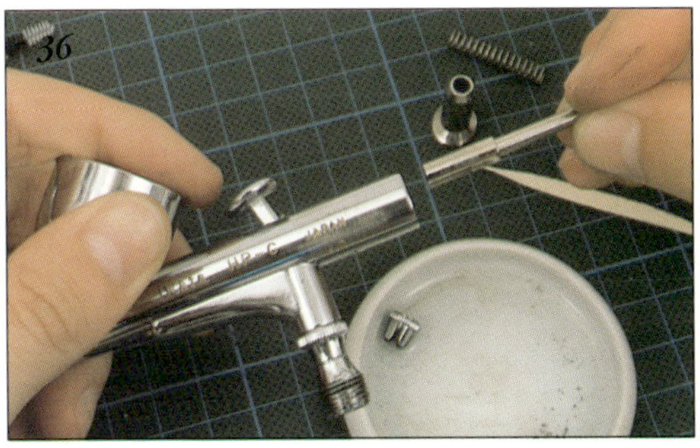

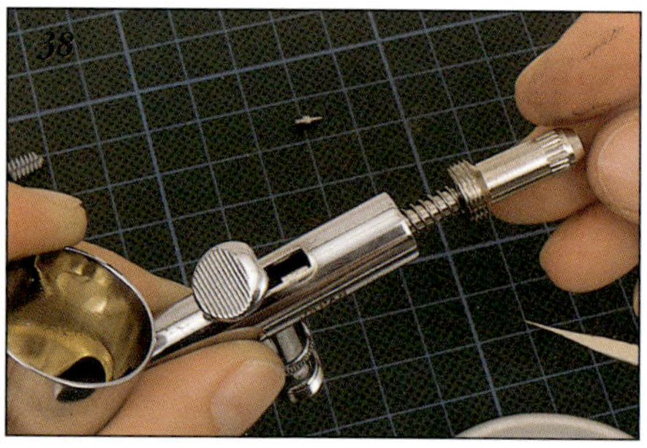
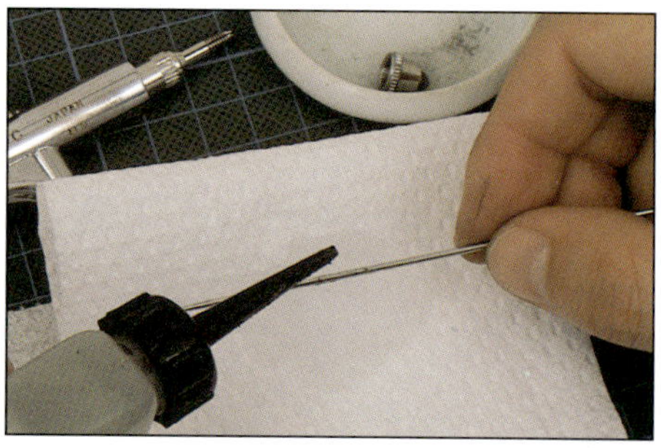

37. Re-introduce the spring by pressing it in with a finger until it wont go any further.

38. Needle mount's adjuster.

39-40. Carefully rub the needle using a thinner soaked tissue. Remember to avoid bending the needle at all costs!

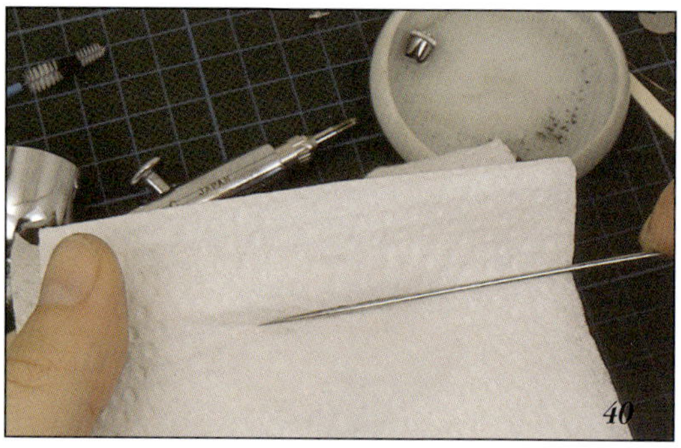

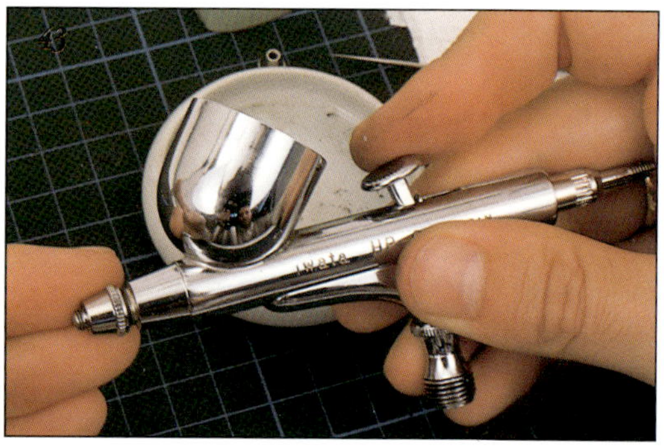
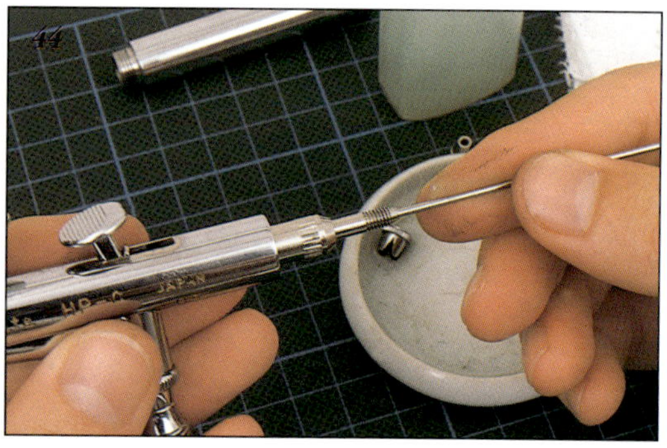

41. Tightening the nozzle using the key. Remember! Do not tighten it too much.

42. Cleaning the nozzle cover with a thinner soaked tissue.

43. Completing the job by screwing down the crown cover.

44. Smoothly, re-introduce the needle…don't force it.

45. Screw in the needle's adjuster.

46. The needle must be seen from the nozzle.

47. Adjusting the nozzle cover, or crown.

48. Closing the handle.

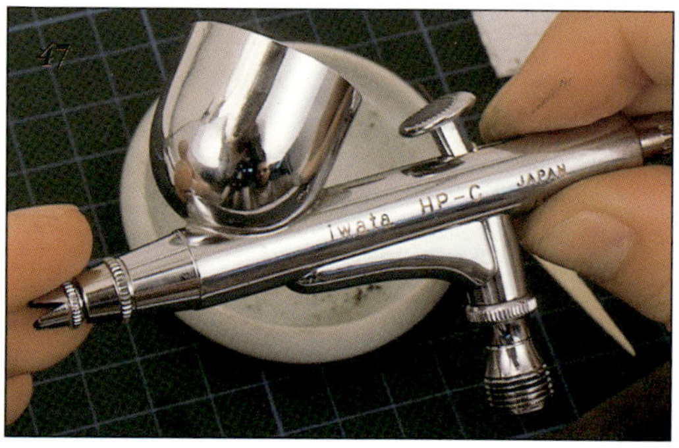

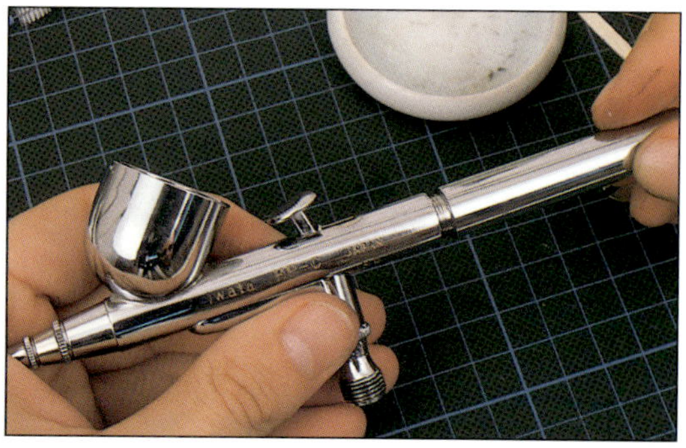

Foreword

Many modelers, on hearing about photo-etched parts, think of something that bears little relation to the hobby. They are regarded as something a little beyond their reach that will, in addition, give uncertain results. On the other hand, there are others that are used to using them and swear by them. They feel that the finished model will definitely be the winner, while also feeling that the imperfections of an all-plastic kit can be corrected, resulting in a model that more closely resembles its real life, full-size counterpart.
The incredible detail that photo-etched parts add to grills, fenders etc… certainly contributes to a more realistic portrayal, making the completed model a more exact replica of the real thing. If you then combine them with other parts made from wire (for all the cylindrical parts), we have basically covered all our needs. Other details, such as exhausts, headlights, wheels, etc… can quite often be bought as after-market parts or scratch-built. Once all the extra details are in place, we can begin to paint the model to the best of our abilities, which allows all those details that we bothered to add combine to make an homogenous whole.
Unfortunately, not all modelers excel in the painting department, and it is certainly sad seeing a superbly detailed model spoilt by a mediocre paintjob. In the following pages, we will use all the available techniques in an exhaustive detailing and painting (using both brush and airbrush) process that can be used in the making of a German Puma.

Puma, Detailed Assembly

With the sunlight reflected in the rain puddles created by the intense rain, it seems as though we are sailing on a rough sea rather than moving on firm ground. The irregular terrain also causes us to bounce up and down as if we really are on a turbulent sea. Mile after mile, water, or rather mud is splashed in all directions and reaching as high as my face, regardless of the fact that I am high on top of the turret. The tracks left behind are truly impressive. More often than not, we sink in deep water holes up to the vehicles axles; but we are not worried as our eight wheels work well and soon get us out of trouble. If the situation is not easily solved, we engage the lowest gear and use some gas, making our 210 hp engine roar like a beast, and transmitting enough power to the wheels, coupled in pairs, until the best placed wheels gain traction and we can drive out of the problem. We cut through a small forest, and see a small abandoned town through the trees. We are almost clear when we hear a rumble in the sky. Above us we spot a flight of bombers, quickly identified as Petlyakov Pe-2's. We remain motionless until they disappear to our left. Apart from the aircraft, we have seen no sign of the Soviet vanguard, but we know that they must be hiding somewhere. We climb a tree-crowned hill (the best place to observe without being seen), from which we see several farms and dark green forests. We decide to cover the vehicle with branches, and wait for a half hour. Then, through my binoculars, I see some explosions followed by the customary black smoke columns. A few seconds later, I spot small 'dots' in the air that grow larger as they get closer. This time, there is nothing to fear, as they are a small flight of our planes (Junker Ju-87 and Henschel Hs129) escorted by four FW-190's. And it is truly a small group! If we consider that they may have to face a swarm of fighter planes, and that they have been attacking a column of at least one hundred armored vehicles, it really is a small group!

Ten minutes later, I'm ready to leave. I'm about to tell my fellow crewmen when, suddenly, the driver puts his hand on my shoulder and points at new 'specks' that have appeared on one of the paths. We remain motionless, because they are getting nearer and nearer to our hiding place. They are quickly identified as Russian T-70A's, about ten of them. They move cautiously towards us, stopping around 400 meters from our position. They are examining the surroundings, especially the spot were we are, but we are well camouflaged. Ten minutes drag by, some of their crews climb down from their tanks, while others are busy on their radios. We have to remain here until we see what happens, and then we'll report.

Almost a half-hour passes before some trucks and half-tracked vehicles carrying guns and 'Stalin's organs' arrive. Without doubt they are about to prepare an artillery position in order to bombard the front line, some 15 km away. Once they have finished, the crews begin car-

2. We begin by sanding the edges.
3. We drill through the transmission part with a 0.8mm drill.
4. Using a new blade, cut the center piece.
5. We can now see the separate parts and the drilled hole.
6. We replace the cut part, and insert a needle into the drilled hole.
7. Snip off the ends to get the exact length.
8. We now have a perfectly jointed piece to position as we like.
9. The position of the steering bar must be adapted to the position of the wheels. Do this by pressing with your fingers and forcing them into position.
10. Each bar will have a different angle that matches the position of its corresponding wheel.
11. Fill the 'slots' on the front of the vehicle with filler.
12. After leaving it to dry for a half hour, proceed to sanding the surface.
13. Some plastic strip is glued onto the interior of the hull, for added structural strength.
14. With a rounded blade, remove the hatch handles. They will be replaced later with photo etched ones.

1

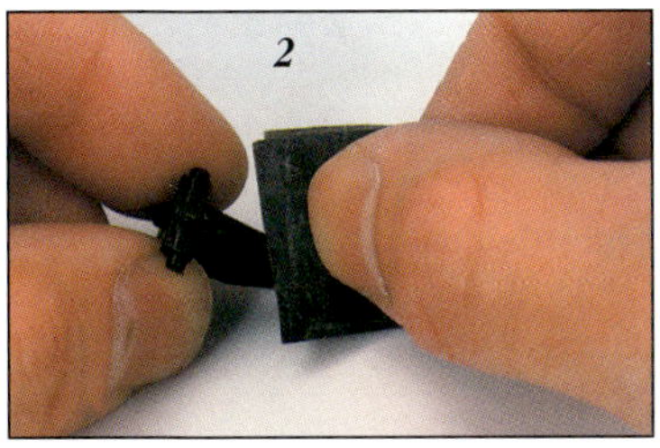
2

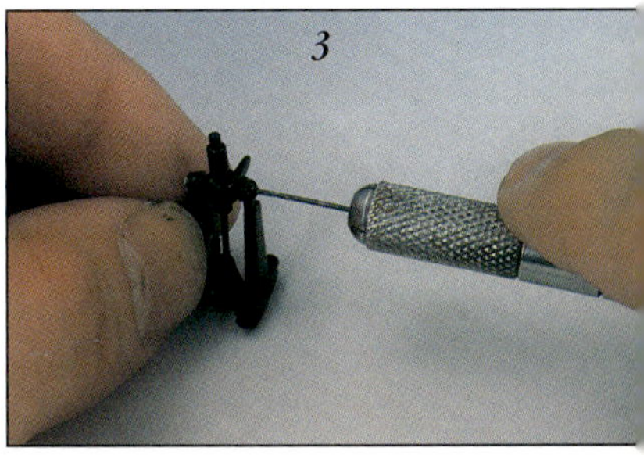
3

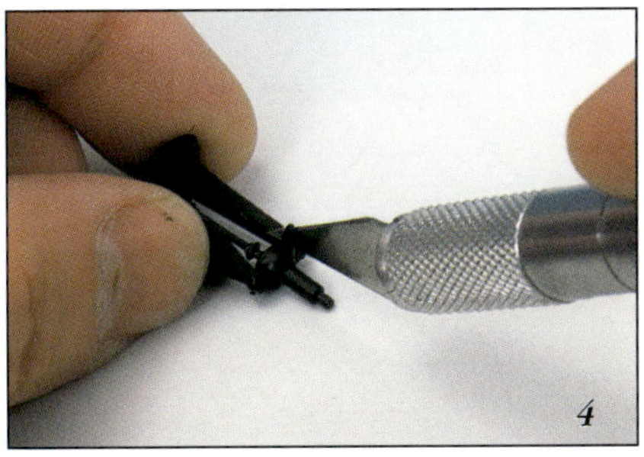
4

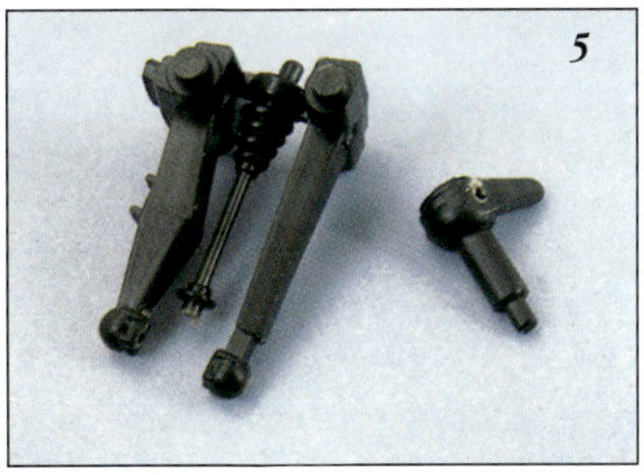
5

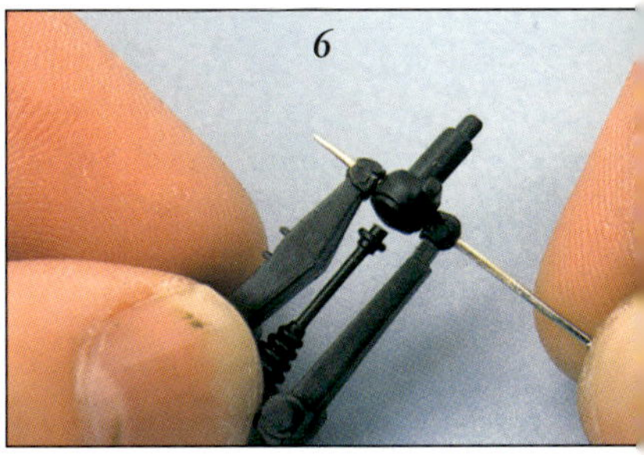
6

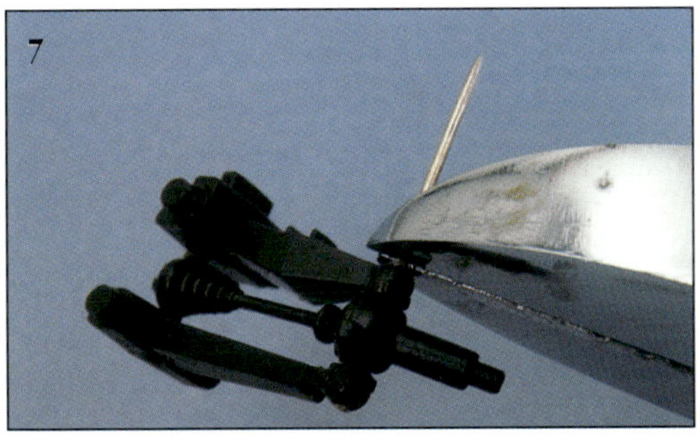
7

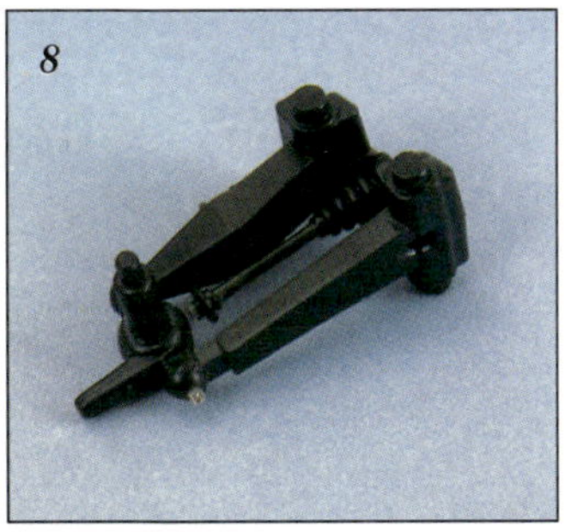
8

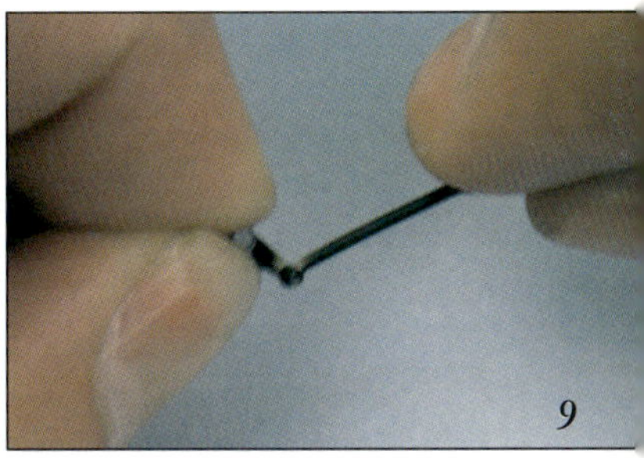
9

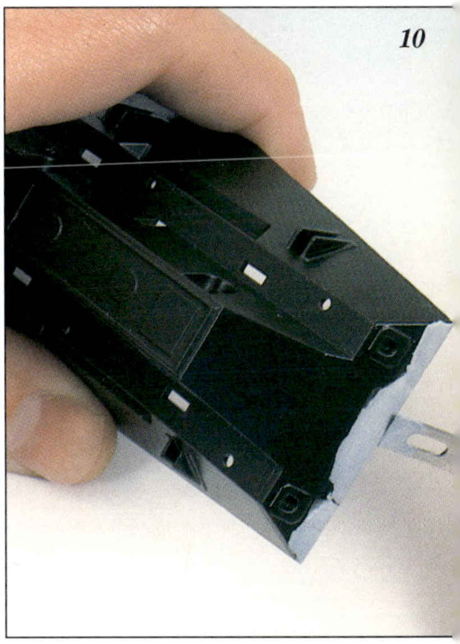
10

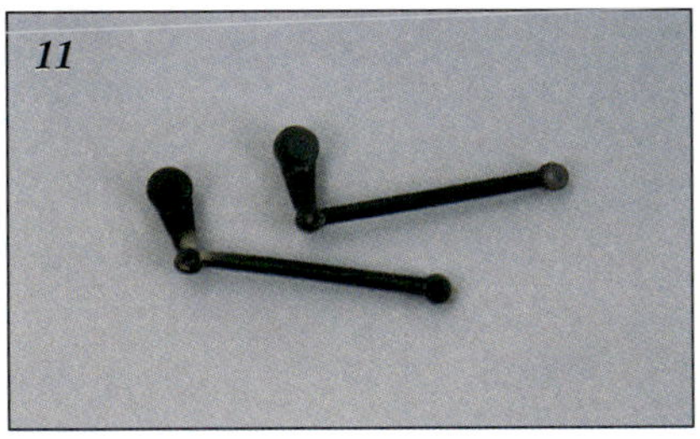
11

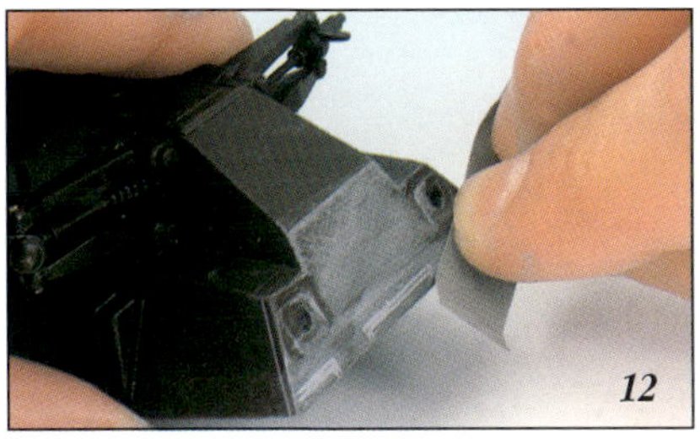
12

13

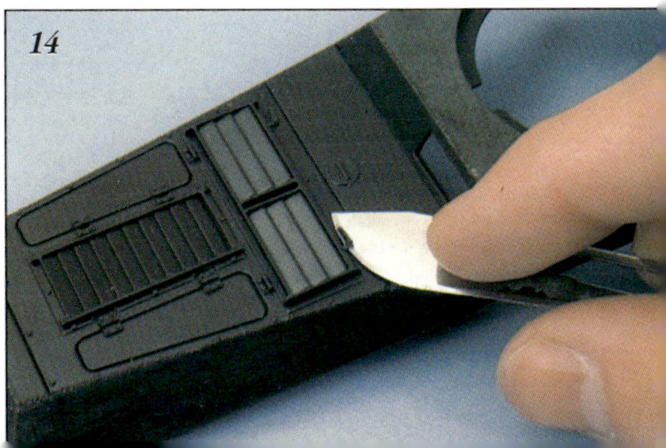
14

rying the shells back and forth. We daren't report in on our radio, as that would mean certain detection. Our only chance is to let our vehicle roll back and down the hill without using the engine to turn around (our vehicle is equipped with two steering wheels) and thus go and report directly. However, we don't move, the temptation is much too strong and the chance is a once in a lifetime one, we won't get a better chance to attack while the enemy is distracted.

I give the order for our 50mm main gun to be loaded with a high explosive and aim directly at the spot were the ammunition has been piled by the Russians. From our actual position, it is almost impossible to miss. The projectile explodes among the rockets. It's a direct hit, the explosion is truly incredible, and destroys just about everything. The next round perforates one of the light tanks. Basically, all the shots are aimed at the armored vehicles that could otherwise have followed us. The crews were outside their vehicles so we have truly caught them by surprise. They do not stand a chance, the field is now a sea of fire and smoke, with distant explosions.

The smoke assists our escape, the driver steers us down the slope using the rear steering wheel. The turret points back covering our escape. We reach our maximum speed, about 30 km per hour that, at that moment, seems too damned slow. We fear that all the hell we stirred up may reach us. We escape by frequently changing direction, and avoiding all visible paths. We have traveled quite a ways before we see the unmistakable rockets' stelae, and hear the 'whizzing' of the projectiles. Some of them pass directly overhead while others pass on either side. We pass through the town that is being bombarded and see how the buildings crumble as if a giant's hand has smashed them. Flying debris from the buildings hits our vehicle's armored sides. Doubtless, the Russians believe they have been attacked by a greater force, when all it was is a small 'sting' from a 'puma' on a big 'elephant' using a gun instead of a trunk. The disproportionate reply was provoked by the action of the finest reconnaissance vehicle of WWII. The above is an account of an actual event that took place on the Eastern Front during the autumn of 1944.

The Puma was definitely the finest reconnaissance vehicle of the war, stealthy, a magnificent suspension and drive train, better armored and well armed. It carried a well-tested 50mm Pak Kwk39L-60 gun mounted in a specially designed turret for the aborted Leopard reconnaissance vehicle, and later used on the Puma. The semi-automatic gun, equipped with a hydro-pneumatic stabilizing system, could be aimed and fired quite quickly, and certainly faster than any contemporary vehicle. The Tatra Diesel 210hp engine was slow to catch fire, and with an effective range of some 1000 km, it was ideal for reconnaissance missions. In addition, each wheel was independently powered and sprung. The front and rear wheels could also be steered independently.

It was the weapon that German units were waiting for. Its only major drawback was its high price and difficult manufacture so, as a result, just 2300 units were made on the Sdkfz-234 chassis and, of these, just a few of them were Pumas. It was the typical German case of too little, too late.

ASSEMBLY

In order to give it a personal touch, we are going to turn the wheels. By doing this, we can break up the vehicle's symmetry, and allow us to integrate it into just about

15. In order to remove the plastic grills, carefully drill the holes to allow the later placement of replacement photo-etched parts.

16. Here can be seen all the drill holes.

17. Remove the part with a knife.

18. Scrape the surface with a knife to make it smooth.

19. This must be done carefully, trying not to cut too much at once.

20. Careful work gives excellent results.

21. Weld seams are done with a knife attached to a soldering iron.

22. This is the desired effect.

23. If we want to make dents on the surface, we can do them with the soldering iron. Don't let the tool come into direct contact with the plastic surface.

24. Once the plastic is soft, make the dent with the end of a brush.

25. Dents can be as large or as small as you want, according to the amount of pressure applied.

26. This particular effect only works on fenders and other thin parts, don't try it on the main armor plating.

27. Holding the knife correctly allows you to scrape the part to make it thinner.

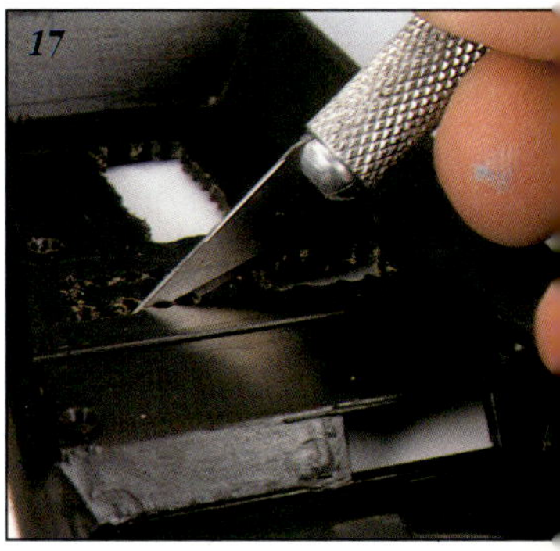

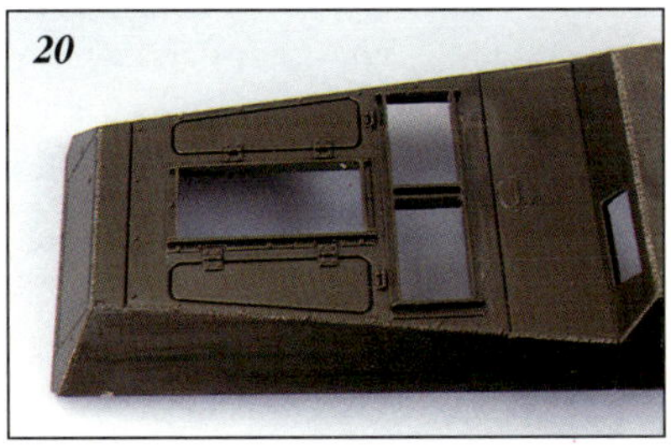

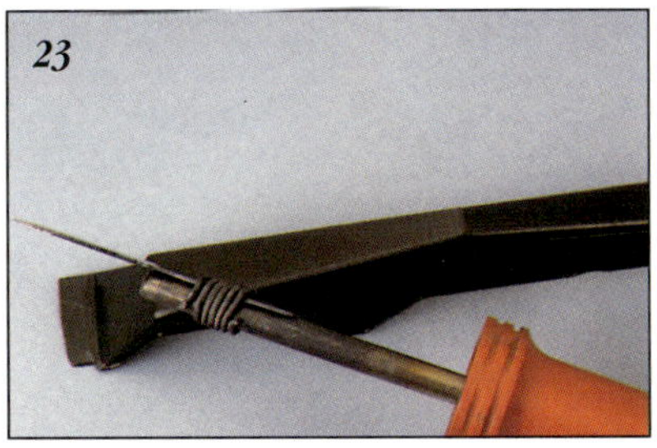

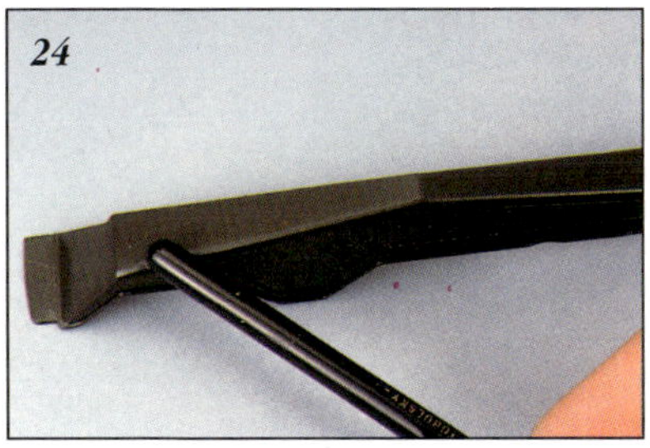

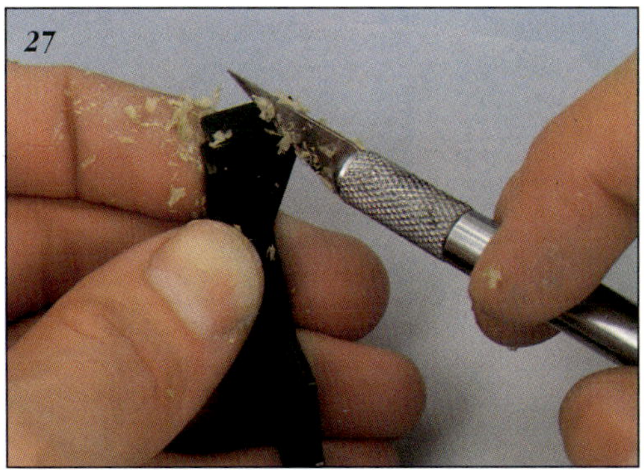

any background. This modification is done by drilling a hole in the wheel's support and inserting a metal pin, which allows the wheels to be turned. Once the wheels are in position, it is best to glue them with superglue.
Before gluing both halves of the chassis, first hollow out the engine grill. Later, it will be replaced with a photo-etched part, making the model look far more realistic. Special care must be taken while carrying out this procedure, as we will be using a mini-drill and if a mistake is made, the kit will be ruined.
Further detailing jobs include adding the weld seams between all the armor plating. A pyrogravure tool can be used, or a 14 watt soldering iron with a knife blade for a tip. The latter is the cheapest option and gives excellent results. There may be some areas the soldering cannot reach. In this case, make the weld seams using thin lines of filler.
The soldering iron is also excellent for making dents in the armor plate. Heat the model's surface with the soldering iron and then make the dent with a brush handle. If the result is not quite right or is too deep, fill it with putty and, once dry, sand the surface flat again.
Once we have made the dents, it is always best to thin the fenders by scraping them with a knife. Thinner fenders are consistent with an actual vehicle and will be in scale.
Just like aircraft, joinlines between the plates must be marked. This is done effectively with a scriber, a tool specially designed for this job. Use the scriber and a steel rule to mark the lines on the model's surface. The tool has a sharp, slightly curved tip that will 'plough' a line on the plastic surface. If a deeper line is needed, simply draw the scriber along the line as many times as necessary.
This tool is particularly useful, but it is not absolutely necessary. To buy or not to buy is really up to the individual modeler.
A detail that can make the model look realistic is to raise the drivers' viewing slot. Do this by placing a piece of clear acetate from another German model kit inside it.
On the turret, the gunner's aiming slot can be opened using a small drill and then polishing it with edge of a knife. The muzzle of the machine gun can also be drilled out. If it is planned to include a figure exiting the gunner's hatch, a knee-high plastic support for the machine gun should be scratch built. Cut a plastic ring (0.13mm thick) and glue it onto the turret's base. The ring will serve to raise the turret slightly, with the result that the paint will not be scratched when turning the turret. The plastic gun barrel can be changed for a Jordi Rubio turned-aluminium one. Of course, you can always eliminate the mold line by sanding it, but the result will never be as good as the substitute.
You might be able to find some 'U'-shaped periscopes in the spares box. If so, sand them down a little and hollow out the spot where they can be attached to the photo-etched grill, and fix them onto the model. The photo-etched grill is there to protect the smoke extractor device behind it.
Pieces such as headlights, crank, and tools can be sourced from other kits, as the ones supplied are not very good. The exhaust silencer is too small, so it has to be enlarged. Glue a piece of Plasticard to the side of the silencer and sand it down. Then, build up the silencer's base with thin Plasticard, and make the exhaust itself from a length of suitable plastic rod. That just about finishes this stage of the assembly.

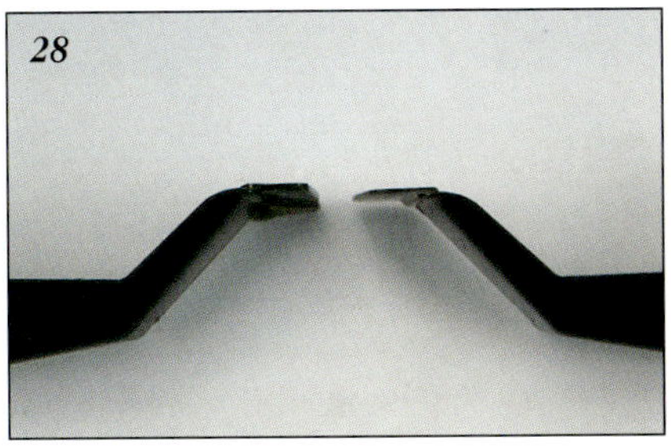

28. A comparison between a trimmed and an untrimmed piece.

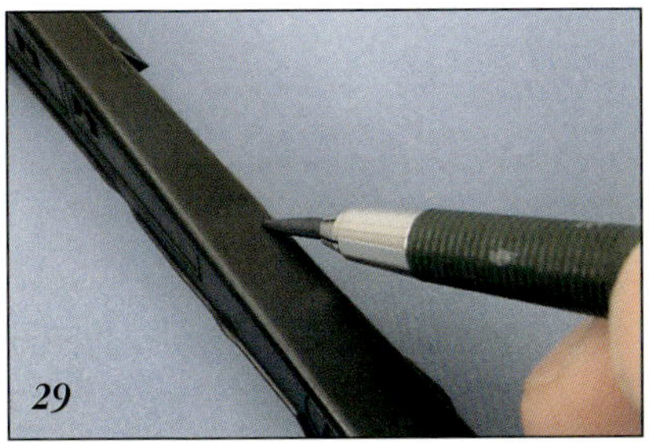

29. The joins between the armor plating are first marked with pencil.

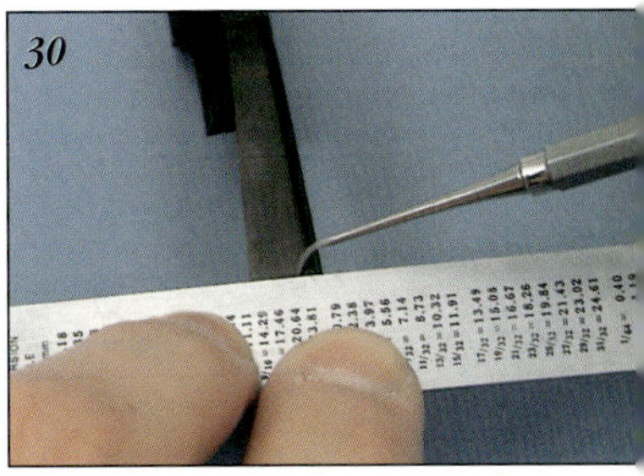

30. The join itself is marked with the scriber, using a steel rule as a guide.

31. The armored glass part is a resin copy from the Tamiya Sdkfz 250.

32. The fastenings and supports for this part are made of plastic rods.

33. Once the fenders are glued, apply some filler, diluted with acetone, and sand them smooth.

34. Use 400grain wet and dry paper.

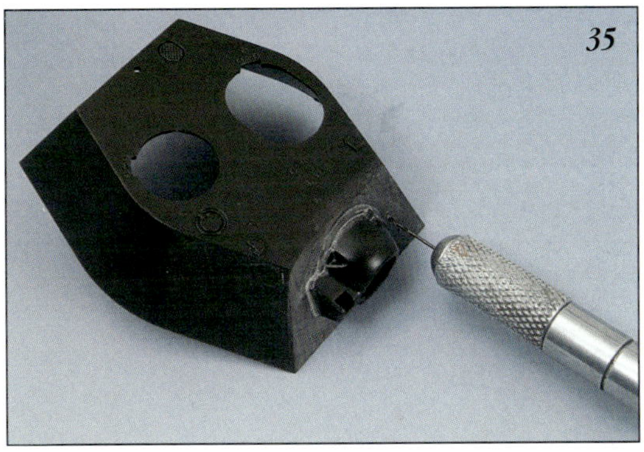

35. The gunner's viewing slot is drilled out.

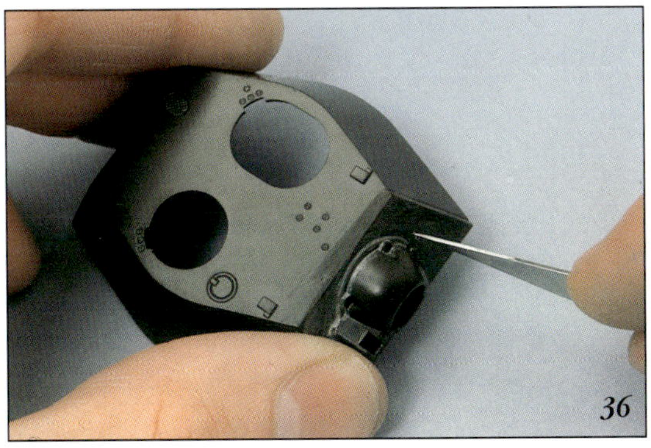

36. The hole should be oval. Make the correct shape with the help of a knife.

37. Finished hole.

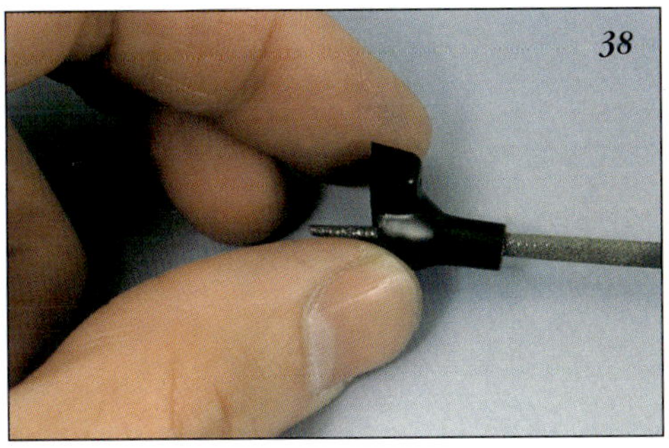

38. The aluminum gun barrel can only be fitted inside if the hole is first opened out with a 'mouse tail file

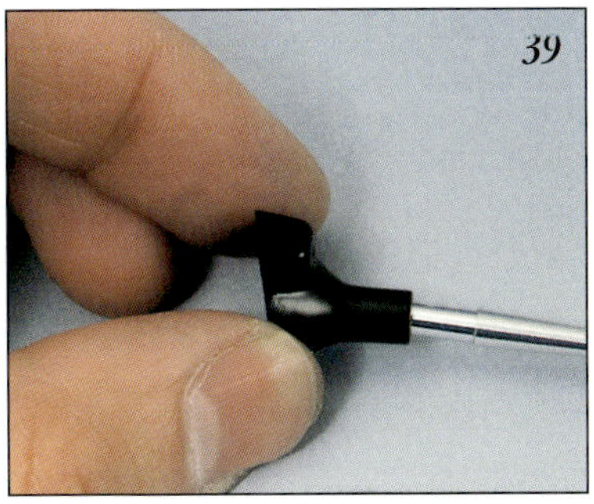

39. Check to see it fits and then glue it with super glue.

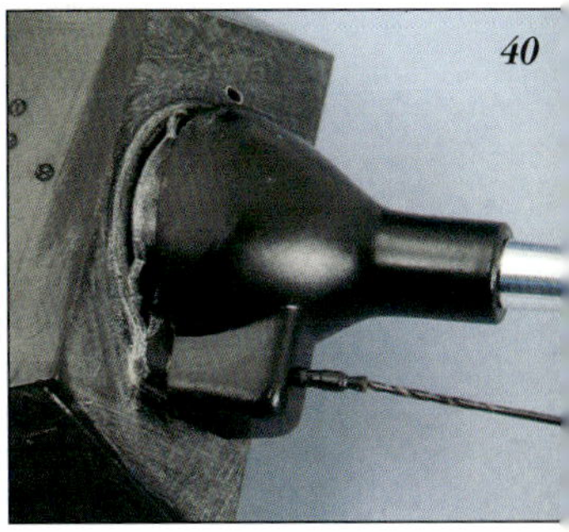

40. The muzzle of the machine gun is hollowed out with a 0.8mm drill.

41. On the lower part, make a plastic platform to support the figure.

42. Glue a thin plastic ring to the turret base. The ring is cut using a circle cutting tool.

43. Once it is set in place, mark the parts that require trimming.

44. The ring will eliminate unwanted paint scratches when rotating the turret.

45. There are some fastening plates on the edges of the shock absorbers that must also be trimmed down as previously described.

46. Using some putty, roll out very thin rod with your fingers.

47. Roll the putty rod onto the shock absorber and thin it down with an acetone-soaked brush.

48. Work it in well with the brush until the sides blend in with the original piece.

49. Using a knife to texture the join in order to make it look like a weld seam. In this way, the same effect can be achieved as with the soldering iron.

50. On the gun shield, make a modified shock absorber along with an unmodified one.

51. The periscope shields must be sanded down… they are too big!

52. Compare the sanded part with the original part.

53. The vent hole on the turret must be hollowed out with a knife.

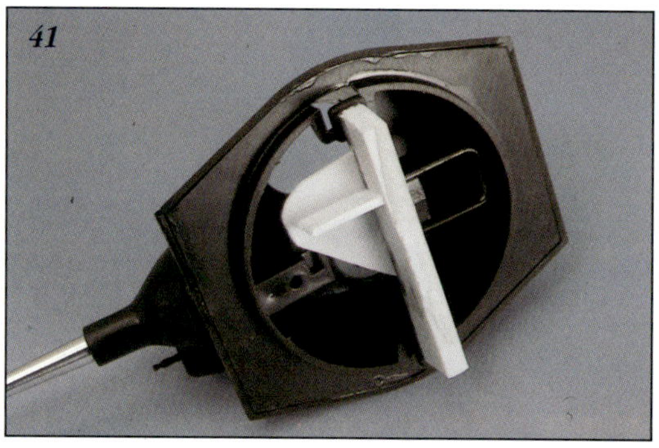

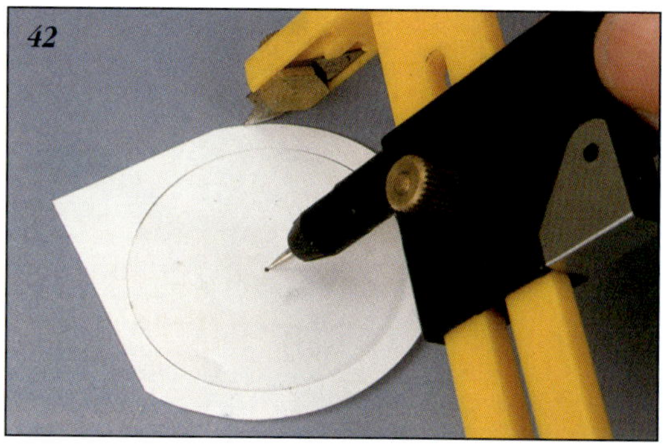

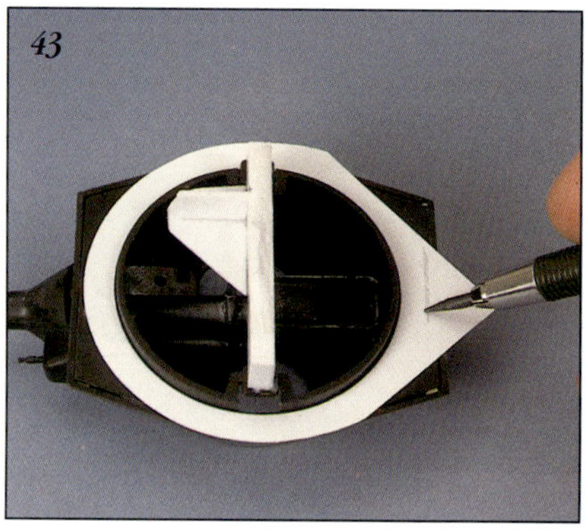

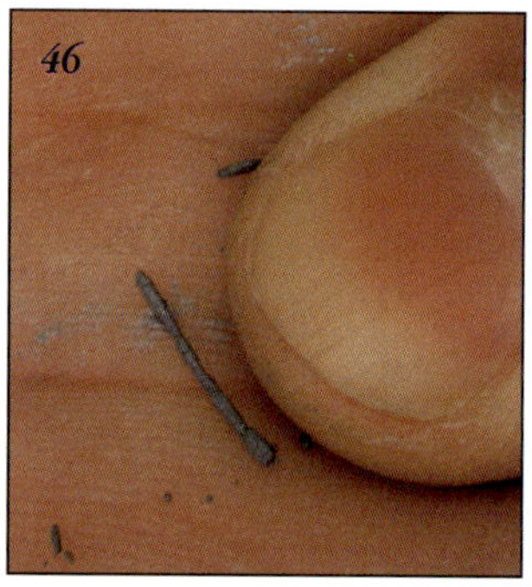

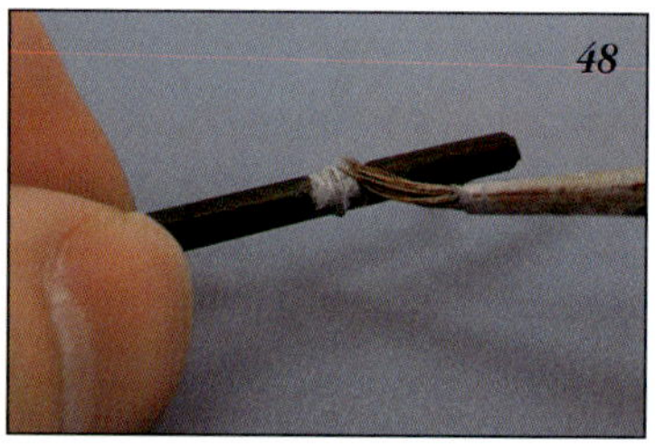

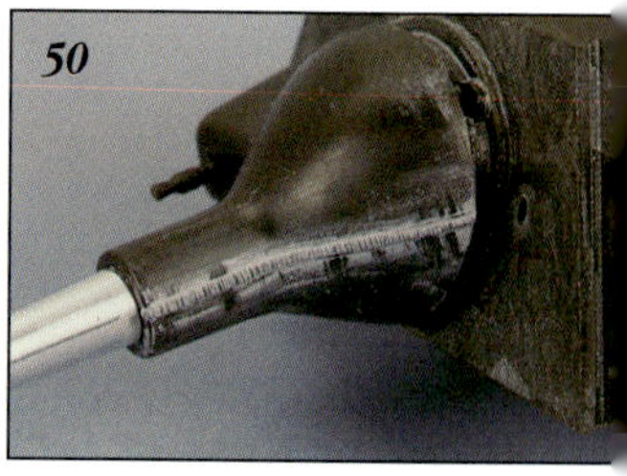

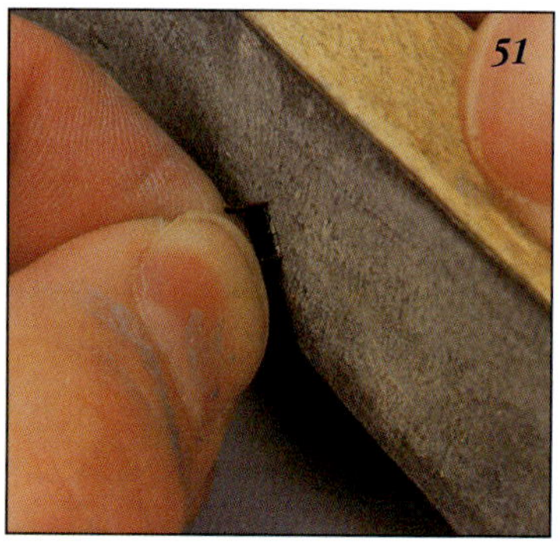

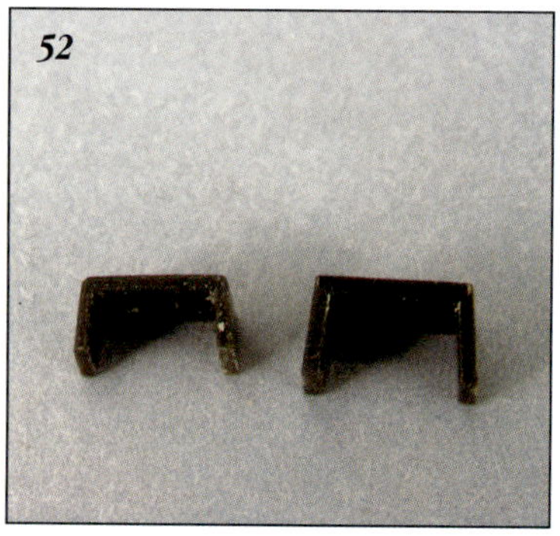

54. The features sticking out of the exhaust must be removed with a knife blade.

55. 1mm plasticard is glued to one side of the part to make it bigger.

56. Glue a plastic strip to the curved part.

57. The exhaust is glued to a thin plastic rectangle

58. Glue three sprockets onto each end of the rectangle.

59. Reconstruct the tube from plastic rod, and then curve it up using heat and pressure.

60. The crank is from Tamiya to which has been added two metal handles and a hand crank from plastic rod.

61. Glue copper wire to the headlight.

62. Two entomologists' needles and a hypodermic needle are used to make the parking bar references.

63. The needles are inserted inside the 6mm hypodermic needle sections.

64. The antenna sported by the command units was made from thin steel rod and six small plastic rods.

65. Draw a cross onto a piece of paper. In the center, fix a rivet. Onto this, you can glue the first plastic rod (use the cross as a visual reference).

66. Following this procedure, and still using the cross as a visual reference, glue the remaining rods with super glue.

67. The distance between each rod must be the same. Use the drawn the cross as a guide. (Note the picture angle)

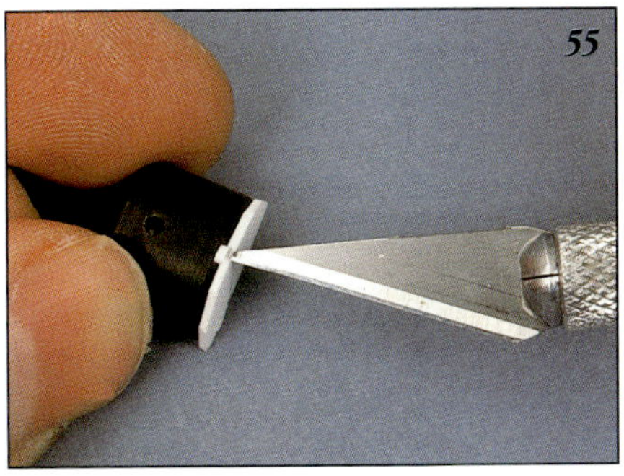

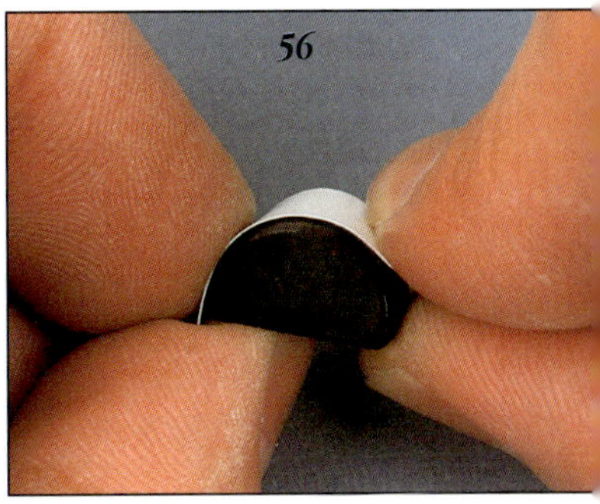

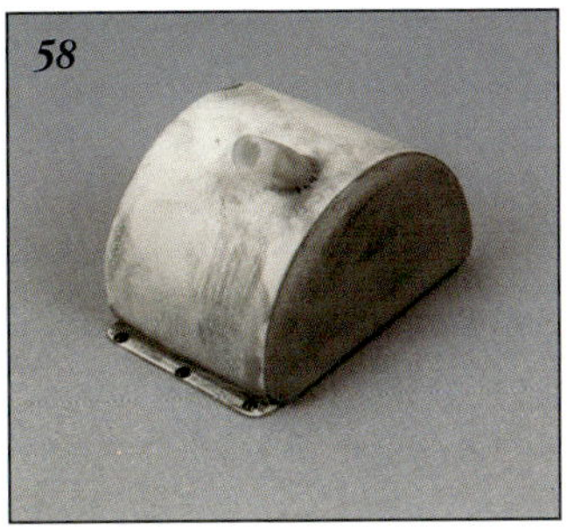

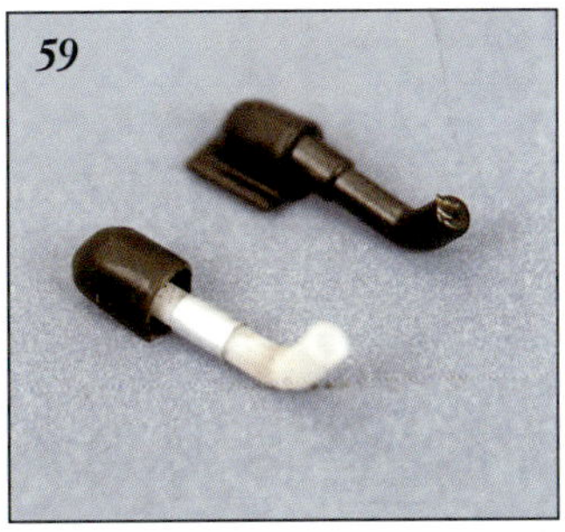

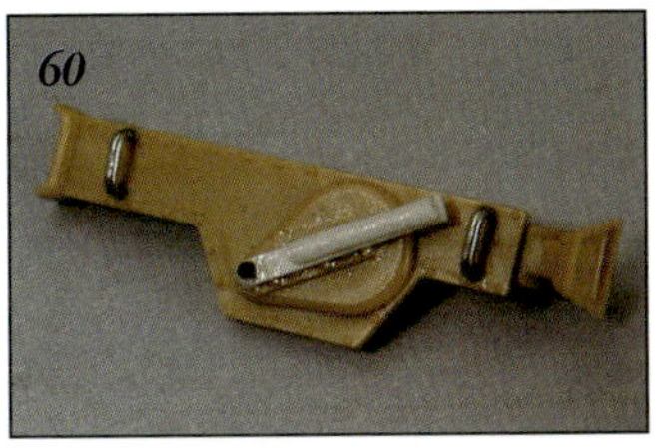

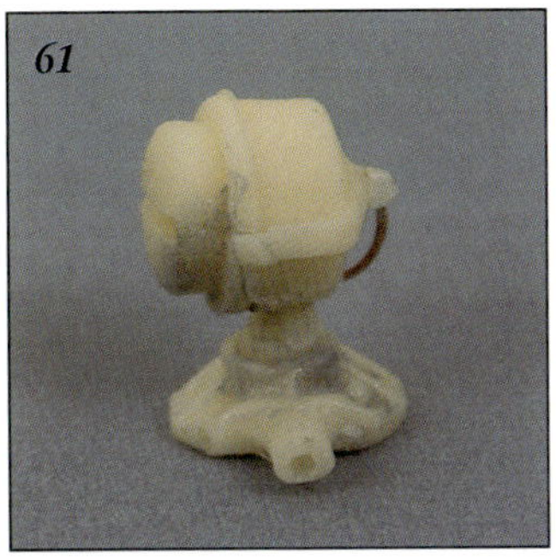

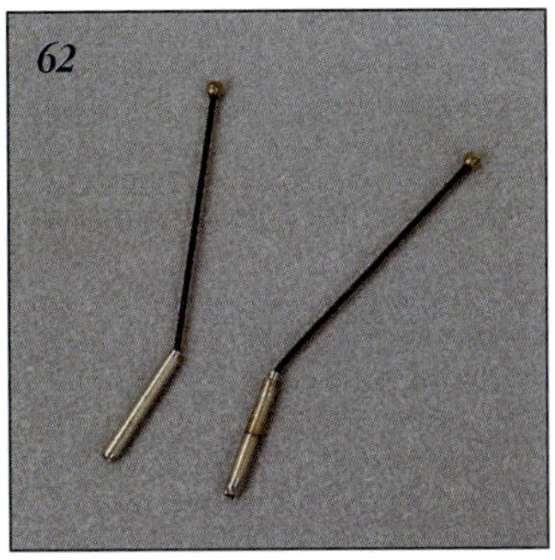

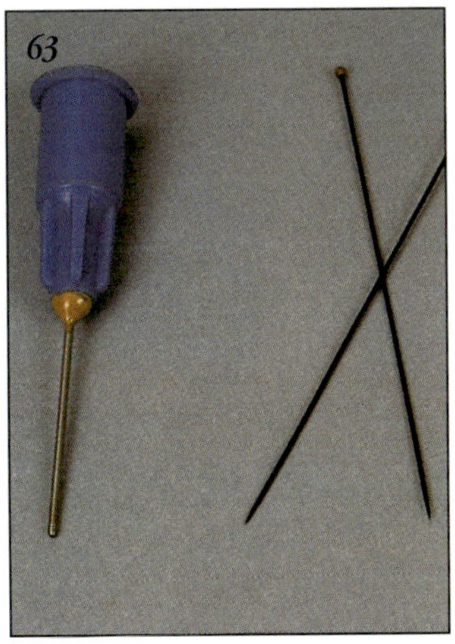

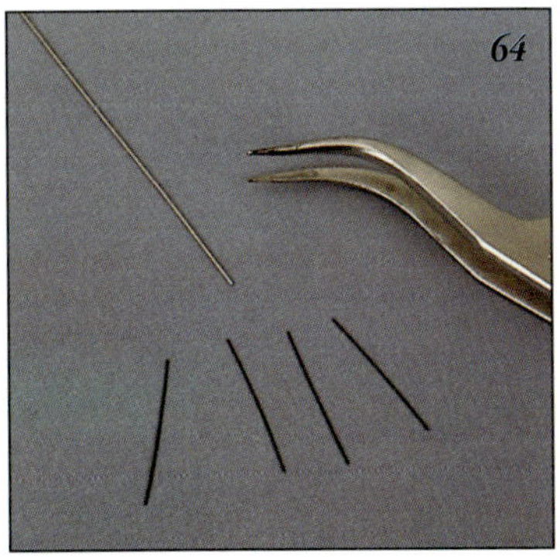

What & How

Photo-etched sheet

Photo-etched sheets are made from steel or brass, and they come with a myriad of different parts designed specifically to improve a basic model kit; grills, fastenings, etc. They are all flat parts with very subtle reliefs. However, once they have been bent into a specific shape, they can be quite bulky. Usually, photo-etched sheets are designed for a specific model kit, but generic sheets are also available which cover many vehicles. These generic sheets reproduce rivets, bolts, lashes, etc. There are also sheets that can be used as masks when painting numbers, insignia, emblems, and such like. These masks are intended for used with an airbrush, and the results are really stunning and realistic. It is very clear that photo-etched sheets are absolutely necessary for detailing a model. Photo-etched parts confer details that are quite simply unattainable in plastic.

There are two ways to remove the parts from the photo-etched sheet. The first one is to cut them off using modeler's scissors. The second is to use a regular X-Acto knife with the photo-etched sheet lying on a hard, flat surface (this will avoid unwanted deformations of the sheet). Each modeler must choose their preferred method.

Once the part has been separated, carefully remove any surplus metal with a file, being very careful not to bend the piece. It is also wise to sandpaper the area to be glued, because this will help the super glue (always use this type of glue) to adhere. Parts should be manipulated with curved-tipped pliers, especially if it is going to be positioned in a 'hard-to-get-at' area.

Parts that require bending usually have bend lines. Smaller parts can be bent using flat-tipped pliers, and larger parts can be bent against a steel rule. Push the other end of the part with the flat side of a knife, until the correct angle is obtained.

As a rule, do remember to be extra careful when manipulating photo-etched parts as they are quite delicate. Also, try not to lose any small parts, because some manufacturers don't 'print' extra pieces onto the sheet, which means you may have to purchase a new sheet.

1. Tools commonly used for applying photo-etched parts.

2. Precision cutting tools are available to the modeler. Great care must be taken during the cutting process to avoid deformation and eventual ruin of the part.

3. Remove any sprue residue very carefully with a file, so the part does not get bent.

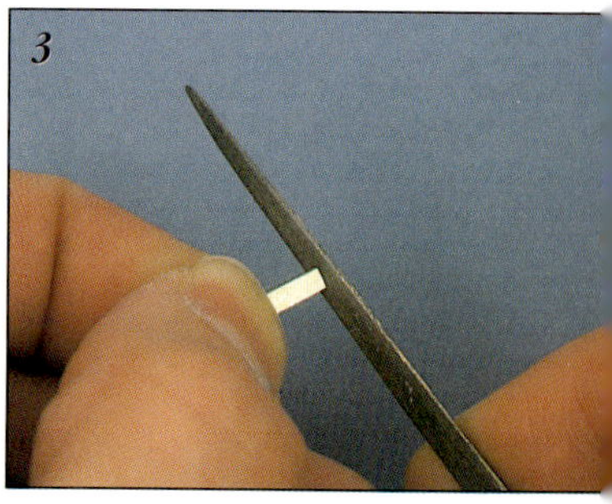

4. Holding the part with flat nosed pliers, place it on the back of a steel rule.

5. Apply pressure against the ruler while turning the wrist.

6. A bent part. This is part number 8 and is a cover for the lower area.

7. The number 2 parts for covering the engine's ventilation aperture. Precision pliers are absolutely necessary for the job.

8. Next, glue parts numbered '1'. Precision gluing such as this calls for super glue in gel form. It allows you to correct the part's position during gluing.

9. After gluing parts 3 and 4, apply a thin layer of putty that tells us whether or not the pieces are properly positioned.

10. In the picture, to the left, can be seen the four rivets added to the upper part.

11. Two hinges have been glued on the rear, number 17. Also glue two small plastic rods and fix six No.12 parts around it.

12. Glue on the plastic rods, Strip No.12 with two plastic rivets.

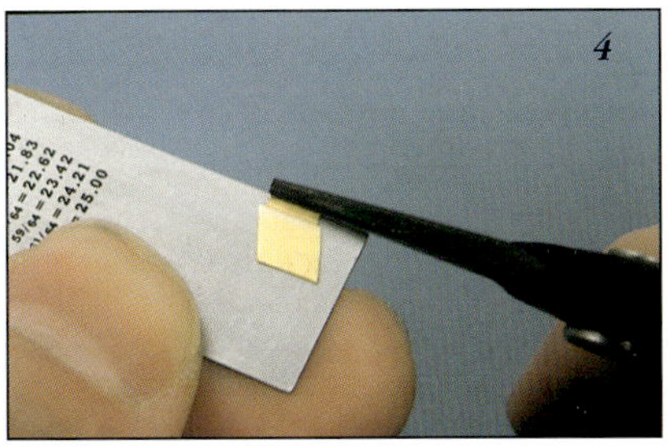

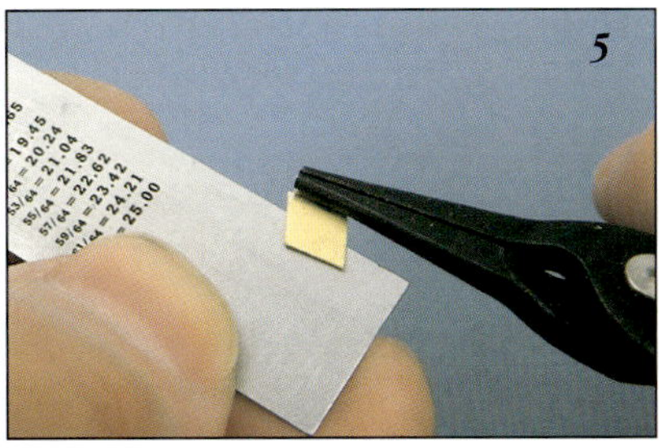

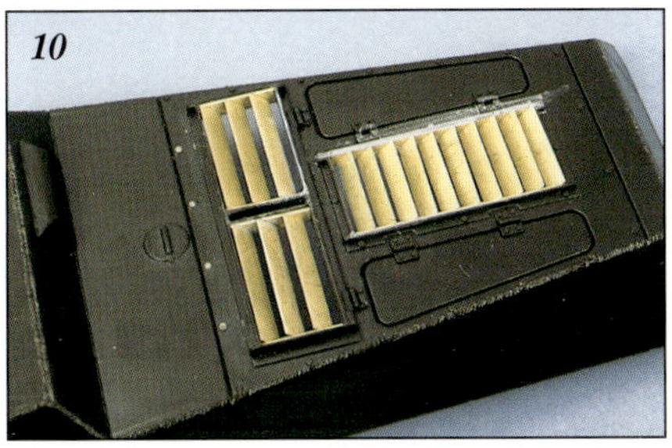

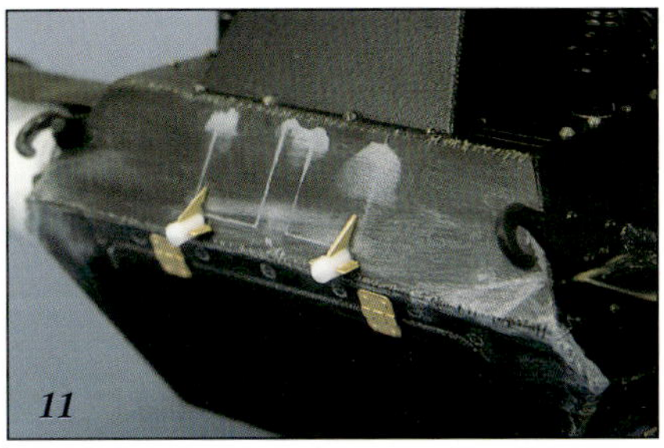

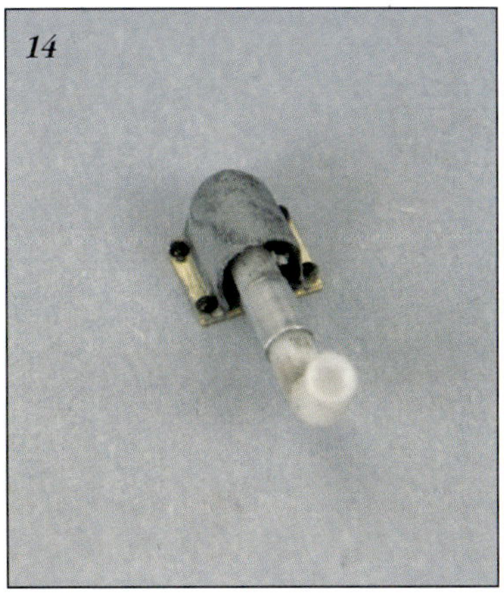

13. Position part No. 9 on the exhaust, the part with the shield.

14. Four plastic rivets are glued to the rear of the part.

15. The box onto which is fixed the antenna base is numbered as part 37. The cable anchors are part Nos. 32 and 33. The photo-etched sheet provides an extra 'butterfly' nut. This is a delicate part, so look after it carefully otherwise it will get lost.

16. Jerry can containers: Two No.7 parts and a No.5.

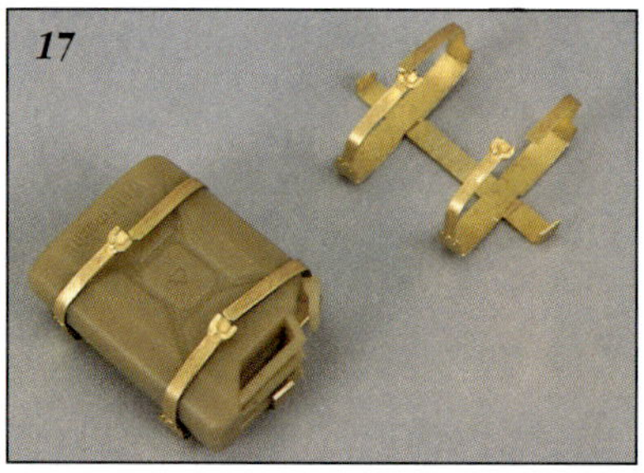

17. No.7 parts must be adapted to hold the jerry can.

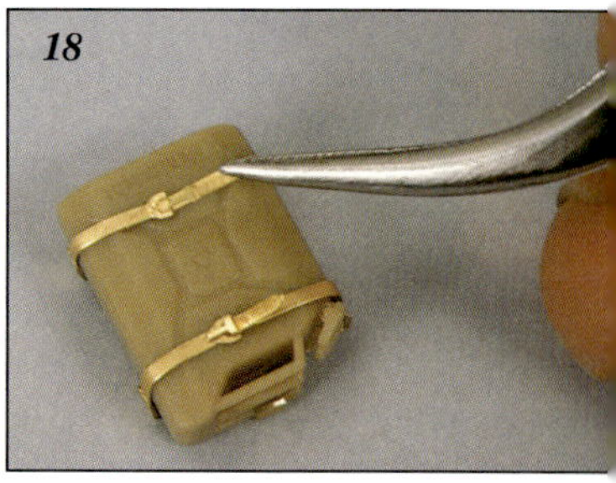

18. The tips of the containers (also parts No.7) should be glued last.

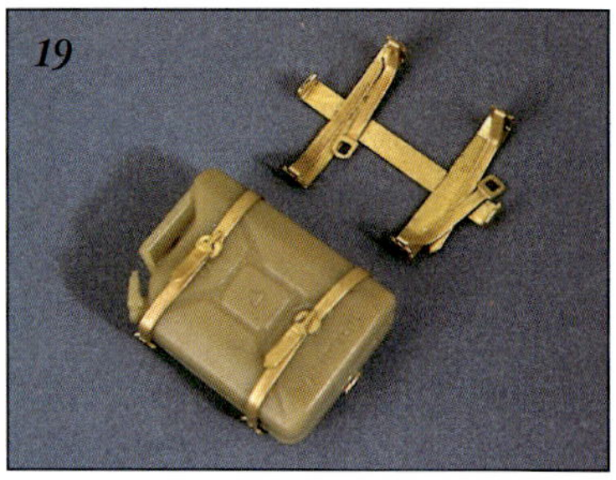

19. If you wish to have a holder without a can, assemble part No.5 along with two No.6 parts, allowing the 'leather straps' to hang naturally.

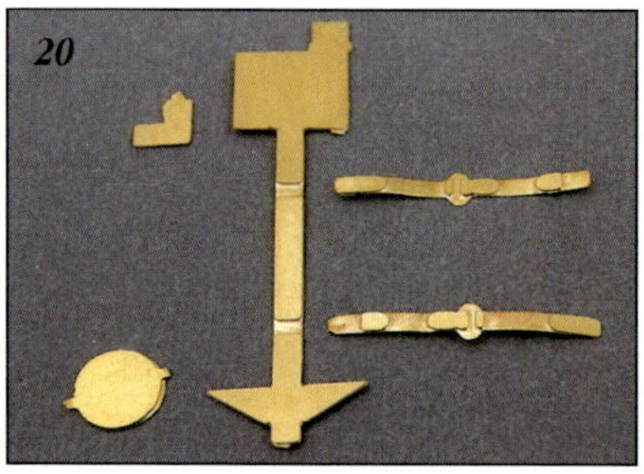

20. The fire extinguisher's straps are 5 photoetch parts, No.13.

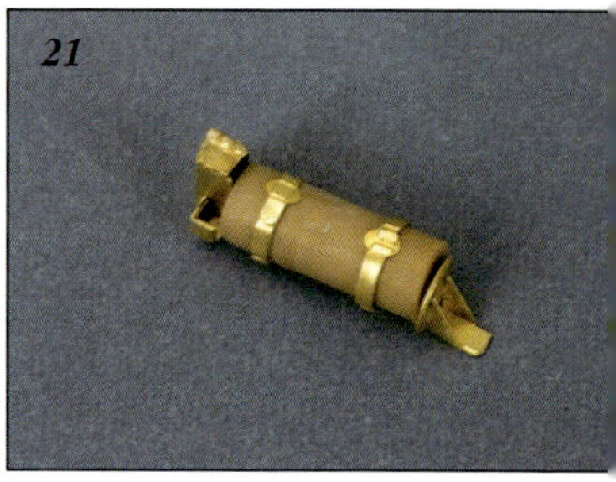

21. A completed part. Note that the straps are not fastened in the same direction.

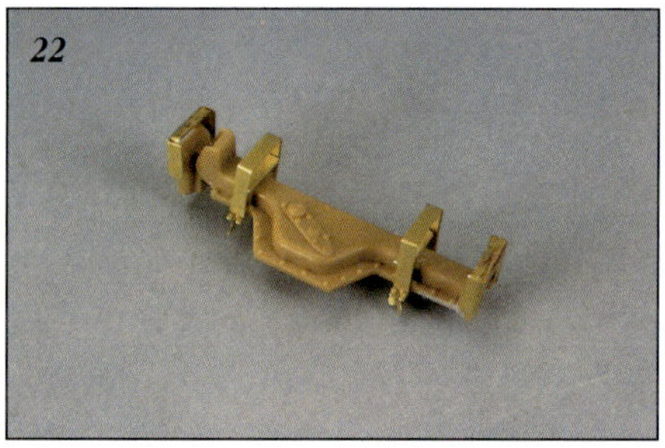

22. On the lower part we have placed two leftover straps, between the crank and parts No.21.

23. In this picture can be seen the result of the work on the photo-etched jerry can straps, fire extinguisher and crank.

24. The small fastenings around the upper part of the chassis are No.20. On the sheet are other smaller fastenings that will not be used as they belong to the Sdkfz 234/3 Puma with the 75mm gun.

25. No.33 parts are reference rods. There's a loose latch to the right.

26. Part No.10 has been shaped using a steel rule and bending it with a knife blade.

27. Shape it by turning your wrist until it has bent through 90 degree.

28. Repeat the process for the other end.

29. Obtain the correct angle by moving your wrist.

30. Shaped parts. This bending method is applicable for all the large parts that can't be bent with pliers. If the part is quite large, use a bigger knife.

31-32. Front and rear of part No.10. Part No.11 must be glued to it. Four rivets, a hinge and four bolts have also been glued to it. The four screwsbolts are to hold the spare tire (made of plastic).

33. The spare wheel support adds character to the rear of the vehicle. Parts No. 40 are the rear position lights and cover.

34. The position lights' support plate is part No.39. The position lights proper are plastic cubes.

35. On top of the toolbox there should be an axe and a pair of cutters. Part No.25 is the axe support.

36. A Tamiya axe was used.

37. The toolbox cover is part No.14. The fastenings are parts No.16.

38. After the shield parts (No.8) are in position, add electric cables to the headlights.

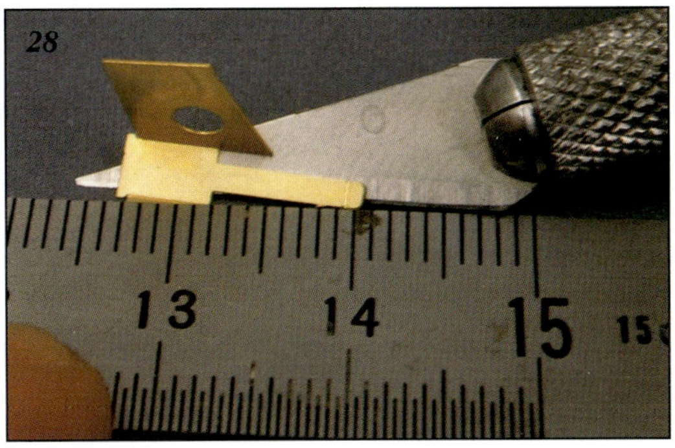

28

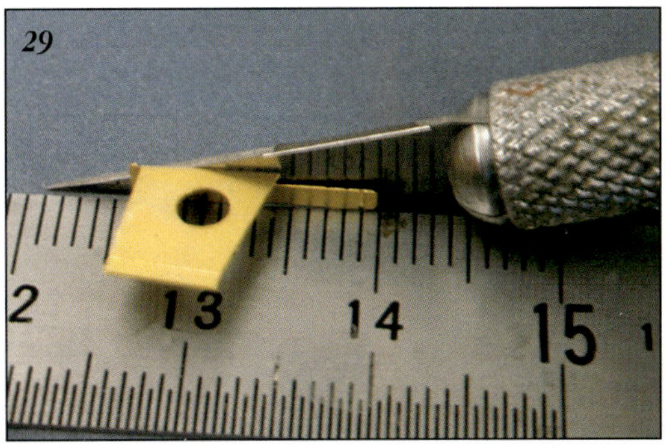

29

30

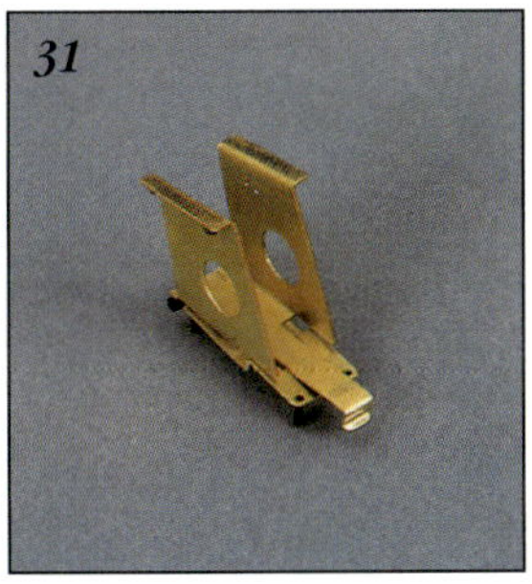
31

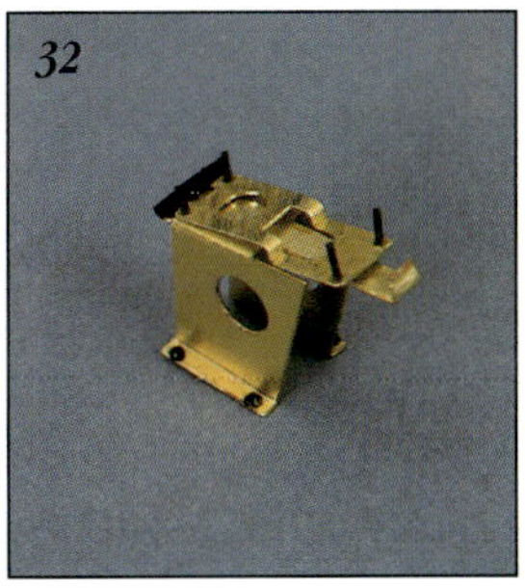
32

33

34

35

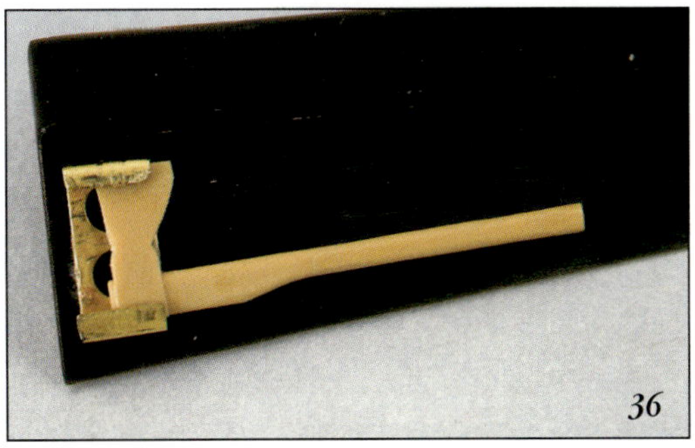
36

37

38

39-40. Parts No.19 are 'fastenings' for the plate holding the smokescreen tubes.

41. The fastenings should be bent as seen in the picture. (This is part No.19)

42. On the rear, glue the rivets that hold each tube in position.

43. The parts for fastening the crank are two No.22 parts plus two No.21 ones. Be careful when bending part No.22, because if you make a mistake, they will be uneven.

44. Electric cables coming out of their respective apertures go back together on the lower slot.

45. On the front, glue a wire that will appear to have picked up the three cables on the back. The wire enters the vehicle on the upper part.

46. By rotating the knife tip, hollow out the three tubes.

47. Completed part. The detail is quite remarkable.

48. There are three fastenings, Part No. 38, on the rear and sides of the turret.

49. On the hatches can be seen the periscopes salvaged from a different kit.

50. On the edge of the gunner's hatch, position parts No.24. These parts were meant to act as fastenings for a lock when the vehicle was stored and out of service.

39

40

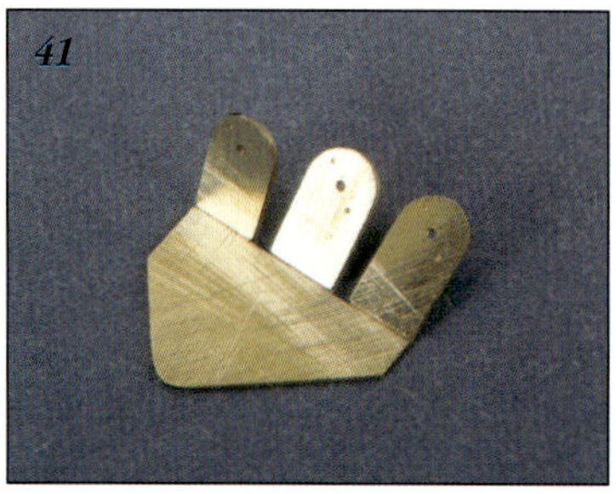
41

42

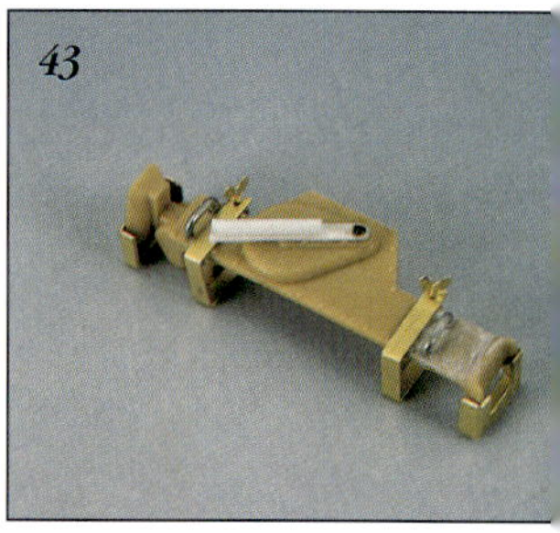
43

44

45

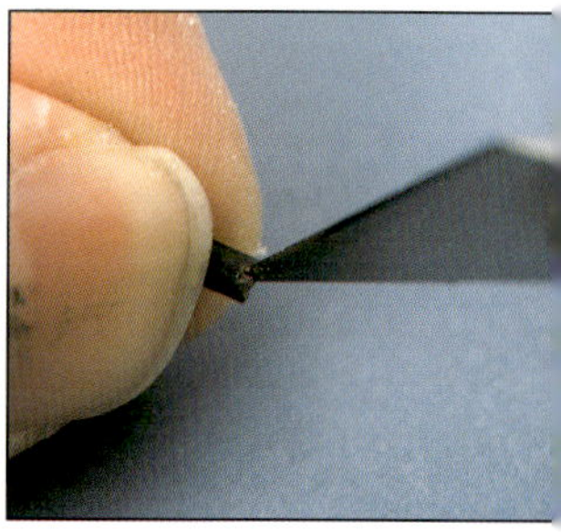

47

48

49

50

19. Using a highly diluted mixture of black and brown, profile all the details and airbrush some dirt. Be very careful and subtle with the airbrush otherwise the model will be ruined. The closer you get, the smaller the dirt spots.

21. Overview of the airbrush 'dirtied' model.

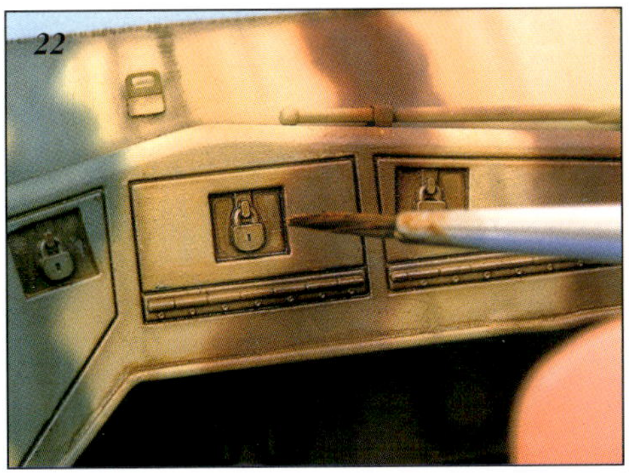

22. Certain areas should be worked with a brush. Do this with highly diluted oil paint.

23. If paint gets onto an unwanted area, remove it with a turpentine soaked brush.

24. Overview of the completed job. Allow a couple of hours to pass before doing any more work on the model. In the meantime, work on the exhausts. Use dark brown as a base color and highlight it with orange. The orange should, at first, be mixed with brown and then the final highlights can be orange alone. That does depend though, on the degree of rust you want to convey.

25. Dry brushing requires one color for each one already on the model.

26. Dip the tip of the brush into the paint.

27. Remove as much excess paint as possible.

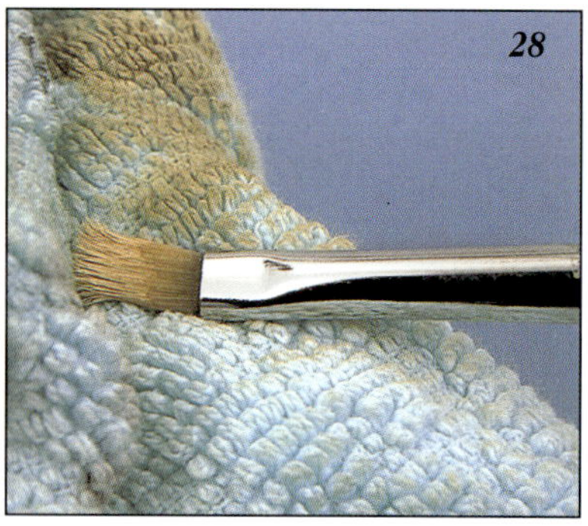

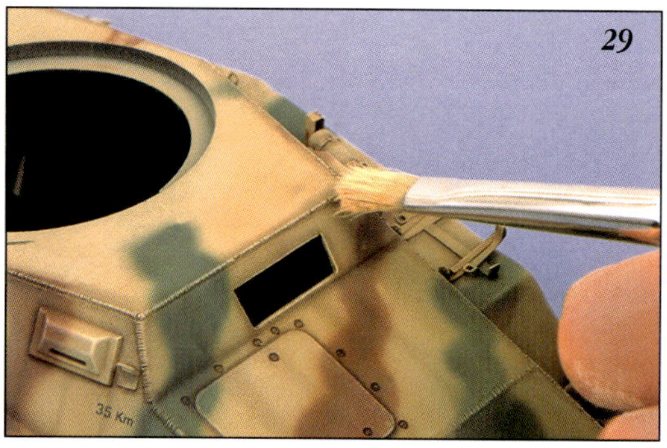

28. Remove most of it onto a clean piece of cloth. Make sure your cloth doesn't disintegrate onto the brush.

29. Brush the edges of the model, leaving just the thinnest film.

30. Do the same with the other colors. Try not to get color on the surrounding areas.

31. On the lower areas, use a mixture of sand and beige.

32. On the right is a dry brushed wheel. Compare it to the one that hasn't been done.

33. Paint peels are applied with a No.1 brush.

34. On the fire extinguisher, apply metal-colored paint on the peeling paint.

35. Peeling paint really gives the vehicle a used appearance. Before 'dusting', matt varnish the model in order to cover the satin gloss of the oil paint.

36. Airbrush highly diluted sand color onto the lower areas to give them a dusty appearance.

37. Once the dusting process is completed, the result is a very realistic looking vehicle, suitable for placing in any background.

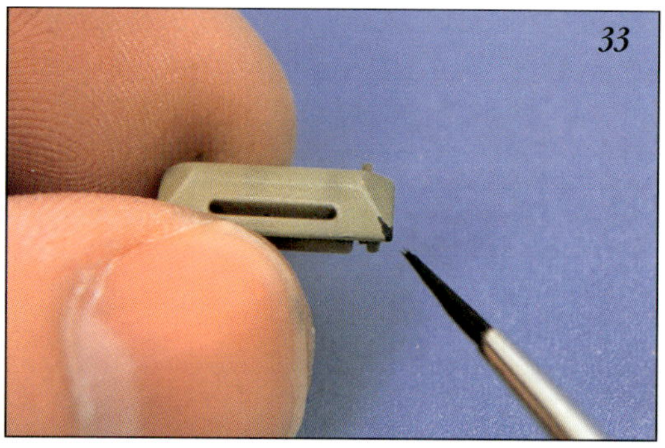

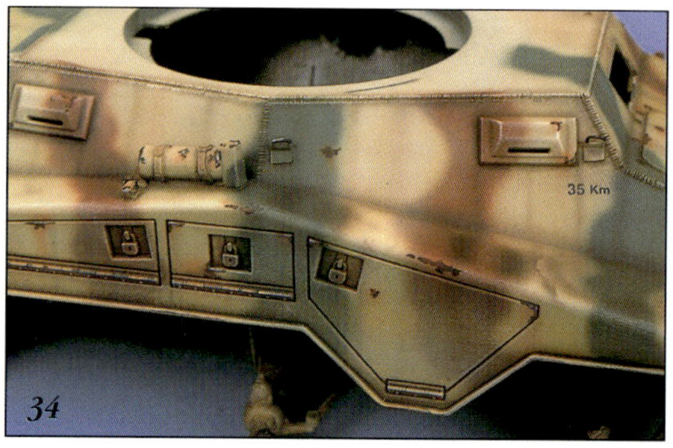

Foreword

Modelers are people with well-defined personalities and peculiar tastes. Some favor the assembly process while others prefer to put their best work into the paintjob. The latter are in the majority as they enjoy assembling the model straight out of the box and then have a field day with the paintjob, thus saving themselves the long-winded detailing jobs, including photo-etched sheets. The first type of person, on the other hand, enjoys obtaining the last bit of detail and modeling an almost perfect reproduction. However, when the time comes to paint, they approach it with trepidation and end up applying some color, a simple camouflage scheme and, maybe, a little dry brushing.

Common sense tells us that both methods are incomplete. The perfect procedure is to combine them both. However, there is a suitable middle course between the photo-etched detailing and a scratch-built part here and there, and an effective paintjob.

In this next chapter, we will unveil a complete study for those more interested in painting and applying all the techniques, and then, on the other hand, we'll explain a process which deals with photo-etched parts and other significant details. Two Soviet vehicles have been chosen, because they are fairly representative of modern tanks involved in today's conflicts and, therefore, they have some history to them. As will be seen, all the related processes can be applied to other models, whether from WWI, II or a more recent conflict.

Operation Desert Storm

Night shadows cover the desert, and the only lights visible are the stars above in a clear sky. Sailing across the desert dunes, the awful armored 'mechanical crabs' churn up clouds of sand along with exhaust smoke. The T-72's jump, they disappear behind the dunes, then reveal themselves again, moving confidently and safely because they have special filters to keep problems at bay. They move as efficiently as they would in the forest or on the steppe.
Along with the first lights of morning, the first explosions are heard which stir up a hornets nest of return blasts, flashes of light, and vast stacks of smoke. Suddenly, the roaring of strange engines mingles with the roar of our own engines. Appearing like bats, we see the A-10's signaling to us to pass. Luckily for our brigade, the Shid Brigade belongs to the Allies, because I certainly wouldn't like to be inside the Iraqi T-72's. Our vehicles are very similar to theirs and were purchased from Yugoslavia for our country -Kuwait. They are also equipped with special filters, firing aids and other western devices.
We are anxious to face the enemy, but when we arrive at the front there's nothing left to fight, just dead soldiers and others waiting to surrender. All the enemy vehicles have been destroyed by the American A-10 tank-busters and A4-64A Apache attack helicopters, so all that is left to do is round up the prisoners.
Never before had the T-80s been in combat, so there's some natural curiosity in military circles as to how the T-72's will perform against the newer vehicles even if it has many things in common. However, the real test between the latest Russian technology and modern Allied machinery never materialized.
The T-72s are not the latest generation but are somewhere in between. They are technologically comparable to the M-60s, but not comparable to the M-1s. On the outside, they are very similar to the T-80s. The T-72s have a diesel engine, while the T-80, like all modern tanks, has a gas turbine one. The latest generation gun can fire both shells and missiles. The firing devices evolved quickly and if they had had the latest on their T-72s, they could have hoped for some success. However, the truth was that most T-72s were safely destroyed from the air. These circumstances also affected some of our own Allied vehicles, including the M1, Challenger, Bradley and other AFVs that were put out of action by mistake, also with the greatest ease. A crew member from a British Challenger commented, 'We were attacked with uranium projectiles by our own planes. Fired by the A-10s, they went through the armor as

1. Not much reference is available on the market: An Osprey book, a Concord book and the Todo Modelismo magazine.

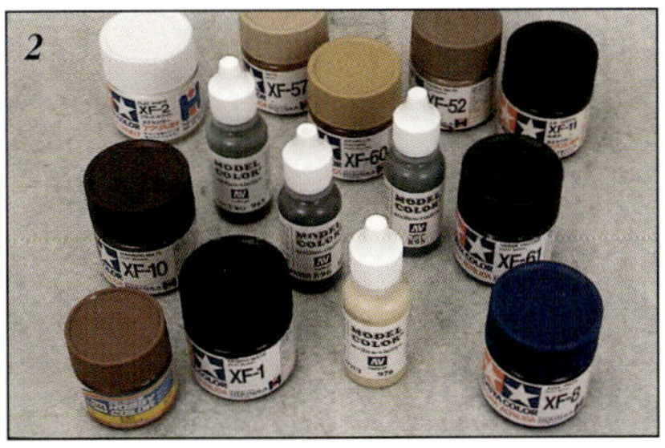

2-3. Airbrush, paint, masking and thinner dispenser.

4. Use an old, thick brush for painting.

5. Put some thinner into the airbrush's reservoir followed by some paint. Stir it well with the brush until you get a milky texture.

6. Test the airbrush first on a piece of paper.

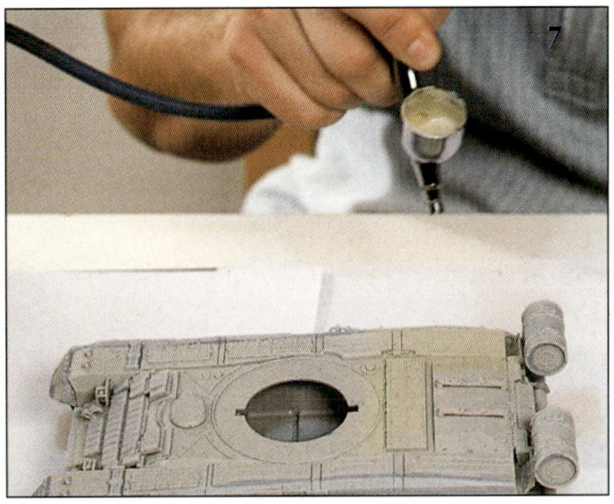

7. Paint is applied in thin coats, constantly moving the airbrush over the model's surface to avoid paint puddles.

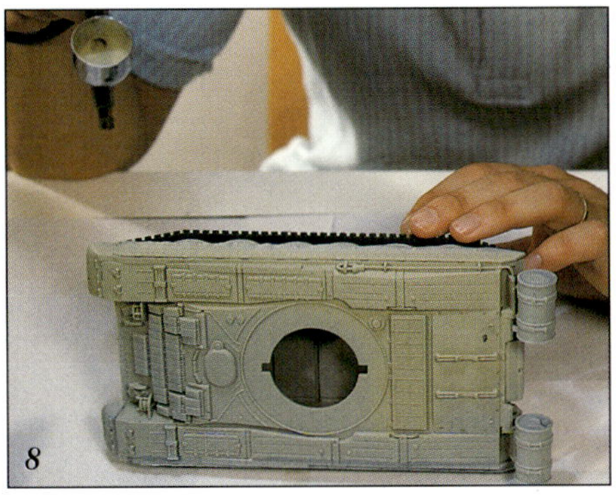

8. Move the model around so it can be painted vertically.

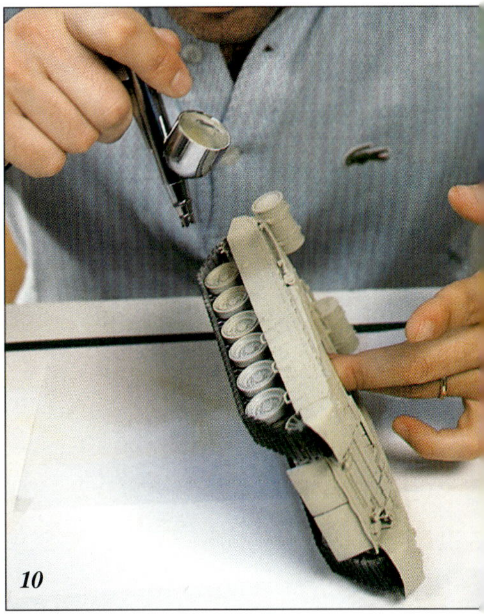

9-11. There are some difficult areas, so you will have to move the model around to ensure the paint gets everywhere.

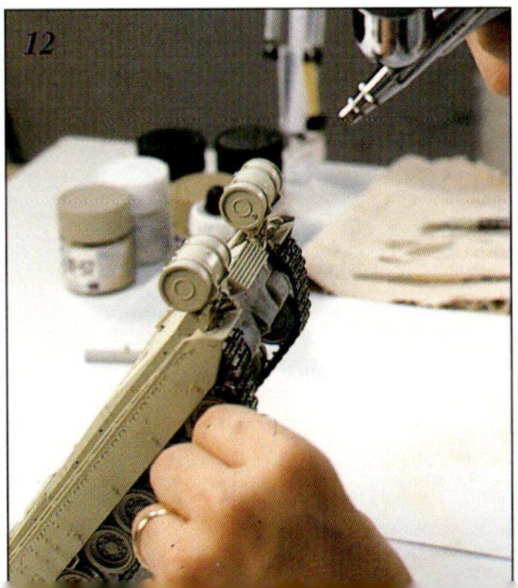

12. Tracks and wheels are particularly difficult: the small gaps between the wheels make them difficult to get behind and all around.

smoothly as they would through wax. If you were lucky to be safe, you still ran the risk of being injured by the radioactive debris. When radioactive debris hits you, you develop very ugly blisters, that wouldn't be out of place in a horror film.'

Officially, there were only two battles against enemy tanks, and both took place at night. During the day, the bombers wouldn't allow a bicycle through. The first one was between the 1st British Armored Division and what remained of the Iraqi Reserve Unit, formed by a heterogeneous mixture of vehicles. The confrontation couldn't even be classed as one, because the British night vision system outranged the enemy's by well over a thousand meters. As a result, they scored direct hits with their first rounds, while the Iraqis were still trying to find the enemy. The other confrontation was much more interesting, because three elite Iraqi Divisions took part, the Republican Guard Medina, the Tawalkanda and the Hammurabi.

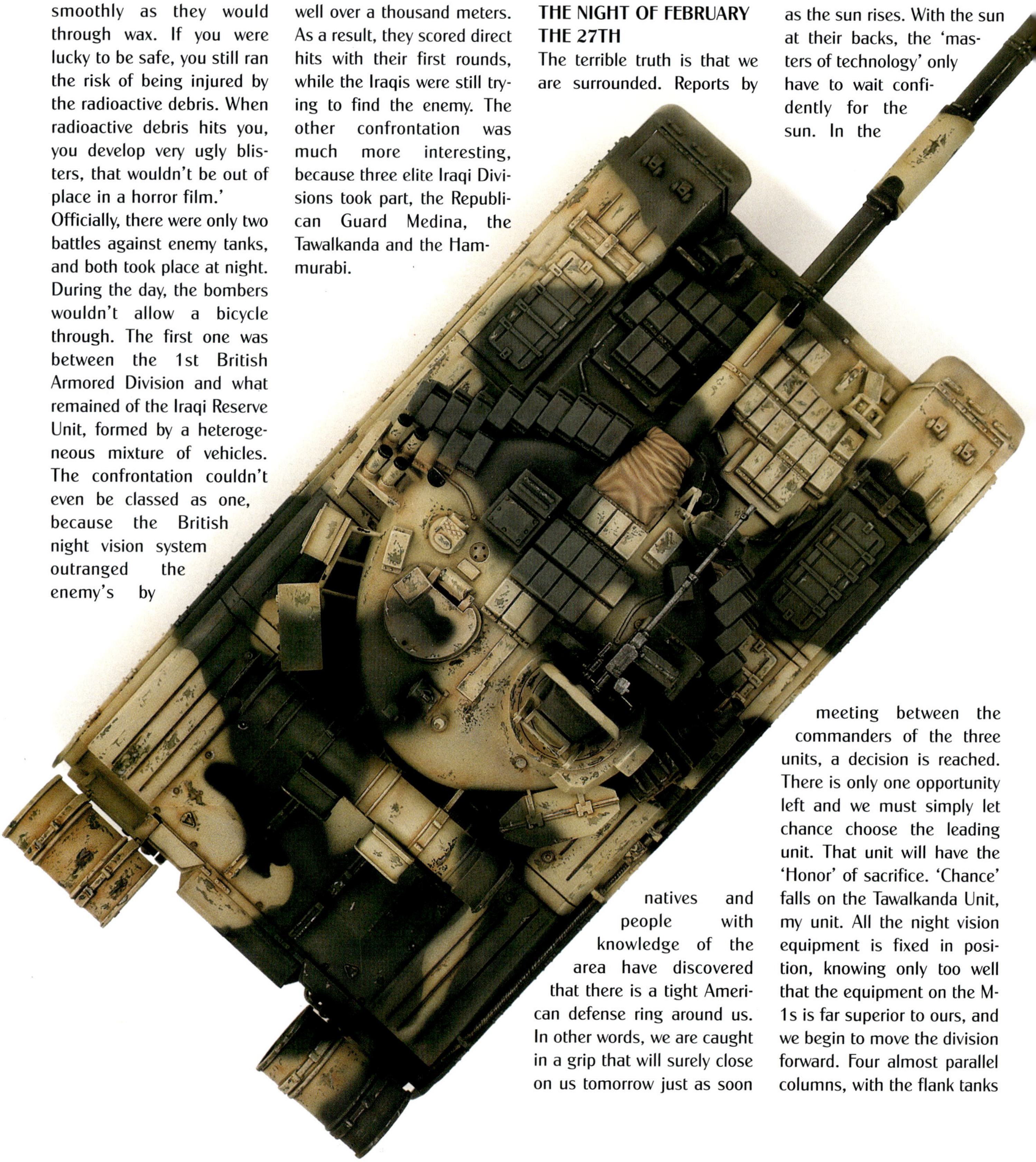

THE NIGHT OF FEBRUARY THE 27TH

The terrible truth is that we are surrounded. Reports by natives and people with knowledge of the area have discovered that there is a tight American defense ring around us. In other words, we are caught in a grip that will surely close on us tomorrow just as soon as the sun rises. With the sun at their backs, the 'masters of technology' only have to wait confidently for the sun. In the meeting between the commanders of the three units, a decision is reached. There is only one opportunity left and we must simply let chance choose the leading unit. That unit will have the 'Honor' of sacrifice. 'Chance' falls on the Tawalkanda Unit, my unit. All the night vision equipment is fixed in position, knowing only too well that the equipment on the M-1s is far superior to ours, and we begin to move the division forward. Four almost parallel columns, with the flank tanks

13. A dispenser comes in handy for ensuring the correct amount of thinner.

14. The turret has many three-dimensional features, making airbrushing particularly difficult.

15. Something to rest the object on is most welcome.

16. Dealing with the lower areas. Most of the work will never be seen, but it must nevertheless be painted.

17. Use any semi-transparent paper for masking. It can be moved around.

18. Illustrations show us how to cut the correct shaped mask.

19. Draw the shape on the paper and then cut it out.

20.Cutting out the marked shapes with a sharp knife.

21. Keep to the pencil markings and try to cut them tight to the lines.

22. This masking is perfect to get those slightly blurred edges that we are looking for on the camouflage lines.

23. Apply Green paint: XF-11 (45%), XF-61 (45%), XF-8 (10%). Try to get some paint under the edges of the masking. By doing this, we'll get the blurred effect.

24. Once we've finished with the masking, go over those areas that may require more paint.

25. Carefully repeat the process, following the patterns on our reference pictures.

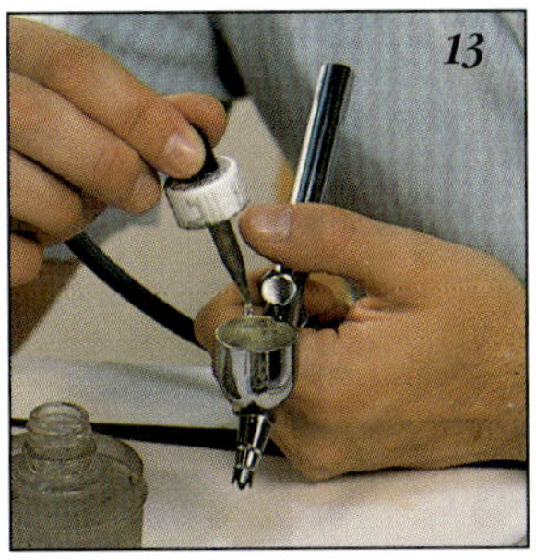

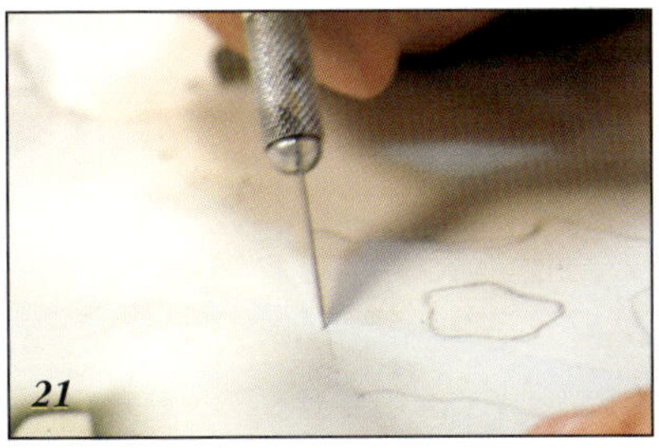

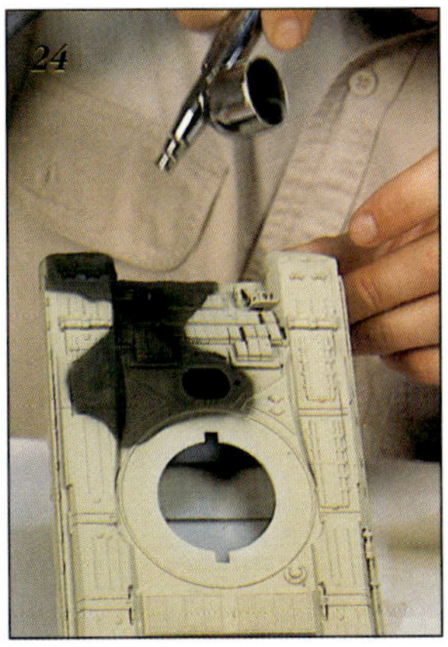

aiming their guns to the right and left respectively, and the ones in the center with the guns aimed forward. I believe that we are experiencing the same feeling that Roman gladiators had when entering the arena. With our vehicles loaded to capacity with ammunition and barely enough gas, we enter the dunes in the most frantic drive, knowing that the faster we move, the harder a target we'll make. The first explosions are not from guns or rockets, they are caused by us going over landmines that blow the leading vehicles apart. In no time, we receive a shower of projectiles of all types that explode everywhere, some only blow off the tracks or the rear parts. Our fellow crewmen run as fast as they can because they know that they may be the next target, as we were soon to discover. Well over fifty tanks in front and on the flanks are burning furiously, the rest of us try to fire as much as we can without even attempting to locate our targets first. The automatic gun fires round after round, we simply fire as much as we can while we can. The area is alight with burning vehicles forming a wall of fire. The survivors feed the fire with fuel, injecting it through the exhausts.

The entire area looks unreal: Fire, blasts in a thousand shapes, fireballs, absolute confusion, dense smoke confusing everything. The enemy is befuddled and blinded by the smoke, firing yet again on already destroyed vehicles. On our side, we don't know whether we've hit our target or not. Our division is undone, and is almost totally destroyed. The remaining two divisions, without firing a shot, pass through the fire, dodging the remains of our vehicles with their minds set on Basra.

This mad run, borne out of despair, shakes our vehicle until we hit a funnel-shaped area that makes our vehicle turn upside down, rendering it useless. I order the evacuation and the three of us climb out wearing our gas masks. Once we're safe, our tank explodes, spitting masses of molten metal. We run the risk of being run down by our own vehicles, and while we hide, we understand the full extent of this disaster: human and metal remains cover the ground around us. The smell of burnt fuel and human remains is unbearable.

We wish for everything to be over and to escape from this horror worse than death. We see something moving among the chaos; it is a BMP transport vehicle that almost runs over us. Suddenly it stops, and someone inside motions us to climb aboard. We leave this burning hell behind us, while debris hits the sides of our vehicle. After a long drive we gain safety, but hundreds of men and masses of equipment from the Tawalkanda Division have perished or been destroyed: 350 T-72's, 275 BMP's, 85 campaign guns and their tractors, 55 AAA guns and some 15 thousand men dead, wounded, or captured. The Medina and Hammurabi Divisions and their T-72's are totally safe and on their way to Basra. The extent of the damage inflicted on the enemy is not known.

PAINTING

We are going to explain the complete painting process

26. To protect small areas from paint, use liquid masking and paper.

27. Make sure you correctly continue a camouflage blotch when it goes, for example, around an edge.

28. On lifting the paper mask, you will find the base color underneath. If the edges between base color and camouflage are too sharp, go over it again with your airbrush.

29. As the turret has complex features, it is advisable to work without masking. It is also necessary to get close to the model.

30. The black blotches are done as previously described. The parts were later shaded using Tamiya XF-1 and XF-10. Gunze Sangyo H-344 was also used.

31. Accentuate the airbrush shading by brushing H-344 over the small crevices, between plates, and on rivets.

32. In order to make the raised features stand out more, apply 968 and 976 on each camouflage blotch.

33. The base of the gun is treated with 929 and 913.

34. The sand color has peeled off a little allowing the base color to show through.

35. The numerals are hand cut from masking tape.

36. This procedure will give the desired results. In fact, the numerals on the full size vehicle are done the same way.

37. The turret with all the treatment - shadows, washes, dry brushing, and paint peels.

38. A final touch: dust on the lower part of the track guards. The mixture used was XF-55 and XF-52.

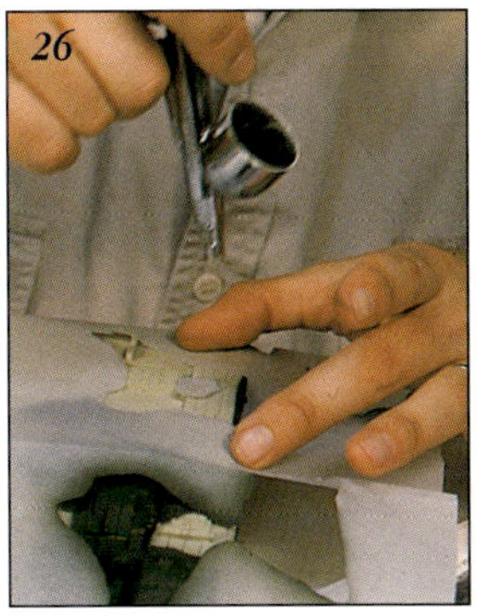
26

27

28

30

31

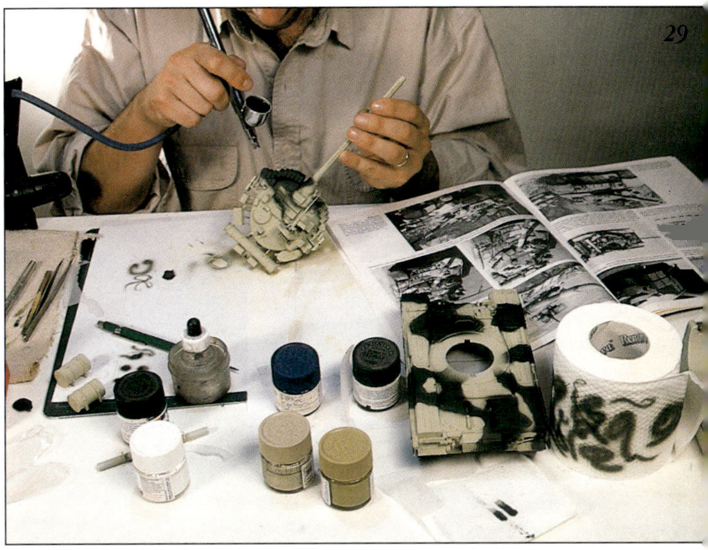
29

32

33

34

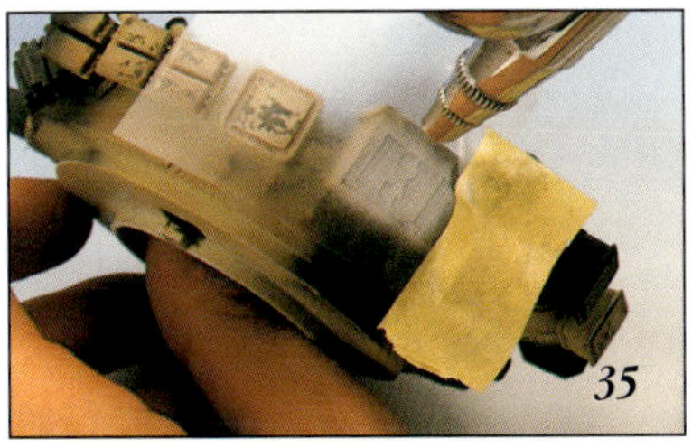
35

36

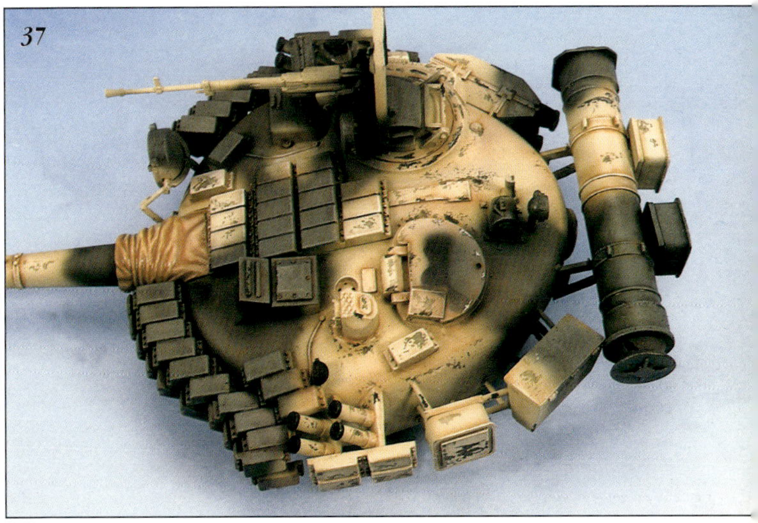
37

and apply all the reviewed painting techniques, airbrush, masking, washes, etc. On the way, we will also the reveal the particular 'modus operandi' for the 'aficionado' so you can see those little tricks used in a process, but usually hidden from view.

The chosen colors are those for the established Russian schemes. They bear little semblance to western vehicles, especially American vehicles. The Russians use a traditional green with sand colored blotches and some smaller black blotches. The idea is to break-up the lines of the vehicle, and to achieve a 'chiaroscuro' effect like the forests of northern Europe.

Wear and tear is conveyed with lots of scratched paint like that seen in all the reference pictures. It is a delicate job, and must be done with a brush. It is, therefore, necessary to be very careful to avoid very thick out-of-scale brush strokes.

COLOR CHART

BASE COLOR (yellow earth)
XF-57 buff (50%), XF-2 flat white (20 %), XF-60 dark yellow (20%) by Tamiya.

CAMOUFLAGE (dark green)
XF-11 J.M. green (45%), XF-61 dark green (45%) and XF-8 flat blue (10%) by Tamiya.

SHADOWS (airbrushing highly diluted paint, next painting washes)
XF-1 flat black, XF-10 flat brown by Tamiya and H-344 rust by Gunze Sangyo.

DRY-BRUSH
976 buff and 968 flat green from Model Color's range.

DUST
XF-55 deck tan and XF-52 flat earth by Tamiya.

39-44. The details of the completed model.

38

39

40

41

42

43

44

Shilka ZSU-23-4

Since it was first released in the 1960s, the Shilka anti-aircraft system has always proven quite efficient, as long as it was afforded minimum protection. In Afghanistan, the guerrillas feared it as much as they feared helicopters because of its overwhelming firepower. In the Balkans, a weapon of this kind could neutralize any building concealing snipers or wipe out a troop formation within the weapon's effective range. During the Yom Kippur War (1973), this weapon was a nightmare for the Israeli pilots.

The system has force cooled, quadruple 23mm guns. It has twin fire control systems, optical or radar guided, designed to destroy any flying object at an altitude of 2-3 kilometers. Its four guns can fire some 3600 rounds per minute that is quite staggering, considering that its immediate-use load of some 500 projectiles per gun is exhausted very quickly. The ammunition replenishment vehicle is the trustworthy PT-76. The continued efficiency of this vehicle was proven yet again during the Gulf War when it accounted for a number of British Tornados.

A TORNADO PILOT

This unique chance will probably never come round again. Putting the Tornados, and its special weapons, to the test in actual combat conditions. Today, we are carrying a load of JP-233's, designed to destroy runways, specifically the taxiways connecting the hangars and the main runway. We are precision flying with the help of satellites and reconnaissance aircraft that relay the coordinates into our flight systems. Even if there are no enemy aircraft around, we are fortunately flying under the umbrella of the F-15's. In the middle of the night, and in the middle of the war, only a few natural reflections confirm that we are airborne. That's how dark it is, and how deceiving distance can be. The reddish-blue spots of the exhausts of the aircraft ahead of us float around like a ghost. We are now just 100km away from the enemy base.

1. Tools and reference material used in the making of this vehicle.

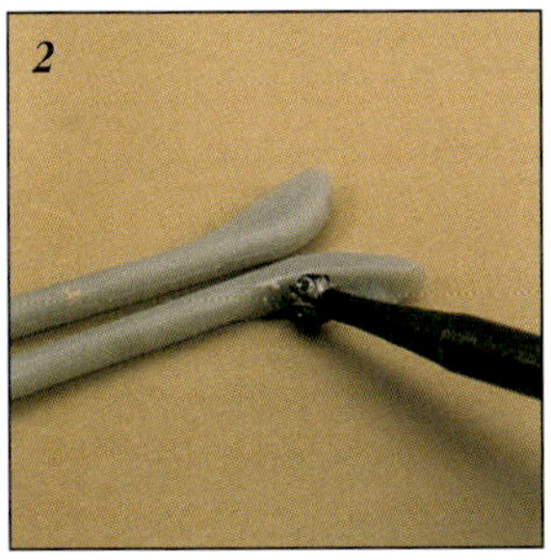

2. Using a mini-drill with a special tip, hollow out the gun's air intakes.

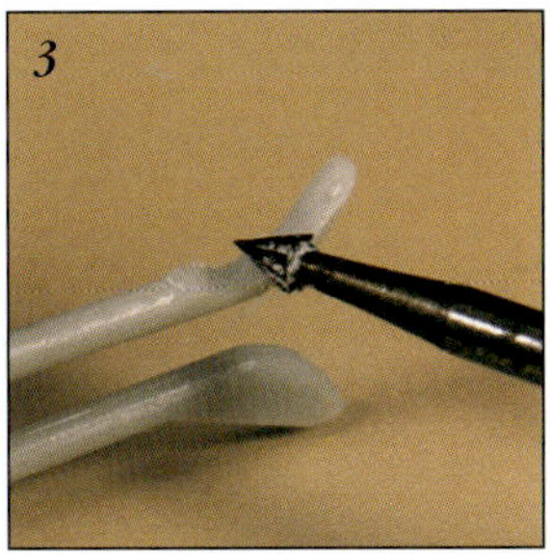

3. Removing the intake sides, as they are not of the correct shape.

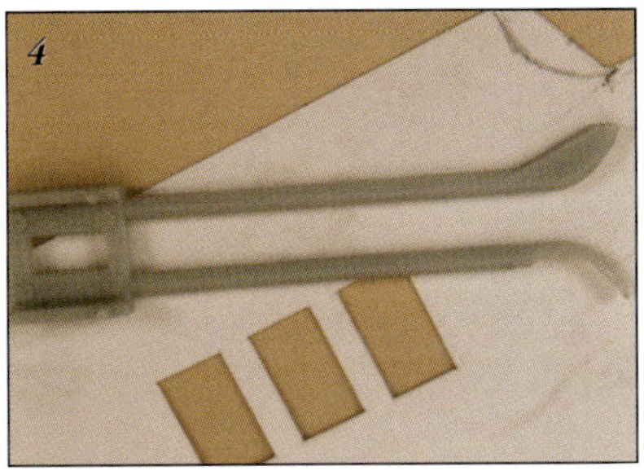

4. Comparing the original piece with the reworked one in the first phase.

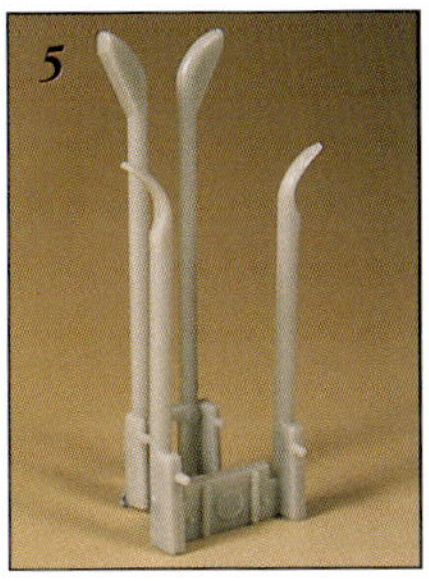

5. You have to do this to all four parts. One per gun.

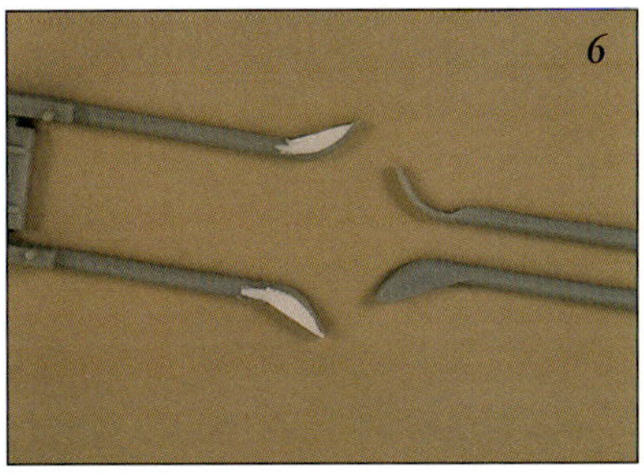

6. Glued small lateral pieces made of thin plastic and cut to measure.

7. Two similar pieces are required for each air intake.

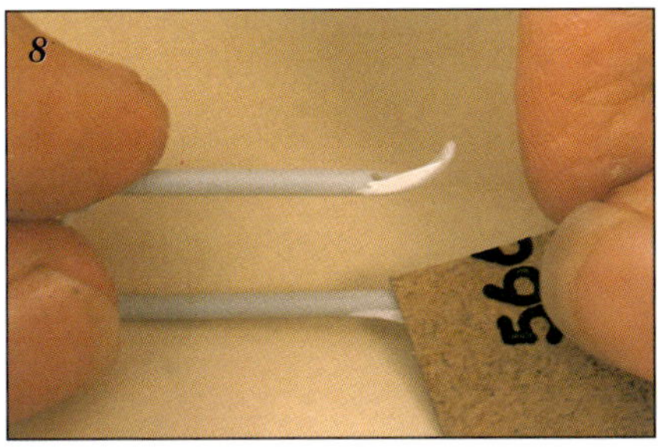

8. Once glued and puttied, they are then sanded.

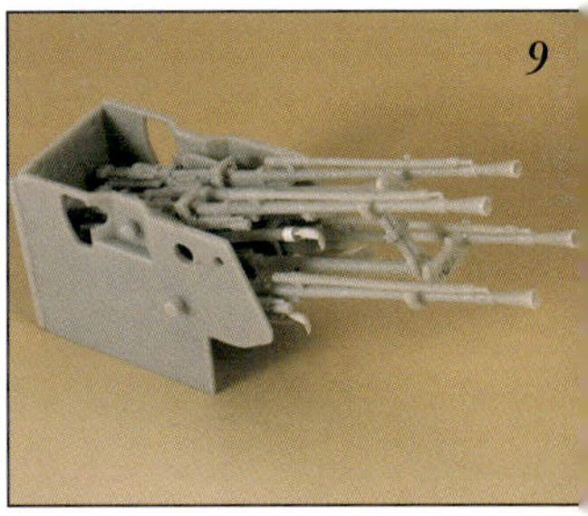

9. All the gun muzzles are drilled.

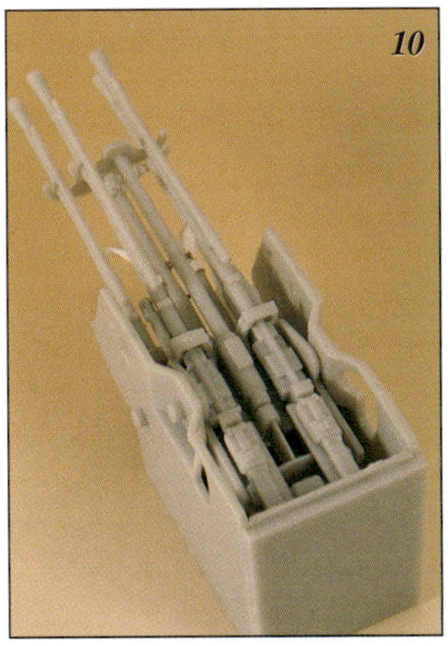

10. The location of the gun parts. On the upper part, complete the assembly with the use a small flexible plastic tube, like the one used for isolating electric wires.

11. Cooling cables will come through the holes we're drilling right now.

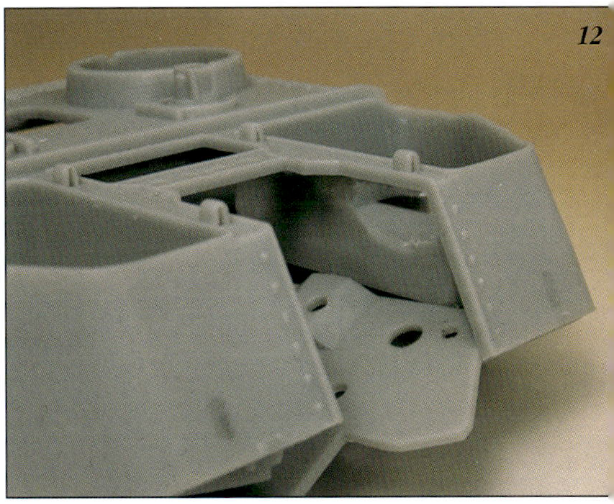

12. The part positioned on the model. Note the holes that have been drilled.

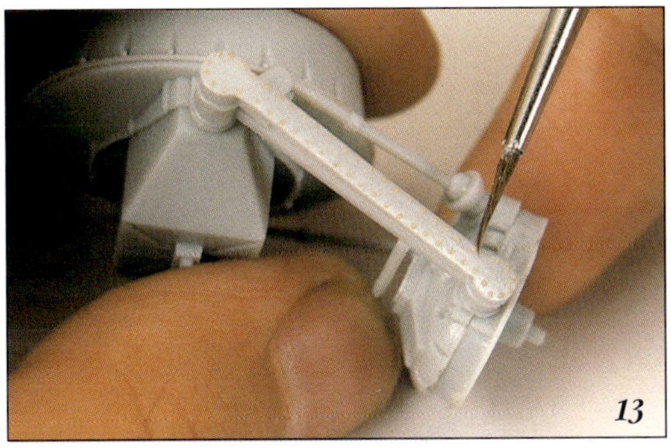

13. Detailing the radar supports with rivets.

14. They are made from heat-stretched plastic and then cut off and positioned at regular intervals.

We make a shallow dive in order to place ourselves at combat height and deceive the low and mid-range radars that may still be functional. The enemy's few remaining radar transmitters only work for a very short time each day to avoid being tracked down. In the dark, they may yet get us with a well-aimed missile. We are reducing the distance to target rapidly, and we're almost on top of them. Our receivers tell us that we are being tracked by a number of small radar transmitters. We haven't even begun the attack, and yet we can see small fires. These have been lit as decoys to get the attention, and deceive any heat-seeking weapon or thermal, infrared detectors. I race up the runway at some 900 kilometers per hour. Our radar lets us fly at the necessary 30meter altitude for releasing the JP-233's. Suddenly, the situation changes, the sky is lit up with strings of light. Lights criss-cross the sky to form a lethal net, light dots occur in pairs forming a fountain of incandescence. Meanwhile, we release our 'load' and the instant it hits concrete, it explodes and the ground is lit up just like the sky is lit with enemy fire. The fire in the sky doesn't seem to lessen, quite the contrary. As soon as I've released, I pull back the stick to regain altitude, climbing almost vertically. Worried, I check the navigation instruments but, Thank goodness, everything is all right. To port, I glimpse a huge fireball climbing rapidly and exploding into endless colored spots.

When we finally return to base, all the surviving pilots count the hits on their 'planes. Each hit is a 23mm projectile hole, so they are quite impressive. In fact, there isn't a single unscathed Tornado. Sadly, one of the planes didn't return, and it never will.

The tremendous crossfire is the work of the Shilkas, firing thousands of rounds per minute, helped to reload while hiding in fixed positions and camouflaged among fake tanks and armor plating, warmed up to the same temperature of real vehicles.

The Tornados suffered ten times more casualties than any other aircraft during the war. As a consequence, those missions that left our planes at the mercy of the Shilkas were eventually abandoned.

ASSEMBLY AND DETAILING

This veteran vehicle took part in many battles and can be traced from Afghanistan all the way to the Gulf War, passing through Lebanon and all the Israeli-Arab conflicts.

The first kit was made by Dragon, but is now molded by Italeri. These two kits are almost identical, apart from a few version details. Dragon also offers a resin accessories kit for detailing the interior. However, in this case we will concentrate our efforts on detailing the exterior using an Eduard photo-etch sheet, and a few scratch-built parts.

TURRET

We'll start with the guns, or rather the cooling air intakes. They should to be hollow, but are not, so we have to take care of this ourselves using a knife or, better still, a mini-drill. Remove all excess plastic with the chosen tool, leaving the familiar curved shape. This operation must also be repeated on the remaining three parts. The next thing is to reconstruct the small lateral plastic parts that have to be cut to measure. They must be glued and than sanded to look like a single piece. If there are any imperfections, apply some putty and sand it down again. Then, using a drill, hollow out all the muzzles. Work will have to be done on the lateral pieces where the guns are to be positioned, making small holes for the electric and cooling wires. Each gun has a tube on the upper part that was, mistakenly, removed. This is easily corrected with a small flexible plastic tube similar to the plastic covering around electric wire. The small flexible plastic tubes should go all the way to the lateral holes (drill them first). Copper wire is used for making the electric wires on the four guns.

The radar has riveted supports that are not supplied with the kit. They are quite small but can be easily made by heating and stretching a plastic rod. Then, cut small sections out of the rod and, using liquid glue, position them at the correct intervals. Our vehicle will have a crew, so the interior will not be visible from the hatches. This is why we have chosen to do all the detailing on the exterior. It will be done using Evergreen strip and a few photo-etched parts from the Todo Modelismo sheet (the one with the aircraft parts). One of the hatches should be equipped with a headlight, not included in the kit, which we have dug out of the spares box and detailed with a Eduard photo-etched part and electric wire. Use the same wire to make the power cables for the radar and then fix the remaining photo-etched parts according to the instruction sheet.

The optical aiming device has oversized cubical shields, and should be trimmed down.

DETAILING THE CHASSIS

The most important transformation is replacing the engine's ventilation grills with photo-etched ones. Remove the plastic grills by drilling small holes around them and then cutting them out with a knife. Repeat this

15. The interior of the turret, everything was made from Plasticard and other Evergreen items.

16-17. Details are provided on a Todo Modelismo photo-etched sheet and small pieces of plastic.

18. Wire attached to the headlight on the hatch. The support is a photo-etched part.

19. Use the same wire for the power cable to the radar.

20. Small pieces of copper wire for the guns' power cables.

21. The position of all photo-etched parts for detailing the hatch.

22. The covers for the optical aiming device are trimmed down to scale.

23. All plastic handles were replaced with ones made of wire.

24. View of the turret from above, showing where we can see all parts have been added, photo-etched and otherwise.

25. Drilling the rear where the ventilation grill will be placed.

26. Cutting away the part with a knife and a steel rule. Concentrate the knife until the plastic has been pierced.

27. Required shape for the access grill.

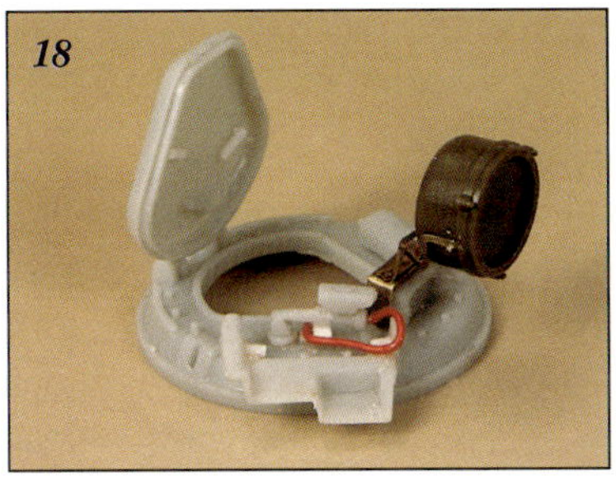

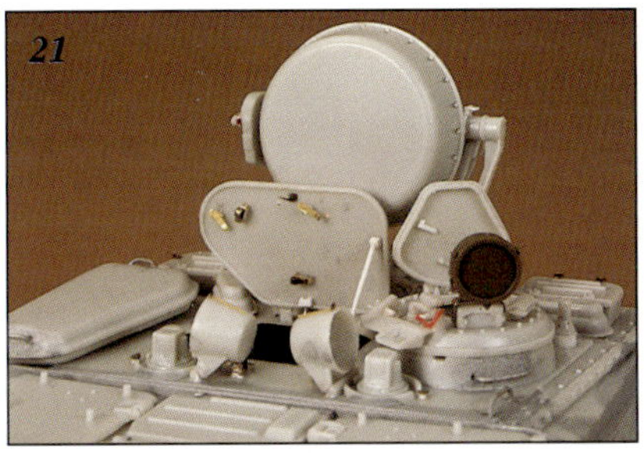

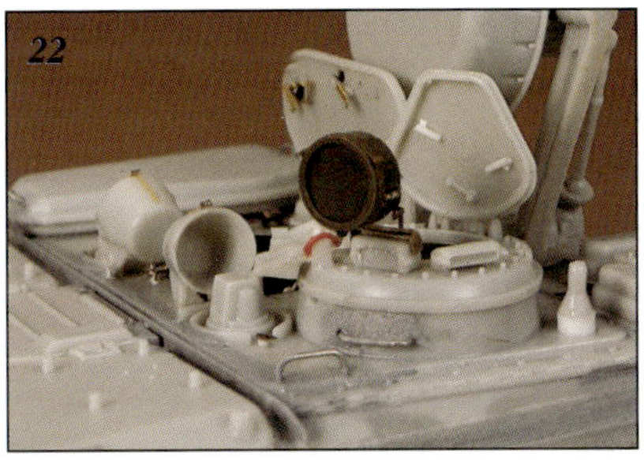

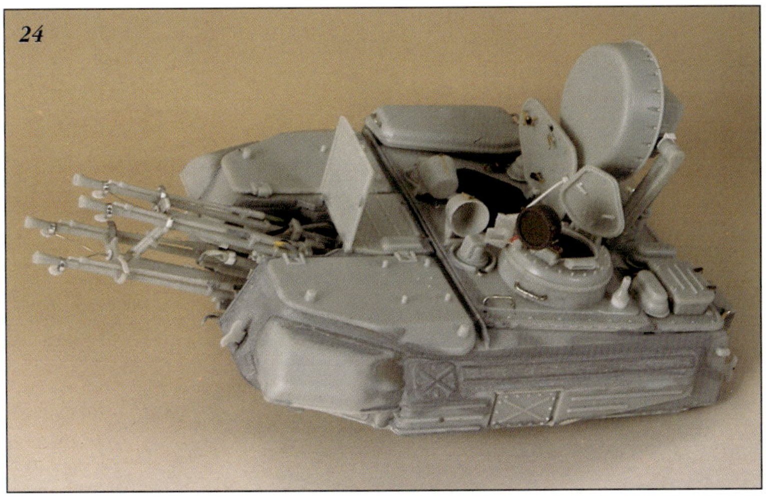

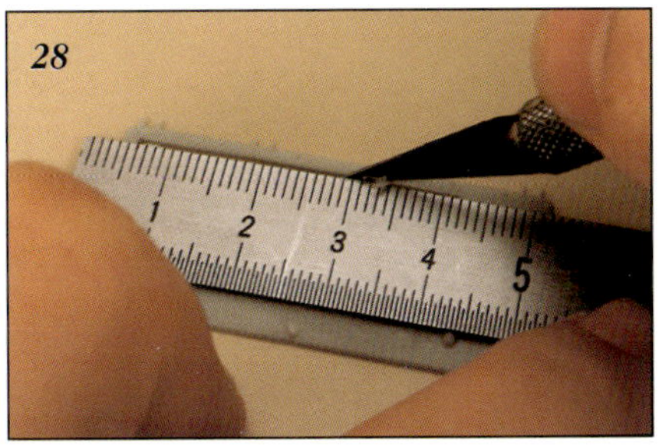

28. Repeat all over on the cover where the grill is.

for the cover. It is advisable to cut the grills slightly smaller than they are, and then file the frame down to achieve a perfect square shape. Now, glue the photo-etched part into position. The photo-etched grill is in two parts (frame and grill). In order to give the grill a used look, press it down slightly against the frame as it is in photos of the real thing. You also have to shape the other grill on the rear. This is done using the original part as a guide. There are also grills on the sides. These require two small plastic strips so you can place the grills on top. All other details are done following the photo-etched sheet's instructions. You can also replace the handles with thin wire. Add some detail to the windshield by adding wipers made from very thin plastic Evergreen rods and a sun shield made of lead sheet. Other details, such as the fire extinguisher duct, can be made from a sharpened plastic rod. Also, place a handsaw, high frequency electric cabling and some chains made from twisted copper wire.

PAINTING

The chosen scheme is the one used in the Afghanistan War. It consists of the classic green base color with irregular gray or pale sand camouflage blotches.

The painting process has been explained at length elsewhere, suffice it to say that, basically, we've followed it to the letter. The masking was made large enough to cover the entire chassis, previously painted with Tamiya XF-62 (50%) and XF-56 (50%). Then, using the masking, apply the gray camouflage paint mixed from XF-53 (40%) and XF-20 (60%). This seemed to be too dark, so we added some white paint to the mixture. We worked on the highlights with Model Color a-77 and a-2, using a subtle dry brushing technique. General ageing of the vehicle was done with highly diluted burnt sienna oil paint.

The lower parts of the vehicle were painted in three phases: use a-82 as base color (this leaves the vehicle quite dark) and then add a-85 to lighten it up. Finally, apply 977 with a brush and blend it into the other colors. In order to achieve this, work fast so that the other colors do not have a chance to dry. Dry brushing touches can be applied later. Division numerals and insignias were drawn and cut from a piece of masking paper, airbrushed on, and then retouched with a brush.

29. Cutting away the plastic part that holds the grill. The part is cut a little smaller than it is shaped.

30. With a small file, leave a perfect surface and then take care of the necessary size adjustments.

31. The two photo-etched parts for the grill and frame.

32. Placing the photo-etched frame on the hole.

33. Slightly sink the grill to make it look like the real thing.

34. The part in its exact position.

35. The part is completed with a frame and small rivets.

36. Bending the photo-etched part to shape on the original plastic part.

37. The plastic part supplied with the kit. It should be replaced with the photo-etched part beside it.

38. The location of the part, behind the armor plating where other items are stored.

39. Plastic parts cut and shaped to accommodate a lateral photo-etched grill.

40. Once the parts have been puttied and sanded, glue in the grill.

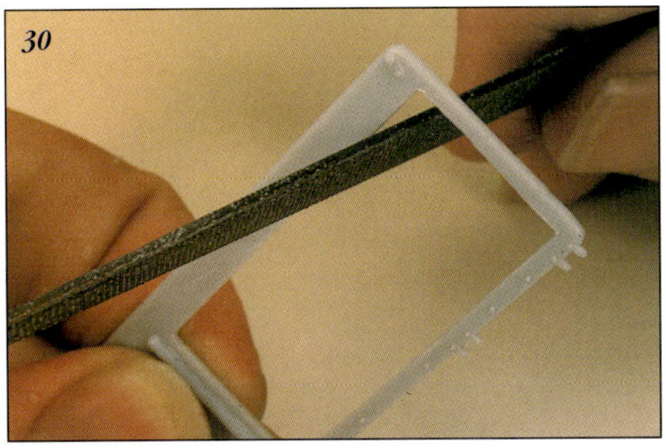

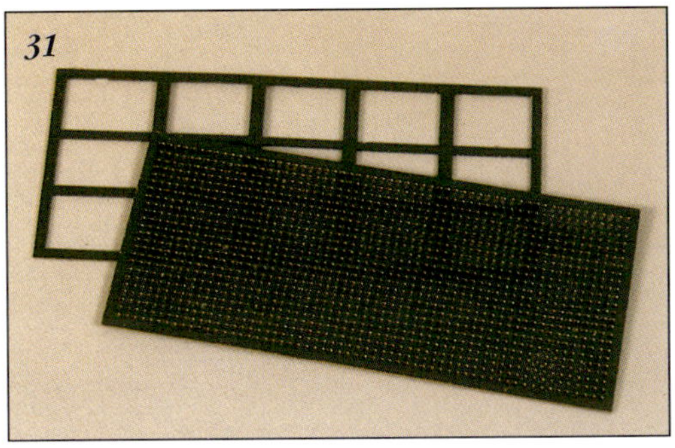

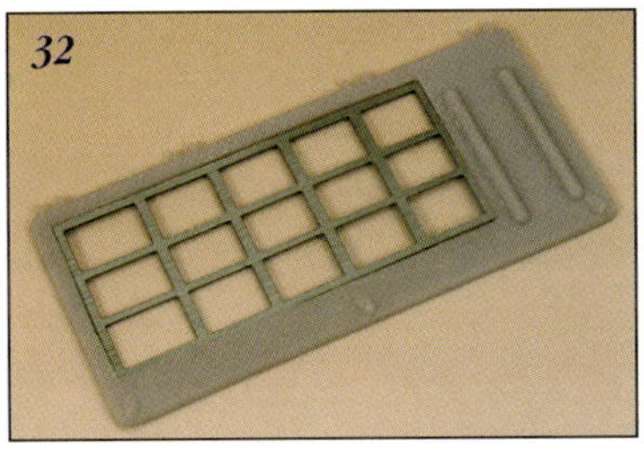

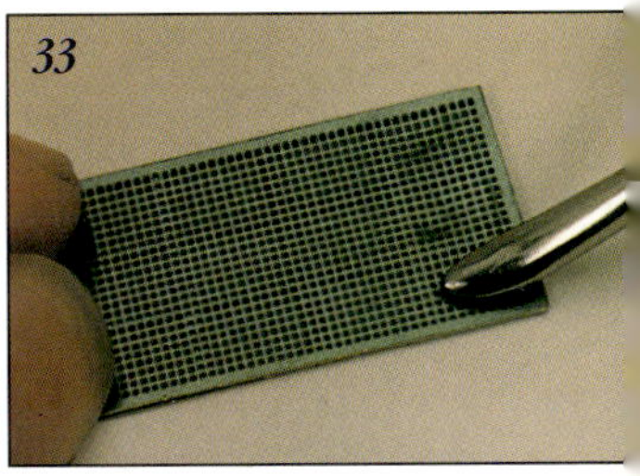

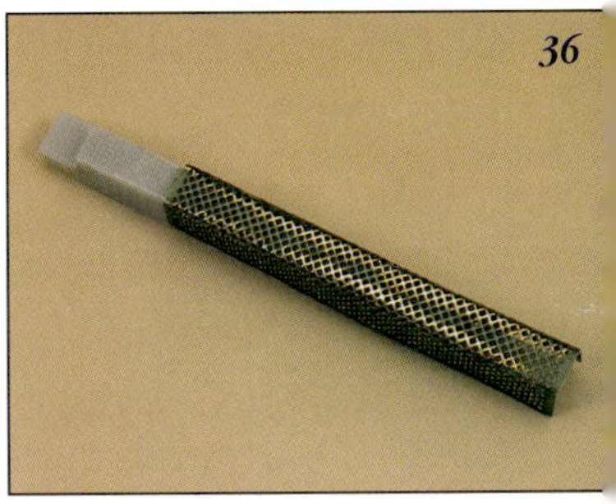

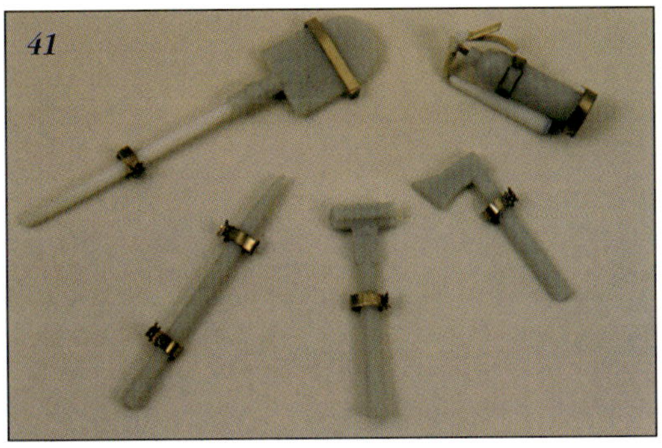

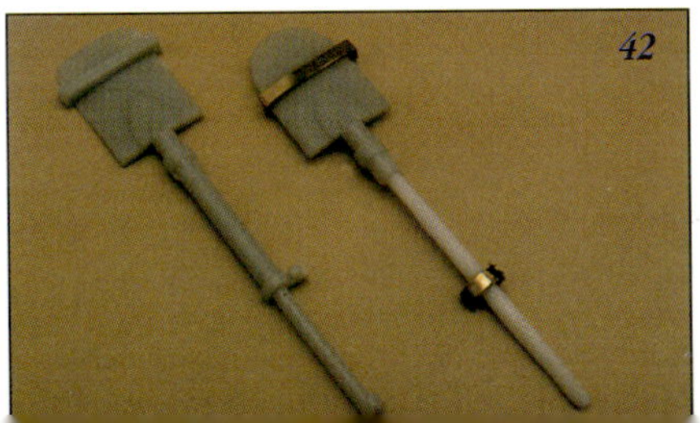

41. The original shovel next to an identical one, but with the plastic parts replaced with photo-etched ones.

42. Different tools with their respective photo-etched parts glued on.

43. Location for the shovel, and other photo-etched parts.

44. Small side window with a windshield wiper and a sun shield made of thin metal sheet.

45-46. Position of several latch supports and cables.

47. Main headlamp with trimmed protection and several Plasticard and photo-etched detailing items.

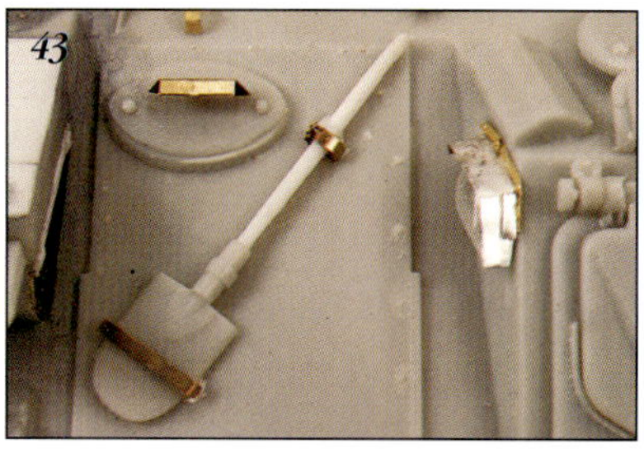

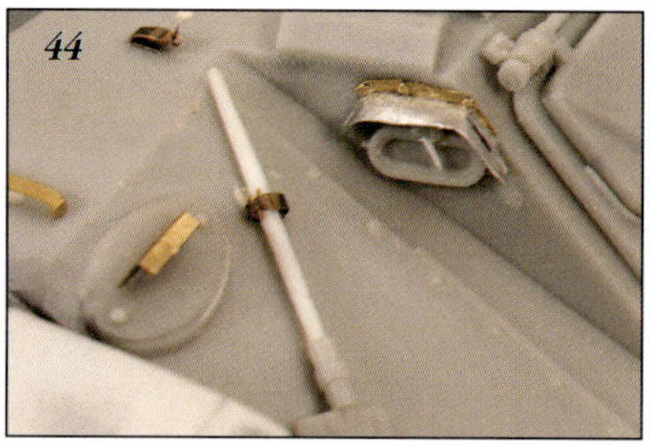

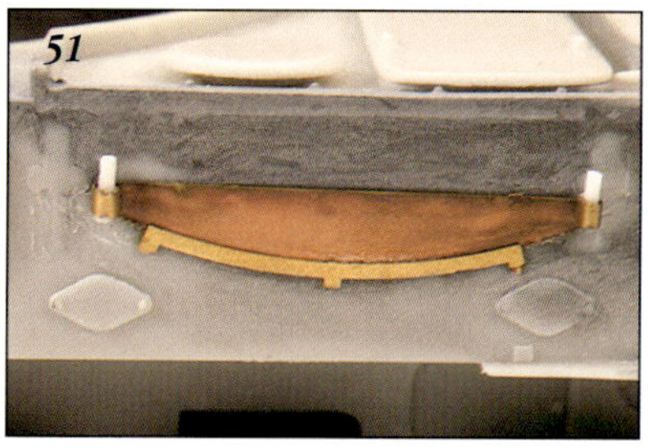

48. The hidden grill that is part of the box where the main headlamps are placed.

49-50. Detail showing the supports and cables for the rear headlights.

51. Hand saw and support. The handles are made from small plastic rods.

52. Placing the links on the tracks.

53. Cable made of high frequency wire. It is comes already twisted.

54-55. A view of the rear, the small chains are made of twisted and flattened wire.

56. Picture showing the complete details on the front of the chassis.

57-58. Rear view of the turret. The fire extinguisher has a conical nozzle made from plastic rod.

59-60. The detailed guns. You can see the muzzle covers made from small plastic sections shaped with a hole punch. They are joined to the gun with aluminum rings and very fine wire.

61. Colors used for the paintjob.

62. A full-size mask has been prepared with all camouflage blotches.

63. The green base color is XF-62 and XF-58. The blotches over the base color are done with XF-53 and XF-20.

64. Highlighting with XF-53 on some areas, allowing some of the original gray color (the darker one) to show through.

65. General oil washes of burnt sand color.

66. First, apply a general wash with thinner, and then apply small amounts of oil paint with gentle brush strokes.

67. The gentle brush strokes should diffuse the oil paint across the surface.

68. Painting the lower parts with a-82.

69. Highlight the area with a-85.

70. Retouching the base color with a-77 to lighten it up some more. The process has been done quickly, in order to be able to mix all the colors together.

58

59

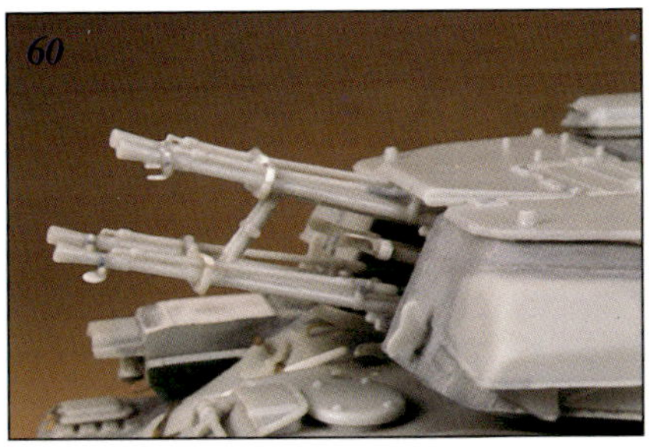
60

61

62

63

64

65

66

67

68

69

70

What & How

Small wire parts

When building model tanks, we often find lots of small cylindrical-shaped parts that are usually poorly reproduced. They may be out of scale, too delicate or poorly molded. After all, there is a limit to the detailing capacity of plastic.

Then, there are other parts, such as springs or small chains that are very poorly made in plastic, or are missing altogether. However, these aren't insurmountable problems, and are easily solved. The parts can be reproduced using wire, preferably copper wire. Copper wire is available in different thicknesses, with or without a plastic sheath. Don't worry, they will all be used sooner or later.

Springs
To make a spring, coil a length of wire around a plastic or metal rod, making it as thick or long as required. If you then pull both ends of the 'spring' you have a telephone wire for wireless/telephone sets.

Handles/moorings
These can be of varying thicknesses and lengths and are common on all types of tanks. They are made from regular wire, telephone wire, etc. Use pliers to first straighten it out and then bend it to shape. You will also need a pair of side cutters and special scissors.

Chains
When making small chains, plait two strands of copper wire or any other malleable metal wire, making sure that they are homogeneous throughout the length. Once that is done, carefully flatten it with a hammer or small pliers. For gluing any metal parts, super glue is your best choice.

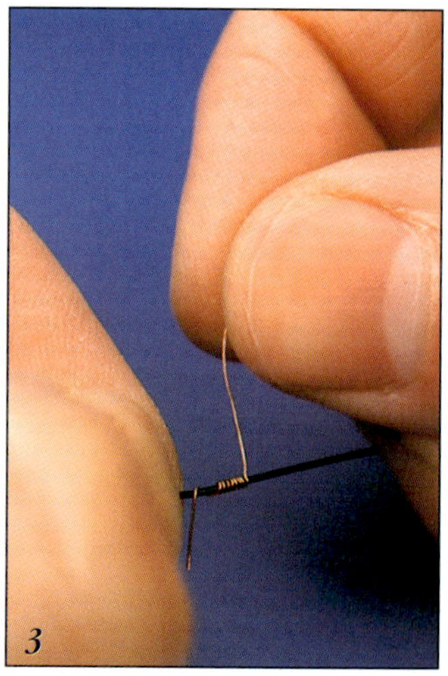

1. It is always useful to have several different diameter wires.

2. When manipulating wire, precision tools give the best results.

3. By coiling wire on a plastic rod, we have ourselves a spring.

4. Length depends on how much it is coiled.

5. Remove the rod and the spring is ready.

6. A typical application for a self-made spring: In the fenders of this Panzer IV.

7. The comparison between a spring and a telephone wire.

8. Pulling the spring apart to obtain a telephone wire.

9. The small chains were made by braiding together two strands of copper wire.

10. It is important to get a homogeneous braid.

11. The looks of the chain are really achieved by flattening out the braid with a hammer.

12. It can also be flattened with pliers.

13. Chain for holding cables on a Panzer IV.

14. Using two pliers, straighten a piece of copper wire.

15. Using flat ended pliers, bend the copper wire at the place where it is held by the pliers.

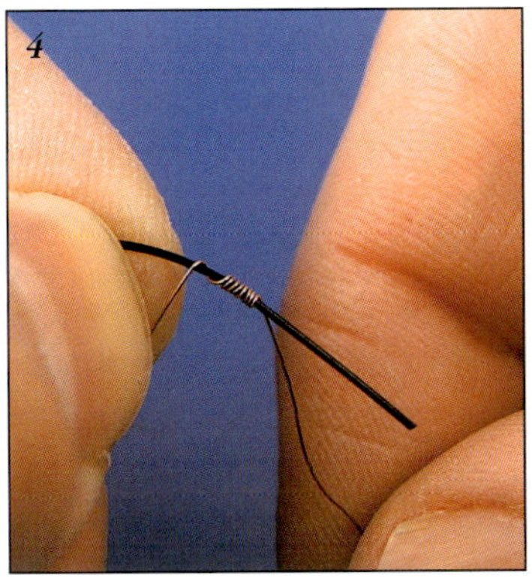

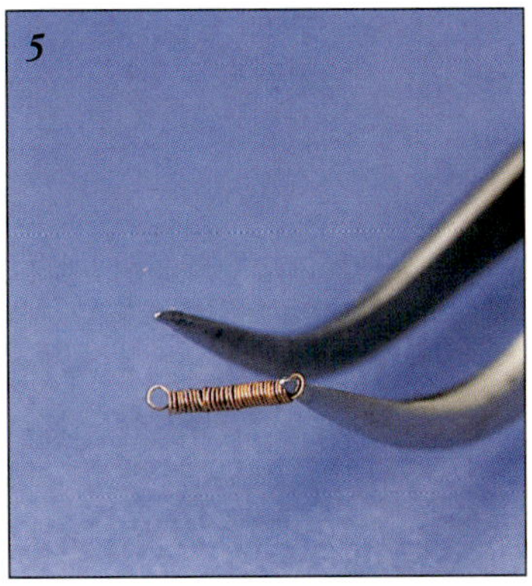

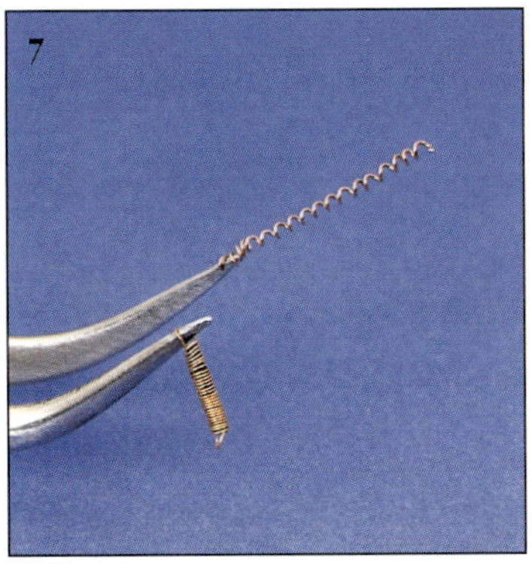

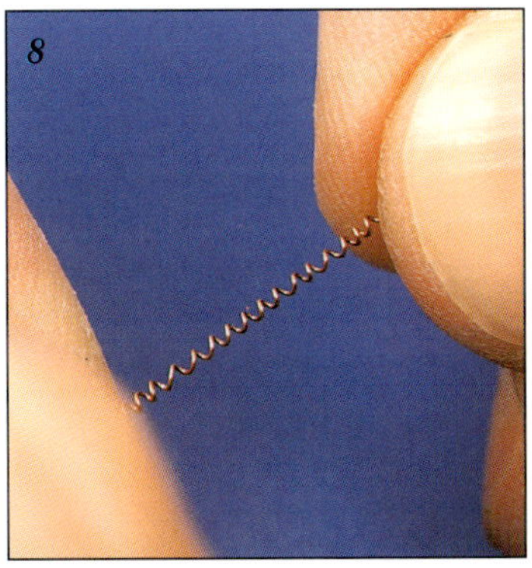

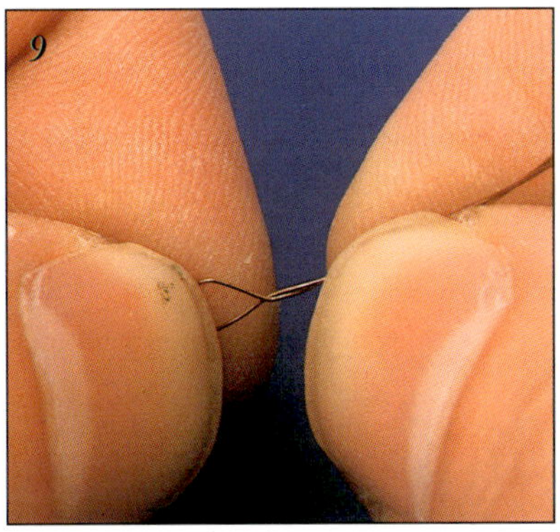

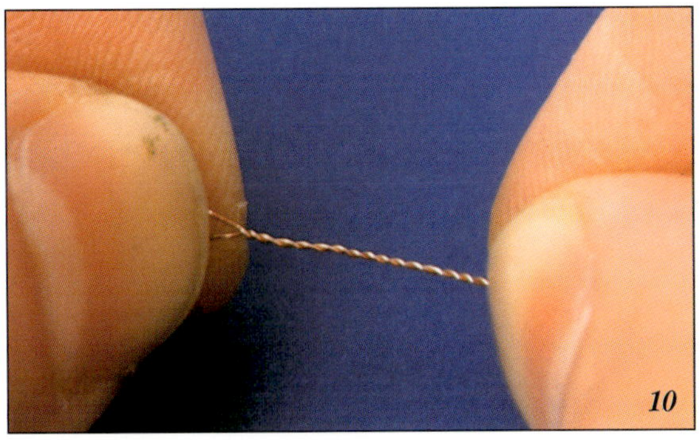

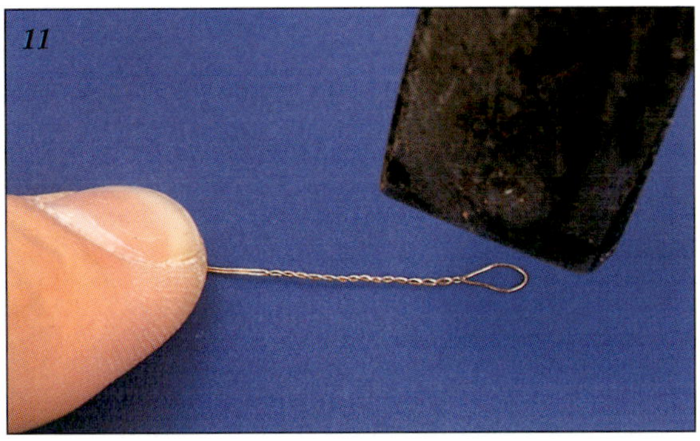

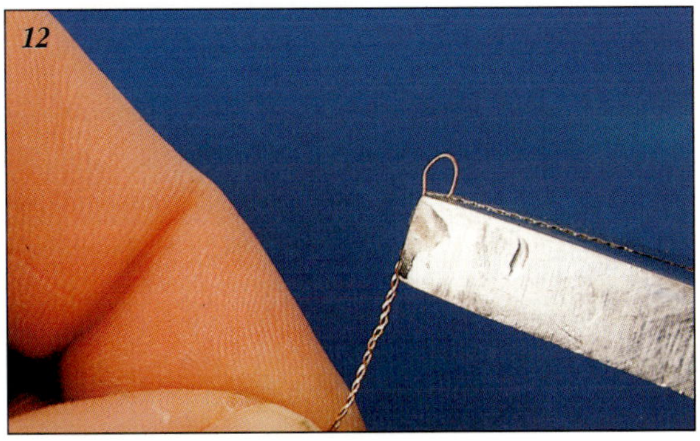

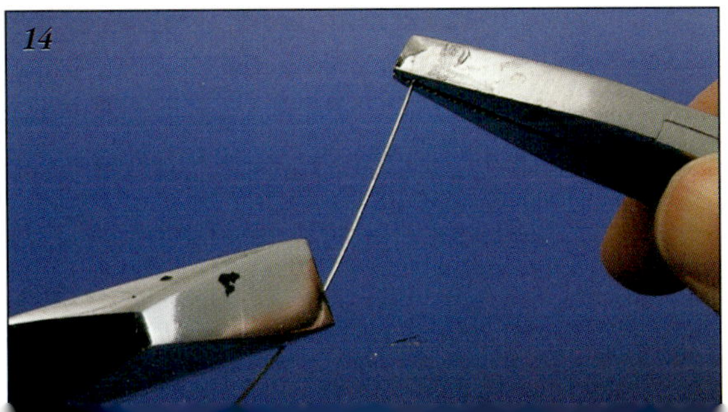

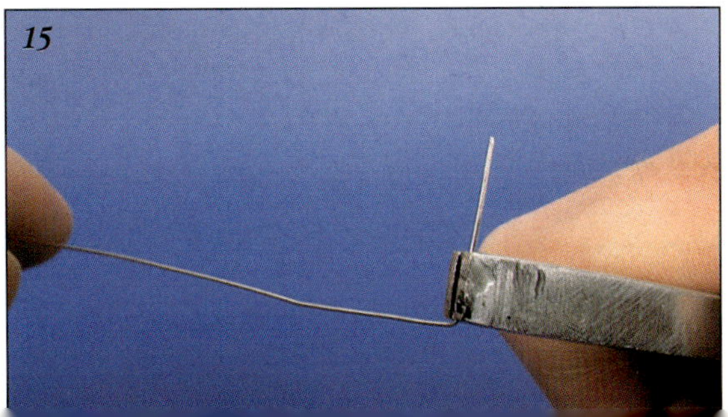

16.Repeat it for the other end of the wire.

17. Cut one end to the desired length.

18. The other end must have the same length.

19. First two bends on a handle with several bent angles.

20. This end should be bent to 90 degrees.

21. The other end is bent the same way.

25. Handles of different shapes and thicknessses can be found on most tanks.

26. Some handles and springs on a Panzer IV.

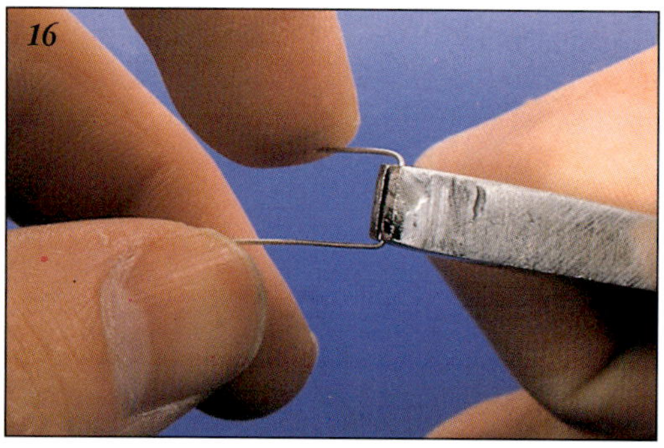

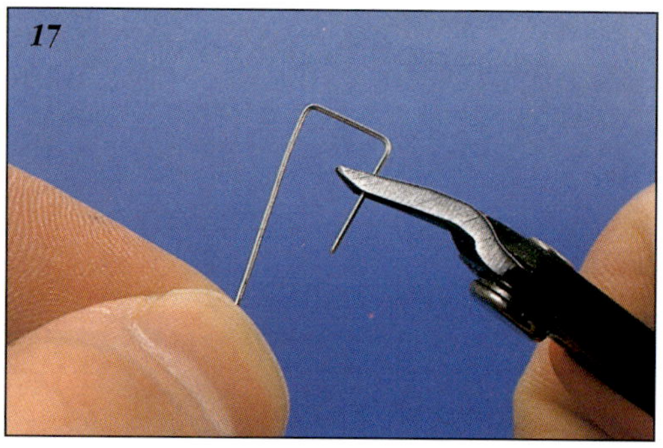

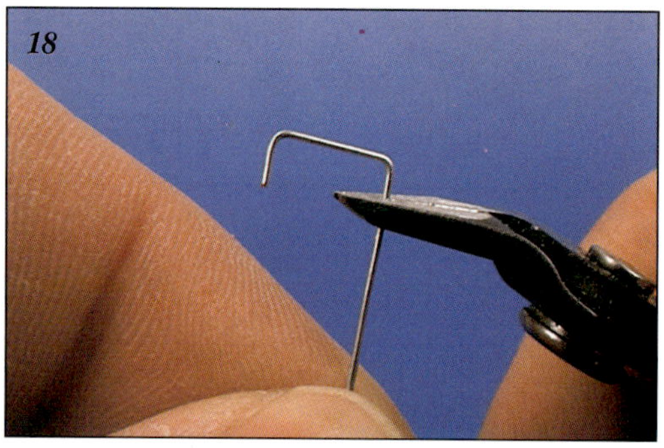

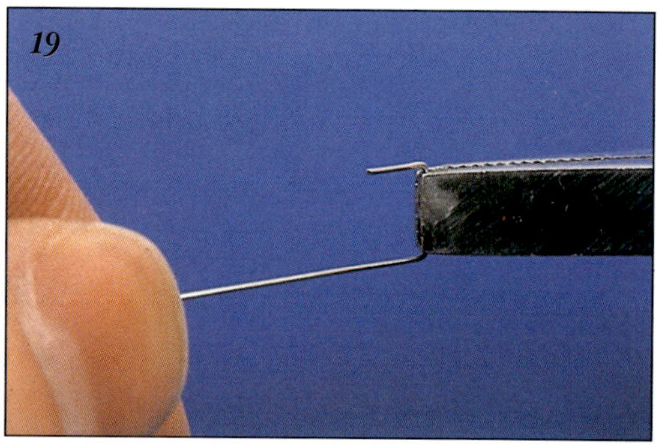

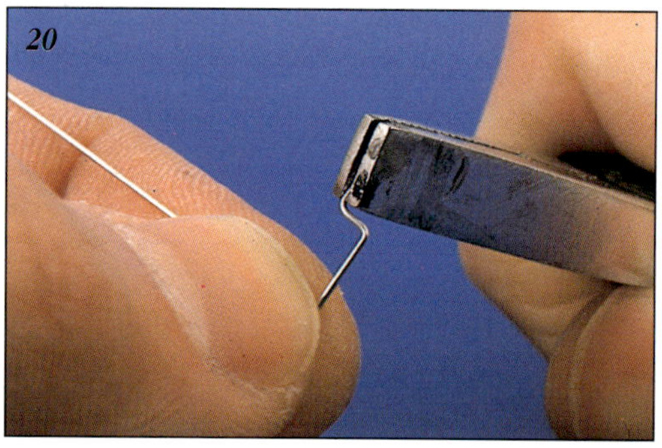

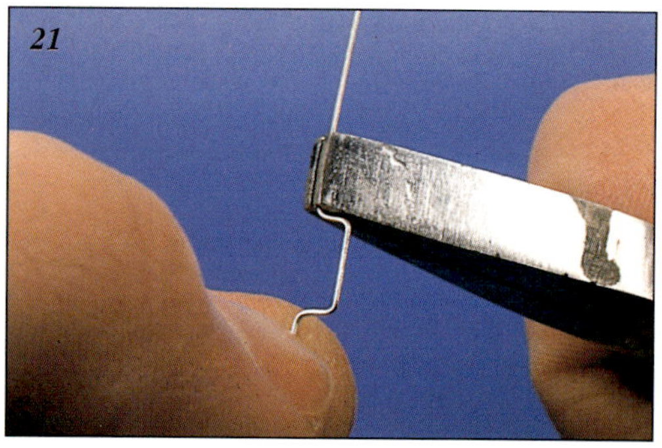

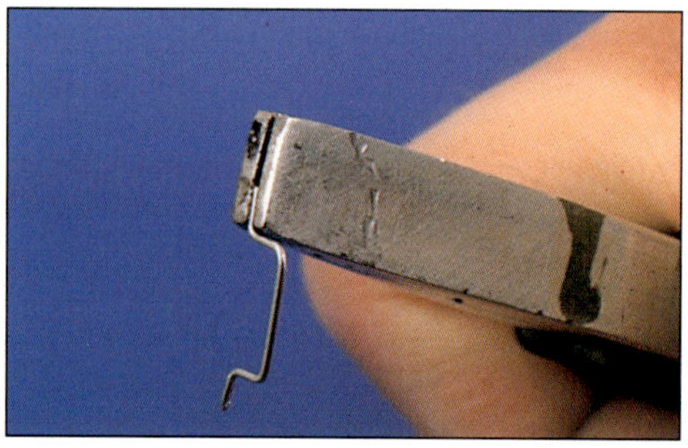

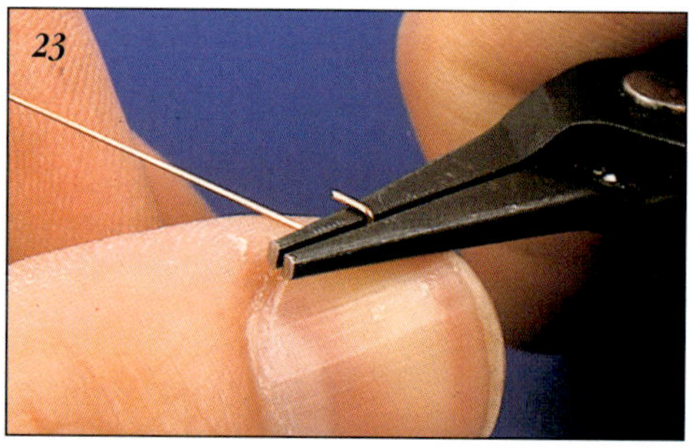

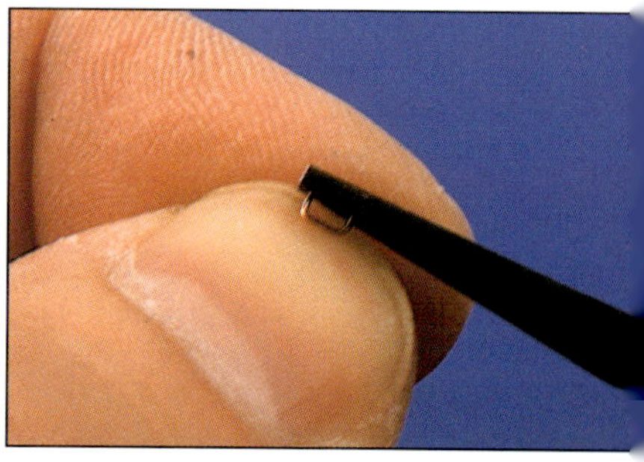

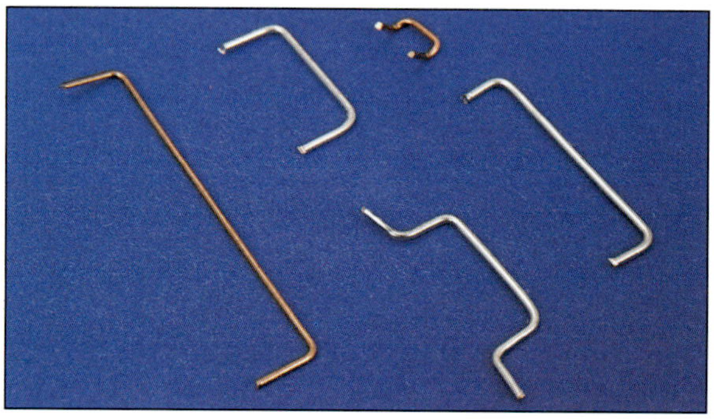

Foreword

The birth of resin kits was not altogether auspicious. It happened just over twenty years ago. The first ones were made of resin and metal and had a brownish look that earned them the nickname of 'soap box kits'. They were made from polyester resin and smelled like it. At first, the quality wasn't very good, so modelers, as a whole, put them aside in favor of the regular vacuform kits.
However, over time, resins improved until polyurethane resin came to the rescue. Detail reproduction improved and became almost perfect.
Verlinden produced the first complementary kits, figures and vehicles. Britain soon joined the ranks and along came manufacturers like Cromwell and Accurate Armour. France (Azimut and Alby) also jumped on the bandwagon, producing accurate, high quality resin kits. The new material actually conveyed detail better than regular plastic. For almost a decade, the more interesting vehicles were produced by the above manufacturers using the new material.
The biggest drawback of quality resin kits is the high price, when compared to the old plastic kits. Assembly and cleaning are somewhat different and, in some areas, they certainly require a greater effort from the modeler (separating parts, sanding, tracks, and having to use, almost exclusively, super glue). Sometimes, parts are a little deformed and require heat to correct them. That said, once the kit is fully assembled, painting is basically the same as other kits.
We propose to exhaustively review two kits that should provide the modeler with some good general guidelines of how to work with this material.

Renault R-40. German Version

WWI was quite traumatic for the French, which in some ways prepared them for the personal disaster they suffered in WWII. However, the success of their own FT-17's was to prove crucial for defense projects. It influenced the thinking of their own High Command, and resulted in such crazy projects as the Maginot line. The design of their armored vehicles was also imbued with this spirit. All vehicles, from the light ones, right up to the heaviest ones, had excellent armor that was far superior to the armor on contemporary British, German or Russian vehicles. However, other things such as speed, independence, and the interior distribution of the crew, were faulty and badly conceived.

The Renault R-40 was the successor of the R-35, which, in turn, had been the successor of the FT-17. The biggest difference rested upon the tracks, the R-35 had a large system of springs with oversized wheels that were quite troublesome. The R-40 version was released in 1940 and, when hostilities broke out, some 90 vehicles had been made and distributed, with 45 going the second D.C.R. and the other 45 going to the 40th. B.C.C. The B.C.C. took very little part in the action, and all their tanks fell, basically intact, into the hands of the Germans. The Germans decided to leave fifty units with the territorial units (Paris in this case) where, eventually, they took an active part during the 1944 liberation battles. The remaining vehicles were sent to Holland, along with some R-35's, and were later used against the British parachutists during the Battle of Arnhem, commanded by 'Von Tettau'. These were only occasions when they were used, apart from a few anti-resistance actions.

The vehicle weighed 10 tons and had armor ranging from 30 to 40mm thick in some areas. The small 82hp engine propelled it at a miserly 20km per hour on a paved road, and considerably slower across country. Weapons included a 37mm gun and a 7.5mm coaxial machine gun.

The German version calls for a double hatch (two armored plates instead of one) and the paintwork is classic Panzer gray with sand colored camouflage lines.

ASSEMBLY

The kit combines plastic and resin parts from the old Heller R-35 kit.

Discard the kit parts acting as reference for positioning the old R-35 plastic parts. Apply a coat of white paint to the inside of the vehicle and assemble the parts that make up the lower, front and rear parts of the vehicle. You will have to use a lot of filler to get a decent fit. Apply a second coat of white paint to the interior of the vehicle and then do some shading with the airbrush, plus some washes and profiling. With black paint and a fine brush, apply the paint peels where necessary. Later, paint some metal color on the inside of the paint peels. That will complete the interior paint job.

The next step is to fit the tracks. Begin by gluing the loose links onto the traction wheel and continue with the links in direct contact with the ground, and work your way along to the links leading to the tension wheel. The upper links must be fitted to the model's surface using heat, and giving them a natural 'drooped' look that is usual on real tanks.

Now glue on the upper part and begin detailing the tank's exterior by building with Plasticard the transmission access hatches, the tool boxes, etc... Glue some thin wire handles onto the rear engine covers. The exhaust was rebuilt using a bent plastic rod and coiling copper wire around it and fixing latches made of two tin straps. These were put into position with the help of curved-nosed pliers. On each end of the straps, glue the plastic rivets. On the right

1. Tools and glue for working with resin kits.

2. Using a knife to polish the plastic surface.

3. Filling joints.

4. The interior is airbrushed with white paint.

5. The interior floor was painted with burnt sienna oil washes. The metal effect is achieved by dry brushing.

6. Paint peels are made with black paint and a little steel paint.

7. The seat is painted a brown leather color.

8. Use sand color for the shadows.

9. Glue several links round the traction wheel.

10. The links are perfectly adapted to the curve of the wheel.

11. The links are easily adapted to the curves.

12. On the rear wheel, glue the links one-by-one.

13. Glue the final links on the upper part of the tracks.

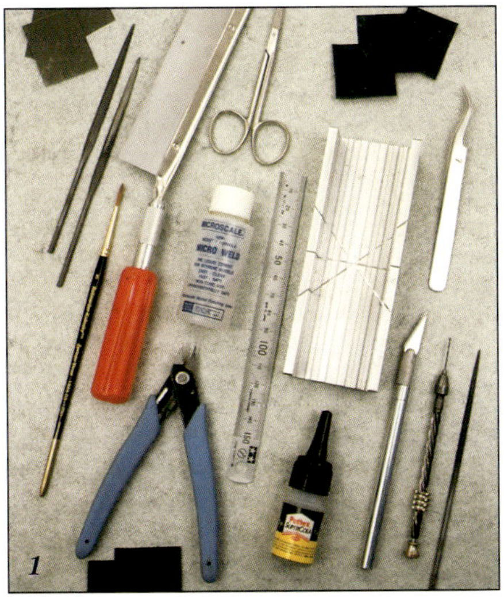

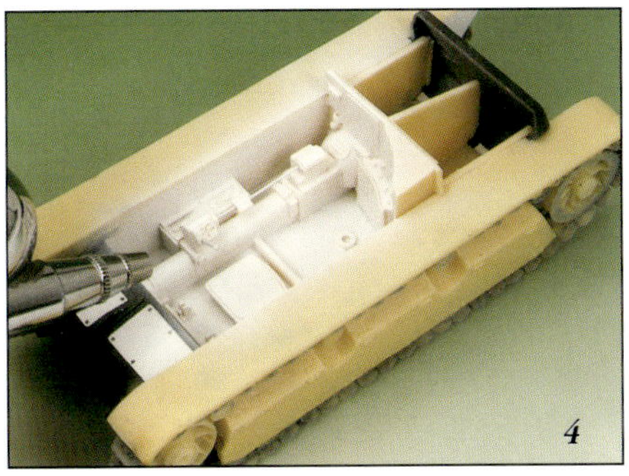

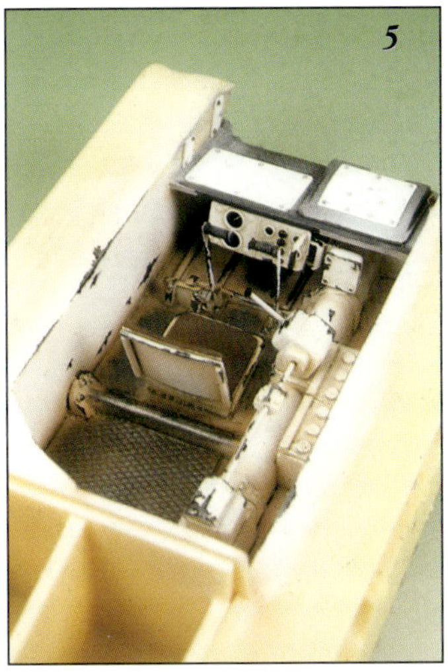

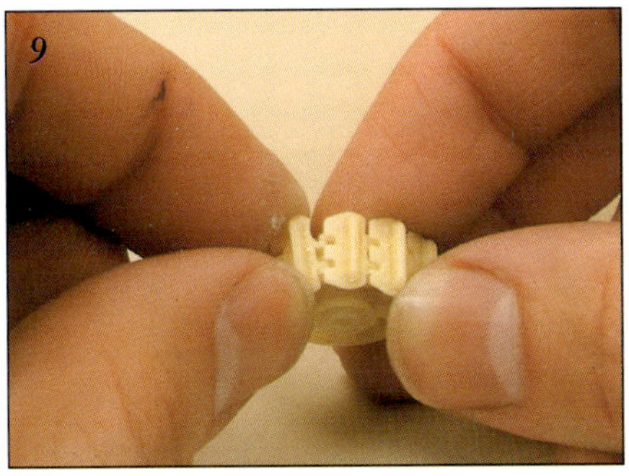

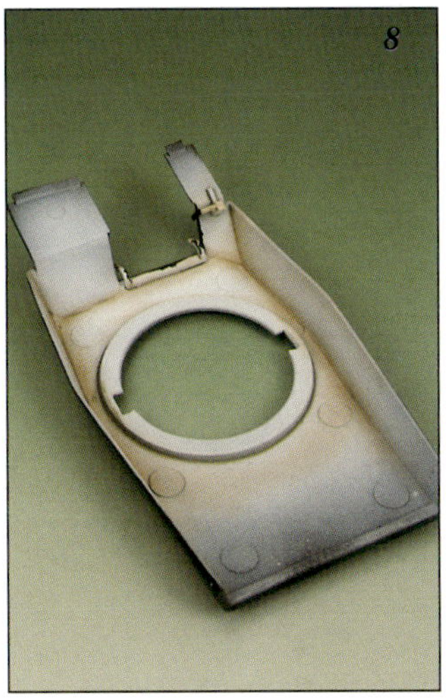

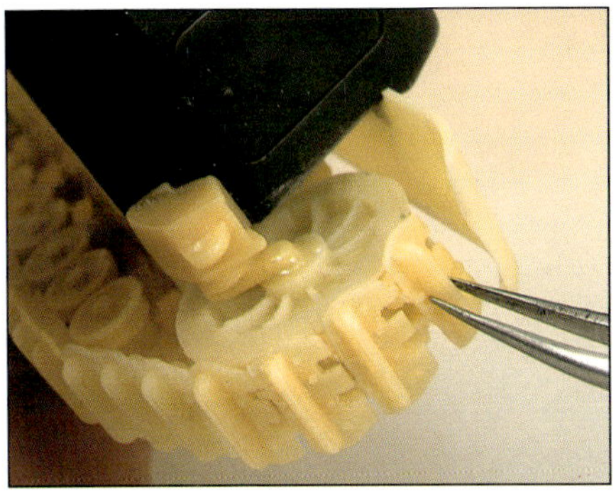

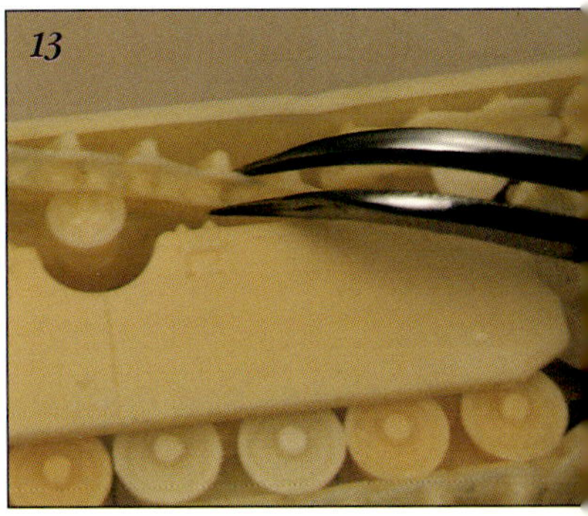

fender, place the folded canvas that has been made of two-part putty. Use a water-soaked brush to shape the creases on the canvas.

If you want to have the driver's hatch open, you will have to carve the inside. Begin by gluing onto the access hatch two plastic "circles" and a small, made to measure, square wedge that are the supports for the three remaining photo-etched straps. Small heat-stretched pieces of plastic are used to form the locks.

The vision slot has to be opened up. Do this with a scriber, after which it can be glued onto the hatch. After the slot has been opened with a scriber, glue it onto the hatch and proceed to detail the inside with plastic cubes and heat-shaped plastic strips.

There are also vision slots on both sides of the drivers' post and they also need to be opened up.

The support that holds the crank's lever is made of Plasticard. The original part supplied with the kit is much too thick and out of scale.

The German rear position lights are made from a small plastic cube with the corners filed off and then detailed with a photo-etched part. Make the four side fastenings using four very thin plastic strips. Six rivets glued onto each of the vision slots on the turret, and also make the four stops on the gun's axis. The stops, made of small plastic 'slices', are housed in specially drilled holes. You also have to make the weld seam that goes around the lower

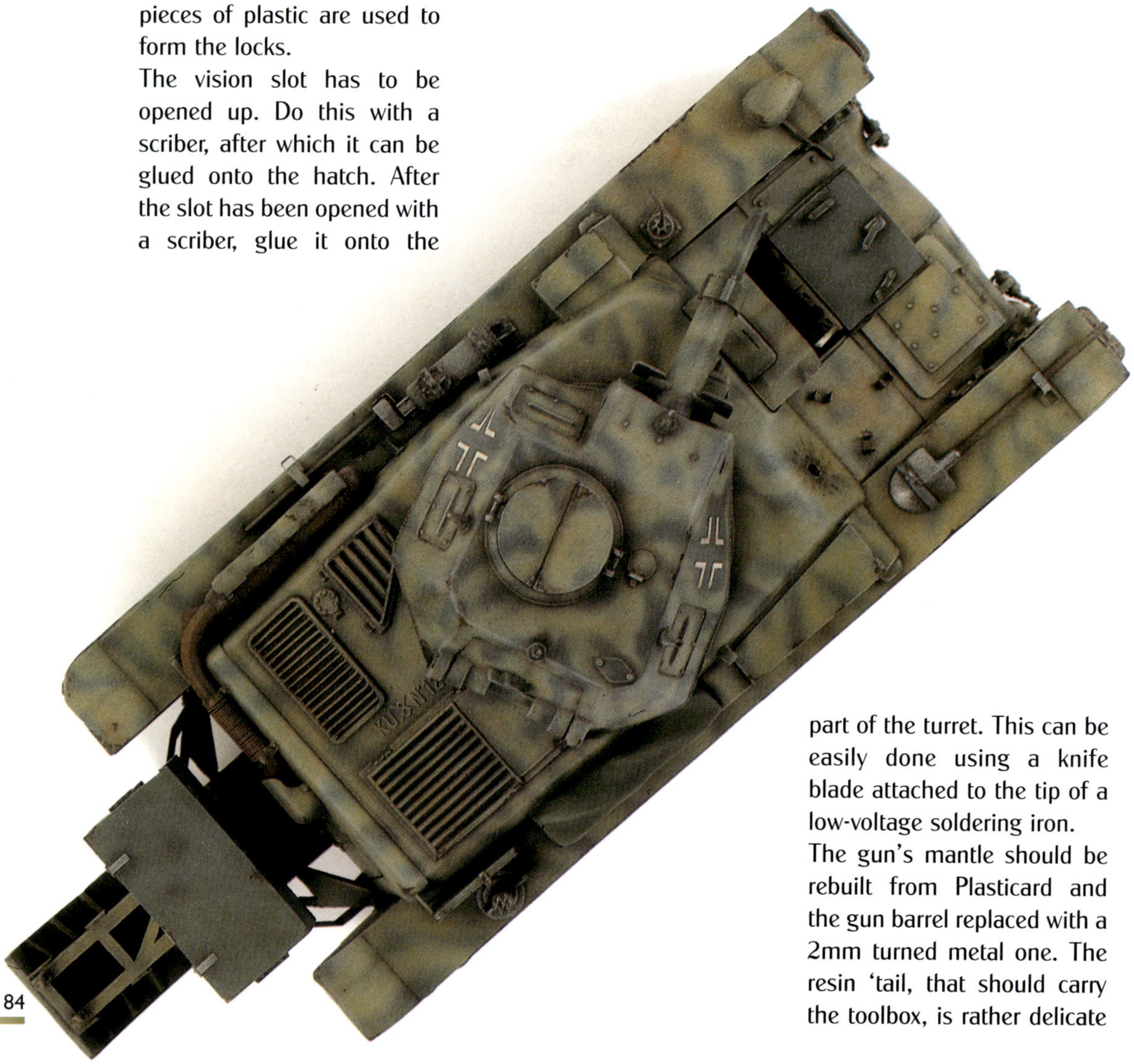

part of the turret. This can be easily done using a knife blade attached to the tip of a low-voltage soldering iron.

The gun's mantle should be rebuilt from Plasticard and the gun barrel replaced with a 2mm turned metal one. The resin 'tail, that should carry the toolbox, is rather delicate and should be cut away from its support using a special cutter. The toolbox itself was scratch built from Plasticard with a couple of photo-etched locks added.

PAINTING

The airbrush applied base color is a mixture of XF-50, XF-18 and XF-63. Add more XF-63 for the shading. Next is the camouflage scheme using a mixture of XF-60 and XF-55. In this way, small gray strips underneath can be seen.

Make the vertical dirt stains with the airbrush using several browns and then profile all crevices. This is also done with the airbrush.

This detail profiling can be enhanced with oil paint after which the model should be left to dry for a couple of days. Then , using light gray enamel, dry brush all the edges of the model.

Wear is simulated by painting paint peels using a fine brush and a mixture of black and red brown acrylics. Follow this by delicately airbrushing a rust color onto the peels for a realistic effect.

Also, airbrush some red-brown on the lower parts of the vehicle. After, apply some gloss varnish to get the appearance of wet mud.

The tracks will receive several burnt sand oil washes and, once dry, dry brush them with steel metallic paint to simulate the polished-worn look on the links.

14. A hair dryer will help soften and, thus, shape the links.

15. Once all the links are in position, glue on the upper part of the body.

16. The white parts are built from 0.13mm Plasticard.

17. The handles on the small doors are built with thin wire bent with pliers.

18. Coil copper wire around the exhaust.

19. Small metal strips are shaped into fastenings for the exhaust.

20-21. The exhaust fastenings are positioned with the help of tweezers

22. Completed part.

23. A small rod, made from two-part putty, is placed on the right fender.

24. A wet brush will help mold the creases on the putty.

25. Detailing the inside of the drivers' hatch. Begin by gluing some small plastic cubes inside.

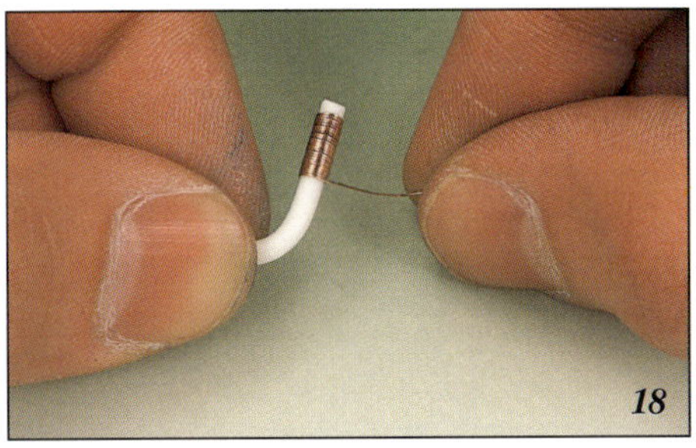

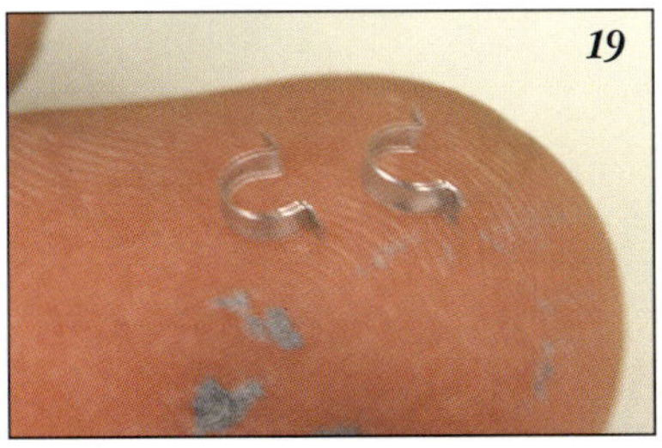

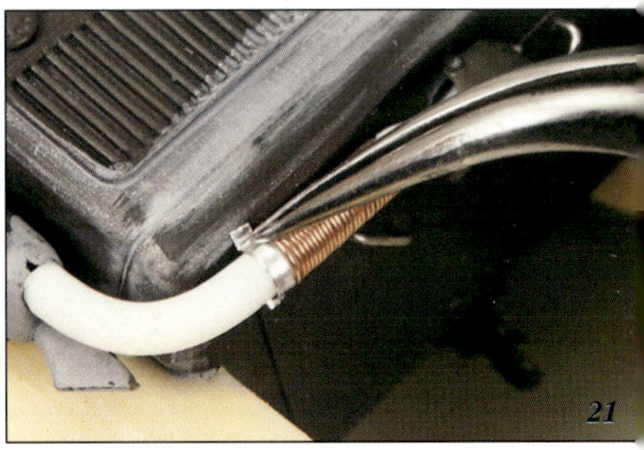

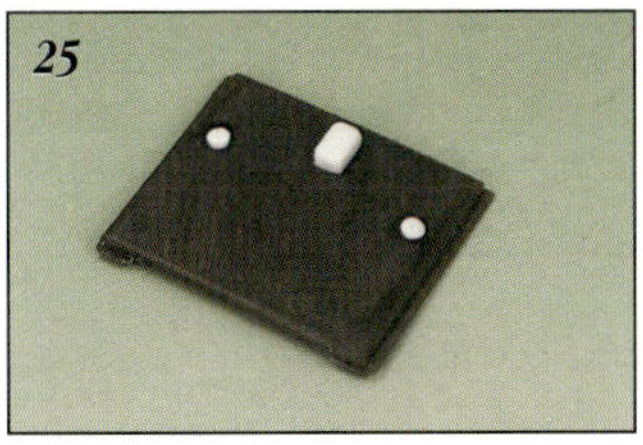

26. Then glue on the photo-etch parts.

27. The handles are made from small plastic rods.

28. The vision slot is marked with a scriber.

29. Note the newly cut slot.

30-31. Front and rear of the driver's upper hatch cover.

32. The support for the drivers' hatch is made of Plasticard.

33. Crank inside the drivers' hatch support.

34. Sanding with a plastic block will result in the correct shape for the back of the rear light.

35. Plastic block and photo-etched part that will eventually become the rear light.

36. Next, glue small pieces of plastic onto the sides.

37. Completed part.

38. Drilling the spot for the guns' axle.

39. Placing a round piece of plastic in the hole.

40. A low voltage soldering iron and a knife will help make the weld seam on the lower part.

41. The mantle is built from 0.25mm Plasticard.

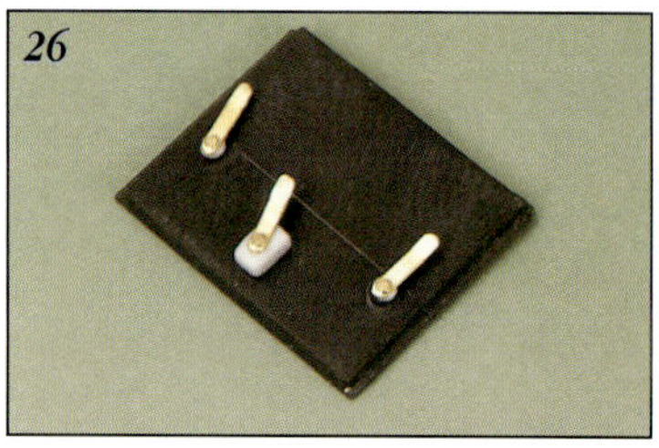

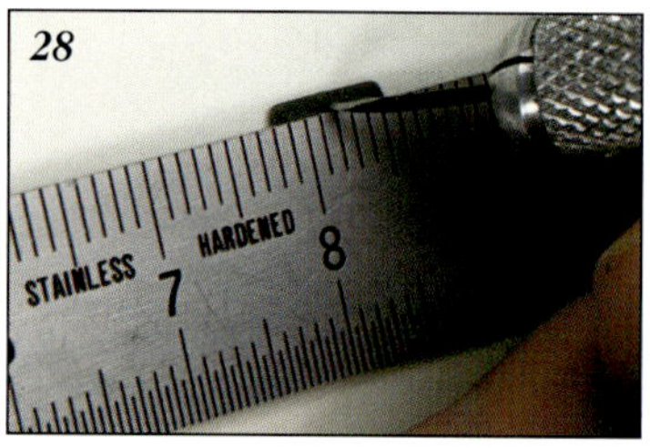

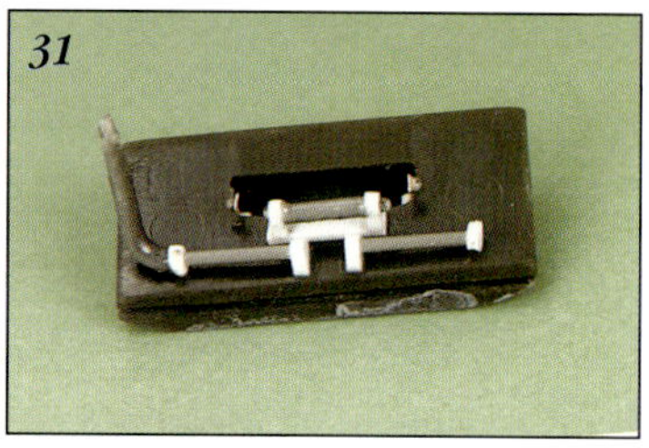

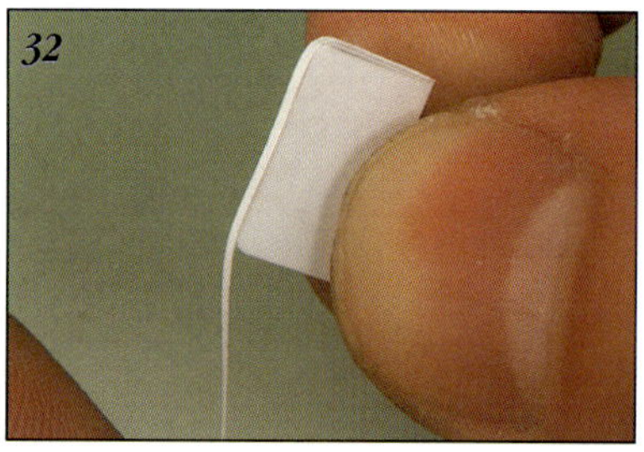

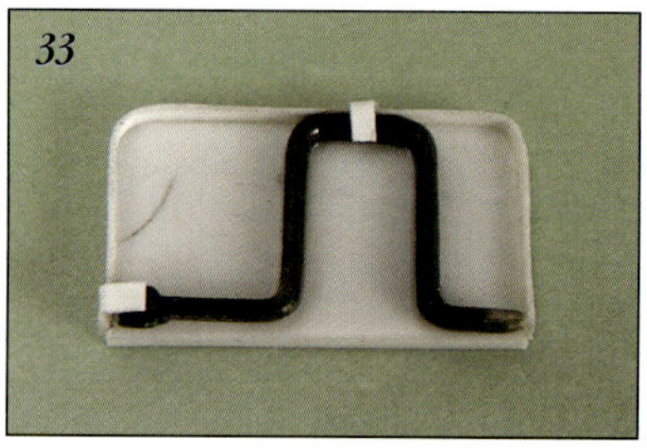

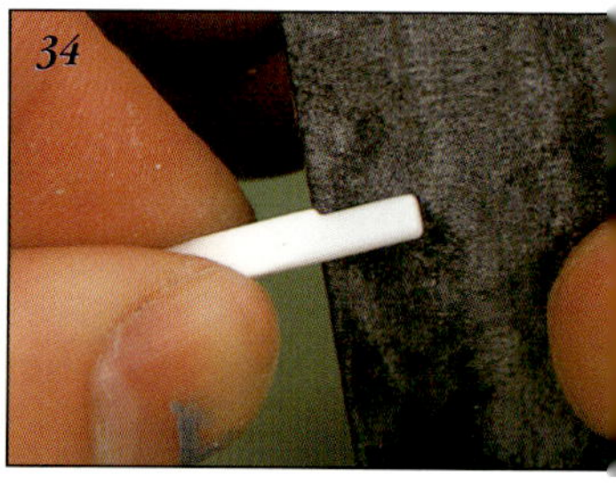

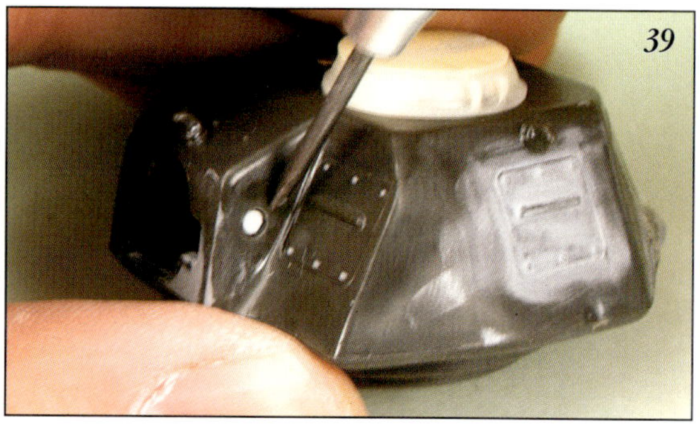

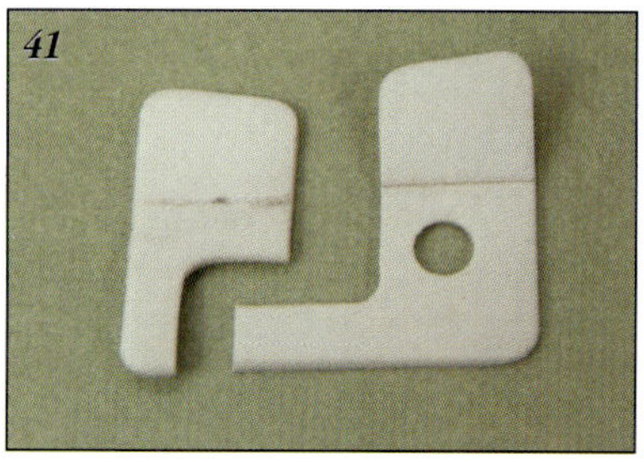

42. The mantle in position. The original plastic gun barrel was replaced with a metal one.

43. Cutting the resin part with a cutting tool.

44. Scraping clean the surface.

45. Clean and ready to glue.

46. Place a scratch built box on top of the assembled parts.

47. The box is detailed with wire, metal strips and photo-etched locks.

48. The box is fastened with two metal strips.

49. The metal part on the resin part (in front of the box) are just regular sewing pins.

50. Obtain a "notek" from another kit and put on it a piece of wire.

51. Some "U" shaped pieces were also made using leftover photo-etch material. The "U" shaped pieces were originally intended to hold a tow cable.

52. A hammer and crank are positioned on top of the left fender.

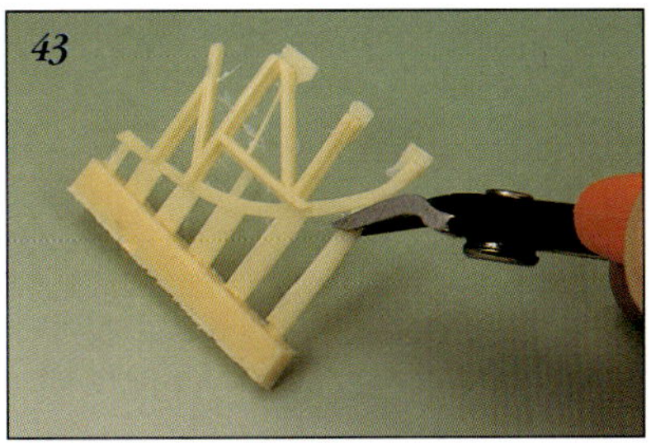

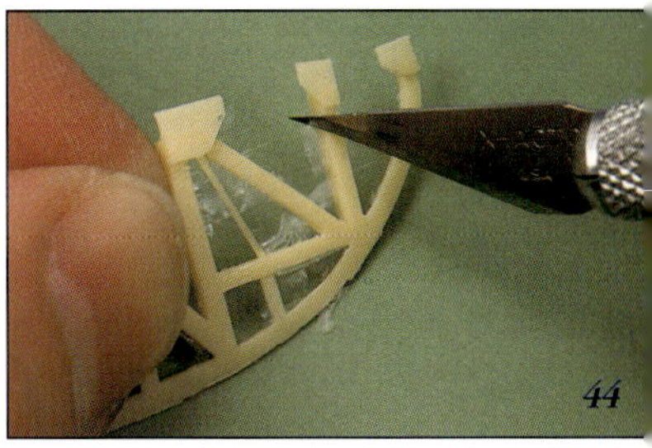

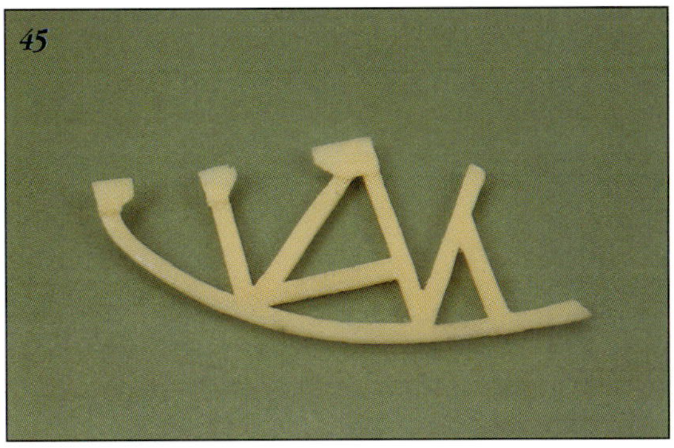

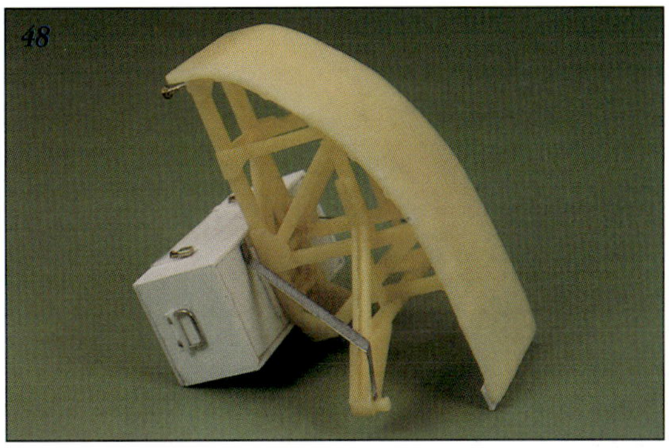

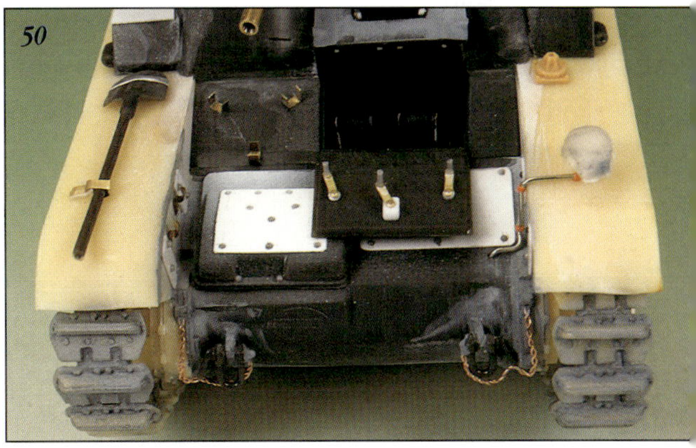

53. The shovel is positioned on top of the right fender.

54. There should be six attachment points on the exhaust silencer. They were made from leftover photo-etched material.

55. The position lights are positioned on the rear of the vehicle.

56. On the inside of the fenders, position some Plasticard attachment straps.

57-61. General views.

62. Make sure to protect the interior of the vehicle before starting to paint the exterior.

63. Acrylic, oil and enamel paints used on the model.

64. The Panzer gray mixture became bluish over time. This effect can be achieved by mixing several colors (the mixture is supplied in the text) and then shading all crevices with a darker shade.

63

64

65

66

67

68

69

70

71

72

65. When applying the camouflage scheme, keep the airbrush just a short distance from the model. XF-60 and XF-55.

66. If the camouflage is too much in some areas, recover it with the original gray mixture.

67. This is the perfect graded effect we are looking for: gray paint is much more visible in some areas. In other areas it is hidden beneath a yellowish tone.

68. This overview shows to perfection the complex shapes of the camouflage scheme.

69. Using a heavily diluted mixture of dark brown and black paint, go over all the crevices and joints and make them look dirty.

70. This mixture applied in vertical brush strokes will help convey dirt quite convincingly. Apply it to the wheels.

71. Highly diluted burnt-sand oil paint is good for profiling all the joints and rivets.

72. Profiling accentuates all the prominent features and gives depth to the model.

73. The wheels are natural dirt magnets. Oil washes will help convey this.

74. Burnt sand oil paint is very good for tracks because, when wet, they are quite dark.

75-76. Highlighting prominent corners is done by dry brushing with enamel paint, HB6. This procedure is particularly commendable for enhancing the shape of all small parts: Handles, bolts, etc...

77. The inevitable paint damage is done with a new No.1 brush.

78. Red-brown and black acrylics are effective for getting the impression of rust.

79. Gunze Sangyo rust paint is used to smear the edges of the paint peels.

80. Red-brown is airbrushed onto the lower part of the vehicle. The paint should be highly diluted and applied in several coats.

81. Once dry, gloss varnish will help give the area a 'wet' look.

82. The areas where the tracks are subject to greater friction are dry brushed with gun metal and steel.

Panzer Gray paint is barely visible on top of the vehicle. Mud covers it almost completely on the lower parts. All dry brush treatments are pretty subtle. They just discreetly enhance the volume.

Lack of space forced crews to use boxes like the one seen on the rear. The box is made from Plasticard and copper wire.

Three different color variants can be made: Gray and green or yellow and green, or the classic three-color scheme: yellow with green and reddish brown distributed in diffused blotches.

Light Vehicles in Battle

The howling of the sandstorm obliterated all other sounds, and left us almost blind. We were going to a fortified Italian encampment with the help of a compass and some maps, while trying not to crash into the leading vehicles. It is frightening not to be able to see anything. However, the sandstorm also prevented the deadly Italian artillery from firing at us. We are reaching the first outer defense ring and that initiates the first skirmishes. The Matildas heading the formation start to fire; visibility improves a little, and I'm able to see the Matilda and a hull down M-11 Italian tank firing at each other simultaneously. The Italian is unable to see his shell bouncing off his opponent's armor, as they have received a direct hit that kills them all instantly.

The whole camp reacts, the Italians open fire with light weapons, and the smoke becomes as dense as the sandstorm just a little while ago. Ricocheting ammunition against the armor of our Vickers Mk. VI reaches a crescendo and the noise is unbearable. I open fire with our machine guns, shooting at anything that moves. An Italian soldier runs towards a Matilda holding something in his hand. He staggers and falls, as bullets from my machine gun hit him. A loud and sinister noise booms on my left, leaving me reeling. When I'm able to react, I realise that my face is bleeding and there is a wound on one side; We've been hit by a 20mm shell, and my face has been pierced by shrapnel.

We are fighting a duel, columns of sand spurt up close by, so I steer our tank towards a barrage of sand-filled sacks. The situation looks ominous; a Matilda fires a couple of rounds, revealing its position. As we approach the interior, the Italian Black Shirts surrender, but the artillery continues its heavy onslaught. A truck full of infantrymen receives a direct hit right behind us. It had attempted to shelter behind us, but, alas unsuccessfully.

The sandstorm has by now ceased completely, but enemy fire increases in intensity. Soon, just the Matilda and us are the only ones left in our position. The firing and the smoke reveal the position of the enemy artillery surrounded and crewed by men reluctant to surrender. They are a whole lot tougher than the Black Shirts. The almost invulnerable Matilda knocks out the guns one by one until it receives a direct hit on its tracks, stopping it completely. As its turret rotates to fire again, it is hit by another shell. Although the shell doesn't pierce the armor, its destruction is imminent. There's just one thing to do, and I don't hesitate. Using the engine's full power we climb the short slope, crash through the sand sack barrier and enter the gun's position, firing our machine guns wildly at the remaining Italians. Surprised by our sudden appearance and caught completely unawares, they surrender. Some raise their hands while others run and hide. At that moment, our infantry arrive. One more Italian camp has fallen.

VICKERS MK.VI A

A direct legacy of the Twenties; the concept of a light vehicle able to accompany cavalry units, resulted in the Vickers Mk.VI A: A light, fast vehicle that could undertake scouting duties. The new concept offered one good advantage; it was able to escape from heavy enemy

1. The reference used during the making of this model.

2-3 Different tools can be used for separating the parts. Here, we are using a knife blade to remove small parts.

4. Be careful when separating each part, you do not want to accidentally remove an important detail.

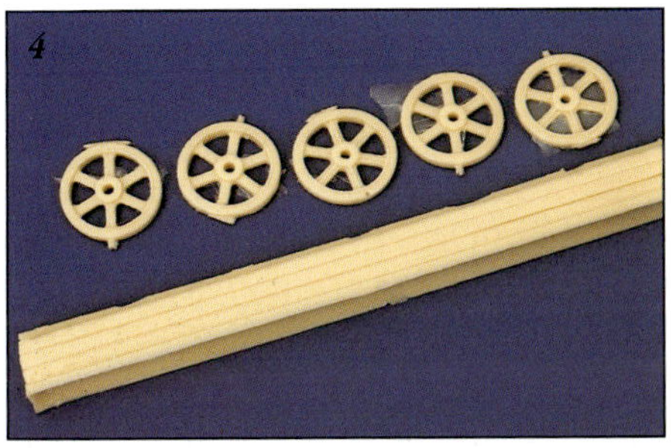

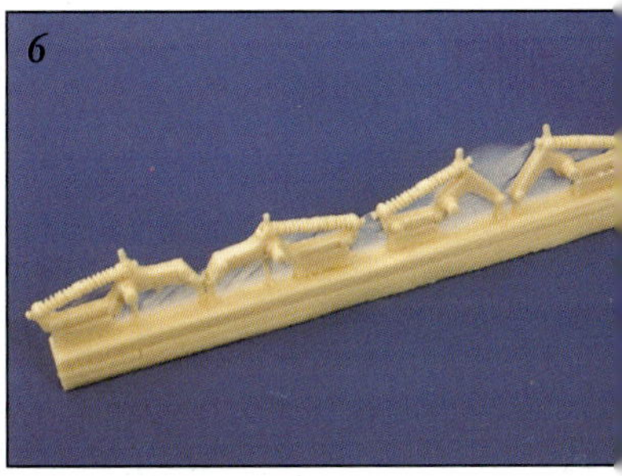

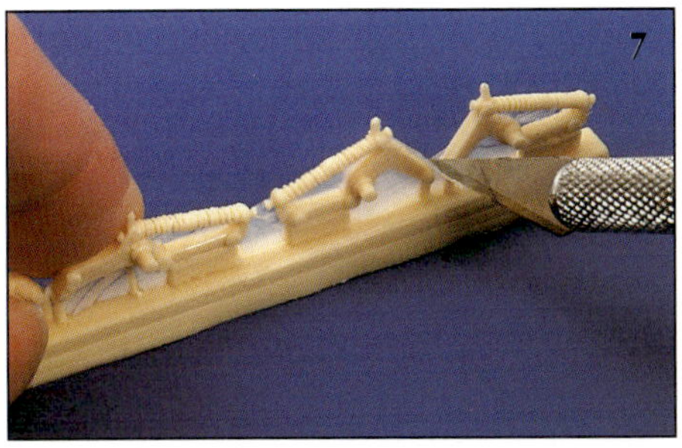

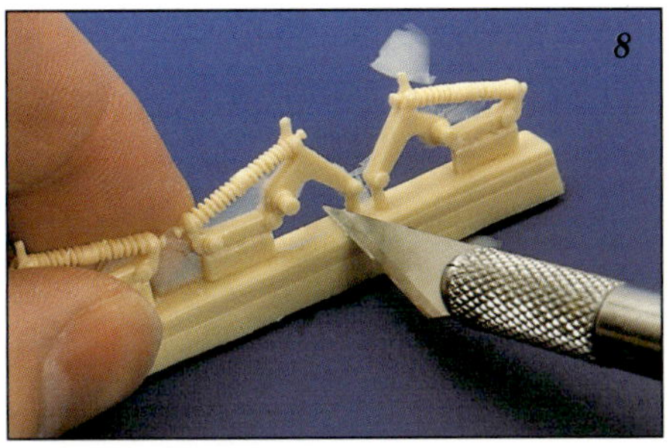

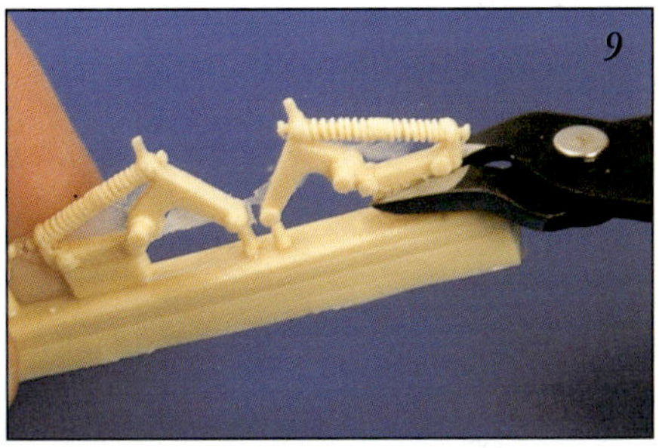

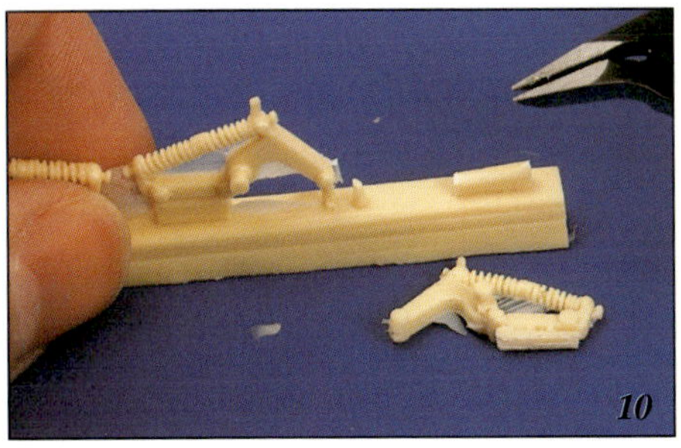

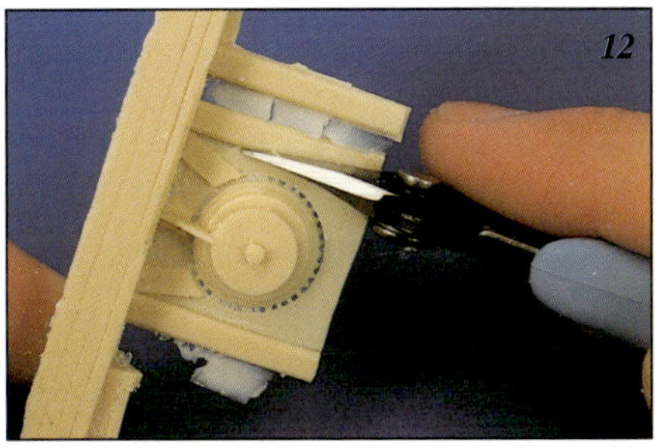

5. The knife is also very useful for cleaning the mold flash off the part.

6. Parts for the wheels, covered in flash.

7. The most delicate parts are removed with a knife.

8. This tool can also be used to remove mold flash.

9. A modeler's cutter is used to separate the piece.

10. The cutter makes a clean cut.

11. When large enough, parts require a small saw.

12-13. Precision scissors can be used for making longer cuts in narrow areas.

machines. As the years progressed, the concept was improved; better armor and superior weaponry was added. When WWII broke out, their debut in France wasn't overly successful. The vehicle was used conventionally and, in consequence, was easily neutralized by the enemy. Anti-tank weapons and the heavy, slow tanks held the advantage. However, when used in the desert, they had an equal share of glory and defeat. Working alongside heavier vehicles, they proved a decisive factor when defeating the obsolete, defensive Italian tanks. The Vicker's high point was momentarily eclipsed by the German victory that echoed the similar defeat in France.

The vehicle we are about to model is one of the final versions. It had a crew of three, weighed almost five tons and was powered by an 88 hp petrol engine. It had a top speed of 51kms per hour. It was armed with two machine guns of 12.7mm and a 7.7mm respectively.

The period paint scheme consisted of three colors. It should be mentioned that when one vehicle was destroyed, its replacement was given the same name. The vehicle we are modeling had at least two 'lives', one life was spent painted in three colors, blue, sand-black and brown, and the second life (the one we're doing) with just two colors. The name for both incarnations can be seen on the rear of the turret.

ASSEMBLY

This is an easy-to-assemble resin kit, and it will be carefully explained how to treat each part, how to separate and clean them. If the kit manufacturer over-uses the molds, as in this case, the natural crevices fill up with resin that has to be removed. This residue, or flash as it is more commonly called, can quite often be found on 'new' copies. For example, the tracks can exhibit lumpy imperfections and these have to be removed. After this tedious job has been done, the next one is to fill all the air bubbles by filling them with putty and then sanding them smooth with 600grain wet and dry paper. When all the parts are clean, assembly can begin with super glue. However, when gluing weak and/or small parts (the bogies on the chassis for example) it might be necessary to use two-part epoxy glue, such as Araldite.

On the other hand, the small weak parts could be replaced with scratch-built ones. These can be made from a variety of materials, Plasticard, copper wire and leftover photo-etch pieces.

Some parts need to be entirely rebuilt: The exhaust, the headlight, the antenna and its base, the hatch on the small turret, etc...

PAINTING

Rough weather along with the rapidly changing temperatures from day to night, as is the case in the desert, have a major effect on painted surfaces. Direct sunshine rapidly deteriorates the colors and they erode quickly. All surfaces where paint is scratched or peeled off, rapidly becomes rusty. High daytime temperatures make rust acquire a particular dark red-brown hue that doesn't drip (as is the case in rainy weather).

We will also have to do the paint peels that uncover the underlying original European theatre colors. We will also have to take into account the general dust/dirt layer that covers the entire vehicle, subtlely altering the color tones. The picture captions explain, in detail, all the steps to follow.

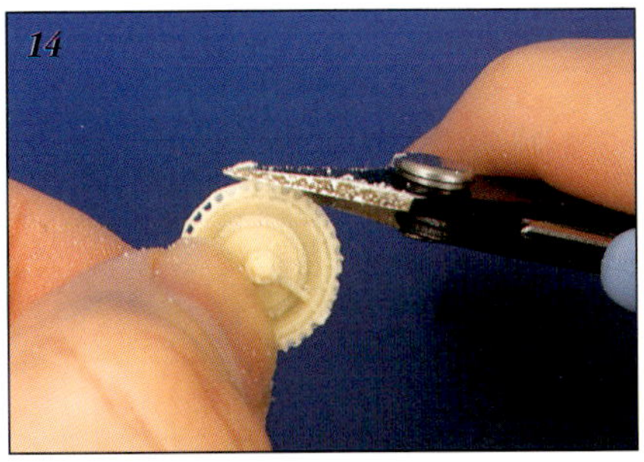

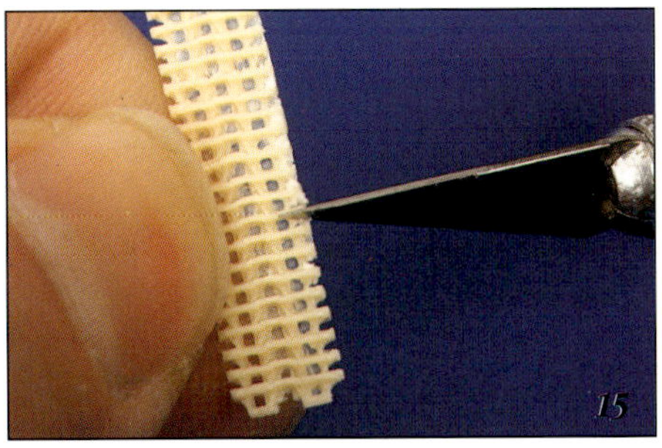

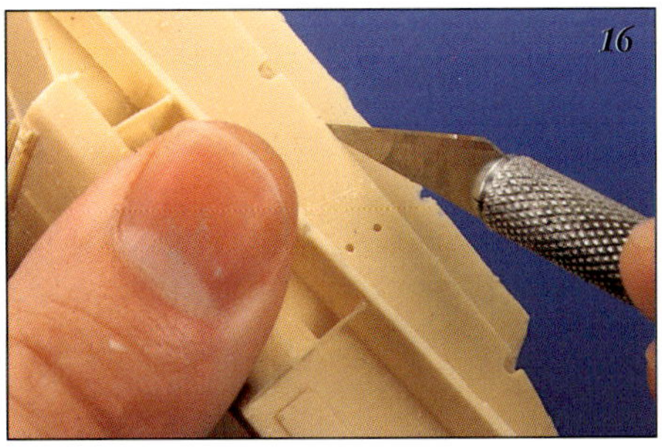

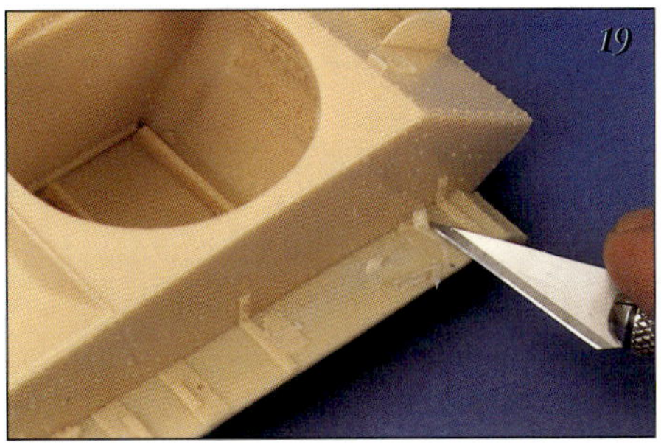

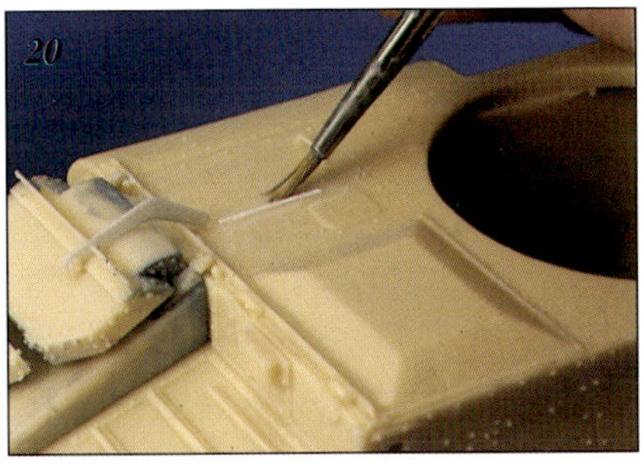

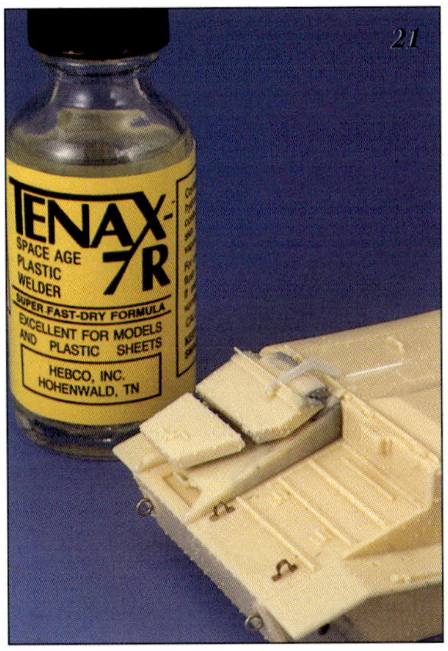

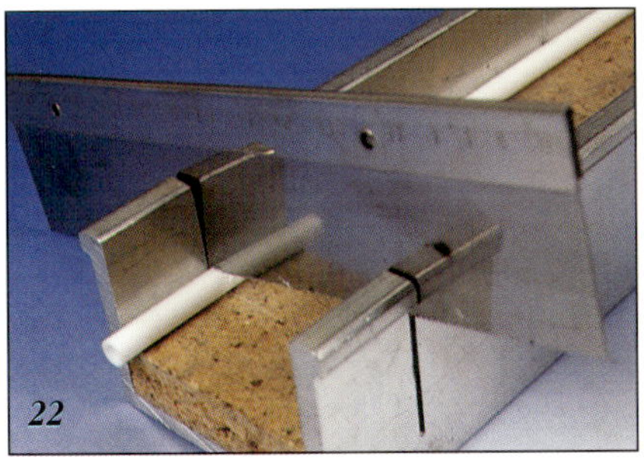

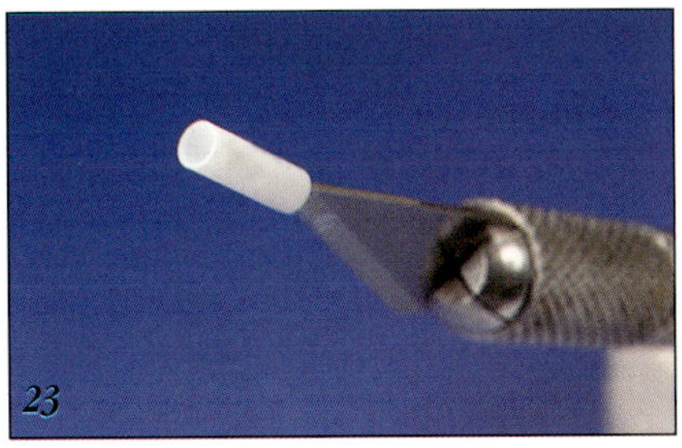

14. The precision scissors also come in useful for removing flash.

15. On the tracks we may find silicone remains from the mold and plenty of resin molding residue covering all details. Clean it all carefully link-by-link using a knife blade. It is a tedious job, but absolutely necessary.

16. On large parts, mark (several times) the cutting line with the knife and then snap it out.

17. Moving the part right and left in order to snap it without unnecessary strain.

18. Use a knife to polish the surface.

19. The area where the box (used in the North African campaign) is positioned must be scraped flat with a knife.

20-21. Super glue can be used for gluing plastic and resin. There are other cements (like the one shown in the picture) that will also weld both materials together. Very little cement, applied with a brush, should be used.

22. The exhaust silencer is scratch-built from Evergreen rod.

23. Fasten the part securely before sawing to ensure a straight cut.

24-25. The round side covers will be punched to measure.

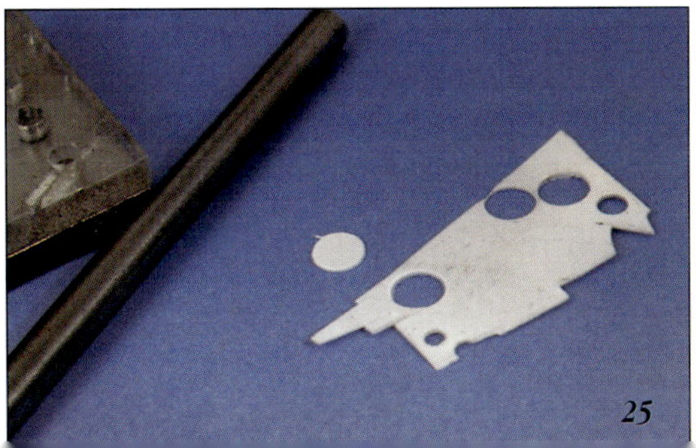

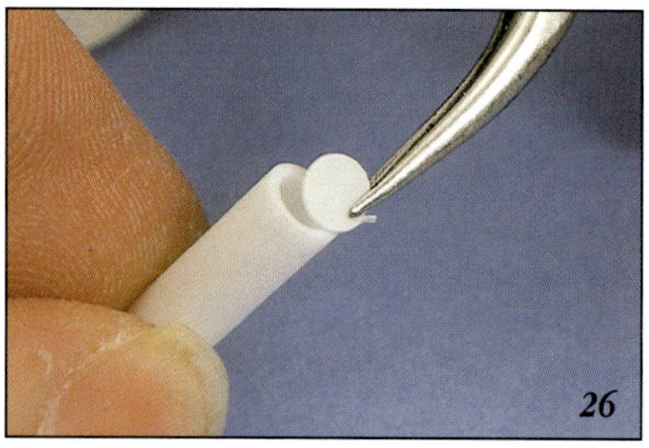

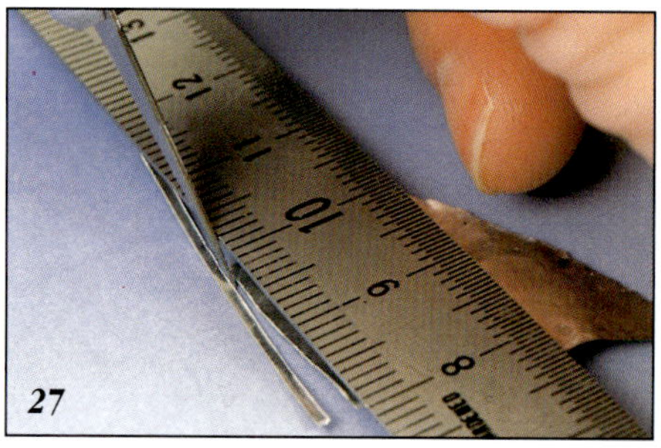

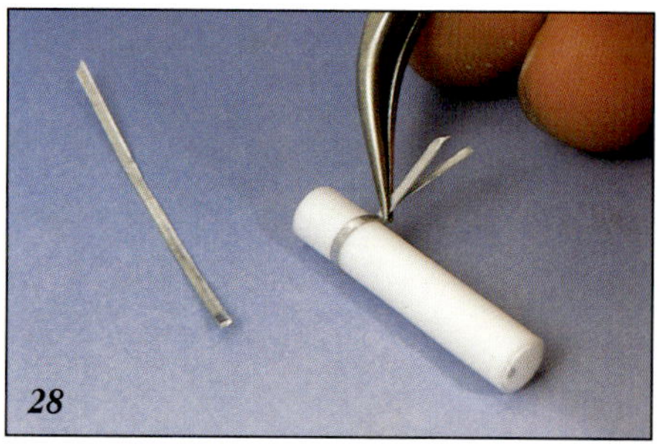

26. Small tweezers will help to ensure that the cover is glued on straight.

27. Metal strips are cut to make the bands

28. The bands are wrapped round the rod with the help of tweezers.

29. Make a new hole with a new knife blade.

30. Comparison between the original and the scratch-built part.

31. The tracks are fitted to the wheels with the help of a hair dryer.

32. First, position the links onto the traction wheel and then work down towards the links that are in contact with the ground.

33. Now, position the links onto the rear traction wheel.

34. Tracks should have a natural droop along the top.

35. Strengthen the join between the tracks and the vehicle with epoxy glue.

36. Use a thin plastic strip and fine wire to make the antenna's tension spring.

37. Position it with the help of tweezers.

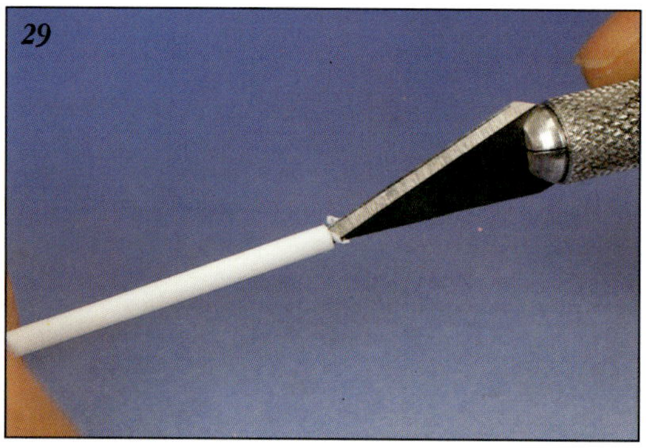

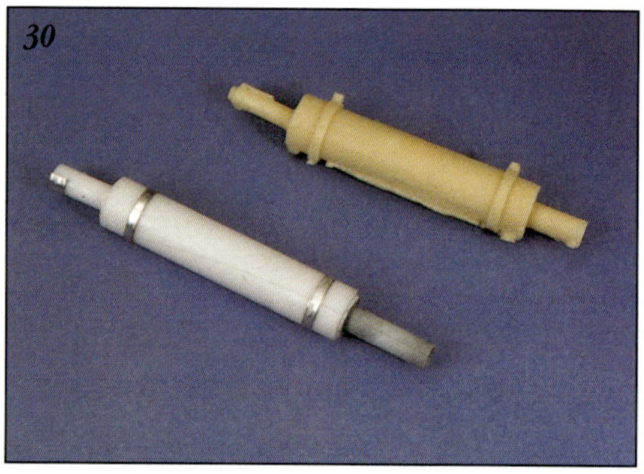

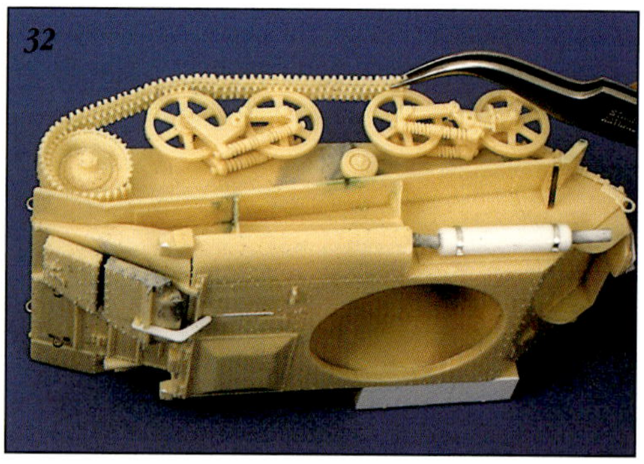

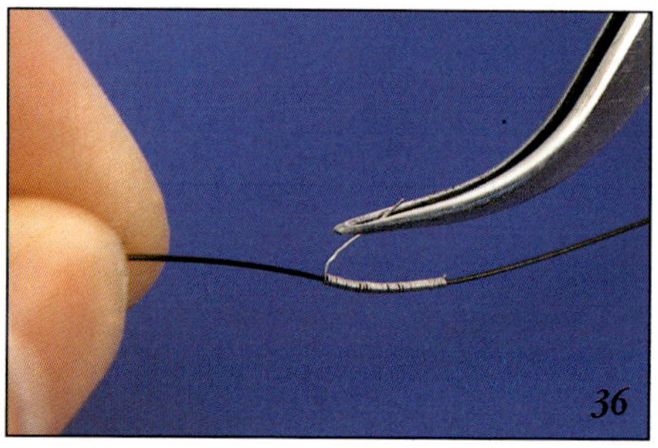

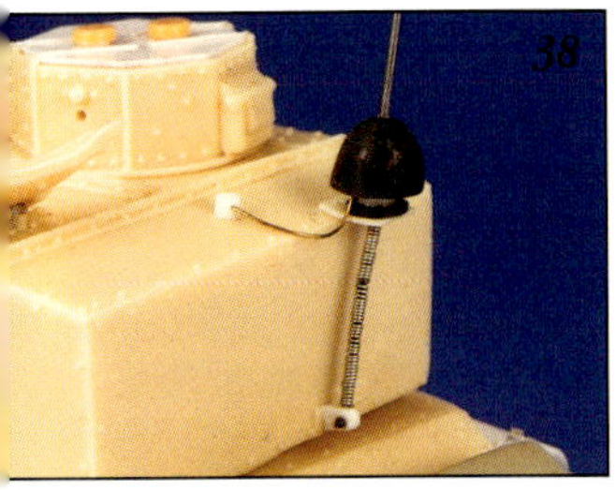

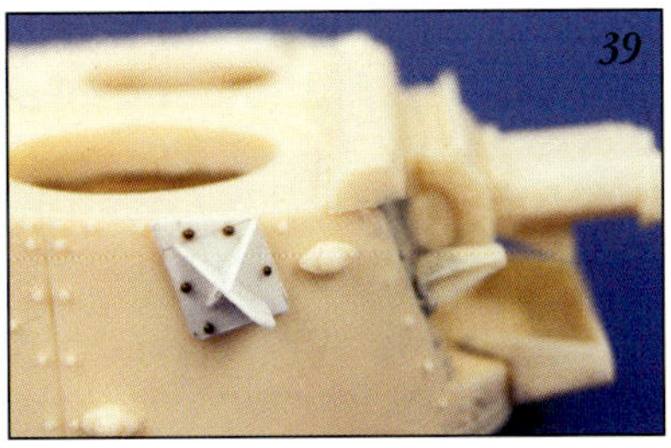

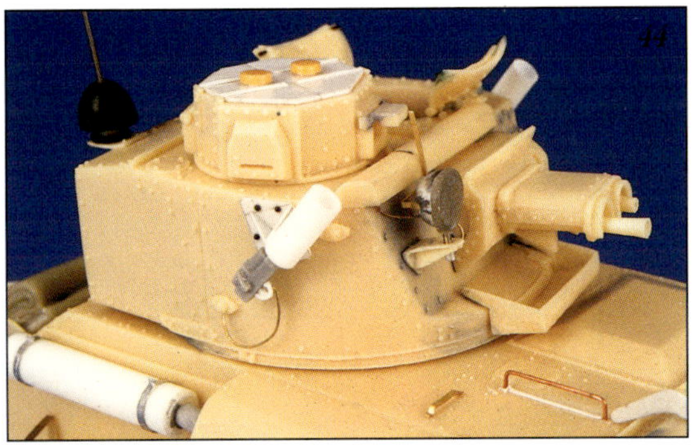

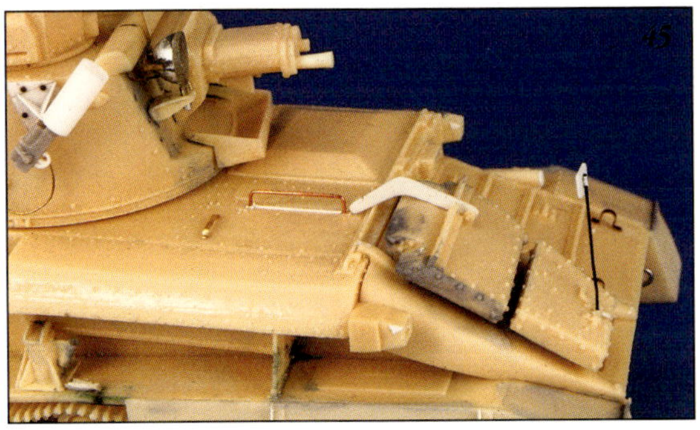

38. The base for the antenna is a headlight from a T-34.

39. The support for the smokescreen apparatus was made from Plasticard.

40. By using a plastic rod and the rear part of a rifle, without the butt, the tube can be completed. Be careful of the cable that is connected to the firing device.

41. The rear of the headlight was detailed with a square piece of plastic with a hole drilled in the center.

42. The license plate was made from thin Plasticard.

43. The hatches on the small upper turret were made of pieces of plastic.

44. The headlight was replaced with one from another kit. The rear handle is a small metal strip.

45. In this view is seen some of the small parts built from different materials, and then glued to the chassis.

46. A metal strip was used to make the part holding the fender.

47. The straps on the upper part were also made of sheet metal.

48. For the rearview mirror, use a entomologist's needle and a small piece of plastic.

· COLOR CHART ·

Tamiya
XF-2 flat white, XF-7 flat red, X-6 orange, XF-10 flat brown, XF-59 desert yellow, XF-60 dark yellow, XF-55 deck tan, XF-23 light blue, X-14 sky blue.

Humbrol
65 light blue, 71 cream.

Oil paints
White, black, burnt umber, yellow ochre, transparent golden ochre .

Vallejo
897 bronze green, 950 black, 988 khaki.

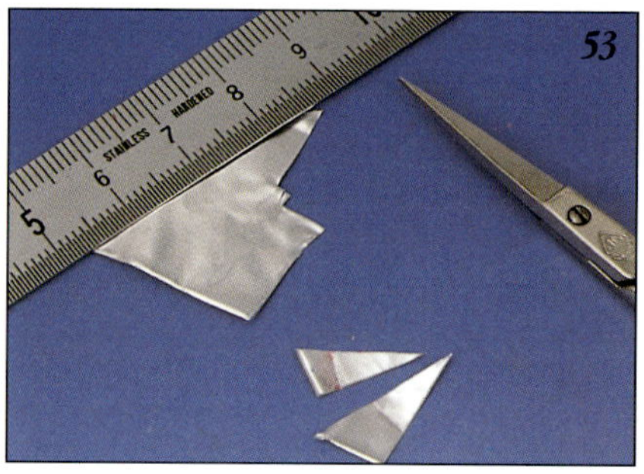
53

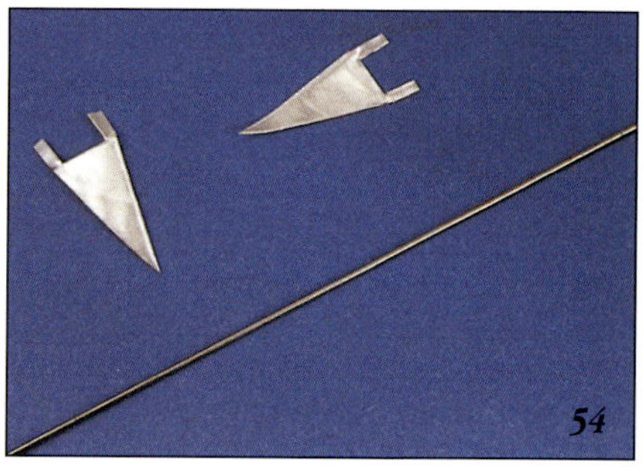
54

55

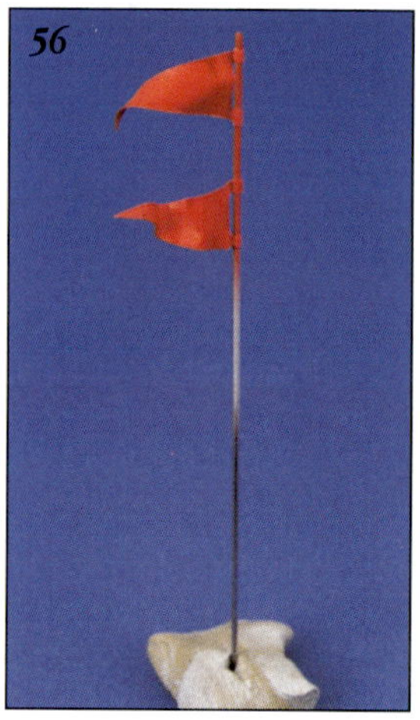
56

57

58

59

49-52. General views.

53. The small flags are made from thin metal sheet. The metal sheet can be easily worked to give it the 'creased' look of real cloth.

54. Antenna and flags.

55. Both pieces were super glued.

56. Red usually gives a lot of trouble unless you prime the surface first.

57. The highlights were done with orange, shadows with red-brown.

58. The base color is a mixture of XF-59, XF-60, and XF-55 toned down with a little white.

59. The acrylic, enamel and oil paints that were used.

60. When doing a straight-edged camouflage scheme, it must first be masked.

61. Our blue mixture contains equal amounts of XF-23, X-14 and white.

62. It is essential to use the airbrush at the correct angle, otherwise paint will 'creep' under the masking and the job will be ruined.

63. Very carefully, and with the aid of tweezers, remove the masking tape.

64. If the process was followed carefully, the result should be perfect.

65-66. Overall views of the camouflage scheme.

67. With a small amount of highly diluted white, the intensity of the blue base will be toned down, and will also turn it a little gray.

68. An overall view of the toned-down gray, the result of direct exposure to the desert's 'blazing sun'.

69. With a dark sandy-gray color, profile all vehicle's features. This will help to simulate the dirt/dust accumulations.

70. Dry brushing is perfect for simulating the fine dust that has accumulated on the fenders.

71. Here can be seen how the peeling and scratched paint reveals the original 897 ref. underneath.

72. Burnt sand and burnt sienna oil paint washes are used for painting the tracks.

73. The numbers and the symbol on the fenders are decals.

74. Paint peels were quite common over the whole of a vehicle in a desert environment. The vehicle's original European theatre color is still visible underneath. 897.

75. Over the grayish-blue camouflage, all the different accumulations of dust and sand can be easily seen. These were done with paint washes and dry brushing.

76. The rust color was used on the exhaust. It also has some burnt sienna oil washes along with some orange and black paint as well.

77. A canvas and a spare wheel were positioned on the rear. It is this type of detail that gives the tank a 'lived-in' feel.

78. Paint peels were done over the whole model.

79. The red square was removed from a square decal that was originally solid red inside.

80. The machine gun muzzles were painted black. They were then dry brushed with metallic gray.

81. The name of the vehicle was done with Letraset rub-down lettering.

82. The headlight is covered with a small canvas. The hatch interior has some leather protection.

Foreword

Zimmerit, or anti-magnetic paste, was an exclusive feature on some German tanks. When the Germans designed and manufactured magnetic anti-tank charges that adhered to the armor of enemy tanks, they also developed the means to counteract the new weapon. The Allies, however, never made extensive use of magnetic explosive charges. While British parachutists and the Russians placed some value on their use and even improved some features of them, they weren't widely used. German armor carried this paste from the middle of 1943 to the beginning of 1945. After that date its use was phased out and the later German tanks never had it applied. The paste looked like concrete, it was gray and would stick quite easily to most surfaces. It was originally applied with big spatulas, and was later textured with different tools to get a rough surface. The most common tool was a rolling pin with lines on it that left the familiar pattern on the surface. Another rolling pin had spikes on its surface, and left rather strange holes on the paste. It was also common to use a plasterers-type float both vertically and horizontally, leaving small squares of different sizes, or even rhomboid shapes. These were the most common textures applied to the paste. However, contemporary photographs sometimes show vehicles without any texture or with random hand-made designs. When choosing the pattern you want to portray, look closely at the pattern and figure the most effective method of imitating it. The most common, and effective means of doing this is with the help of a pyrogravure, or a low voltage soldering iron, on regular or epoxy putty.

Tiger I

Tank chassis' lie among hundreds of parts: track links everywhere, separate turrets, everything scattered in apparent confusion. I say confusion rather than destruction, because we are in an improvised repair shop at the front. Our vehicles, after three months of heavy fighting, are not in the best of shape. The mechanics work day and night, trying to repair and replace the broken parts, a difficult task due to the complexity and weight of the machines. The ground we're fighting over, and the appalling weather condition we're suffering, greatly contribute to the present state of our AFVs. Of the 45 tanks in our Panzerabteilung, hardly ten are in a serviceable condition. We've been forced to cannibalise one machine for spare parts, because the confusion of battle resulted in two of our tanks firing on each other and putting both out of action before the mistake was realised.

From the commander we receive a signal ordering us to advance towards his position. It appears they are in a pretty bad fix. On arrival, we're told that the front line has been broken in several places by T-23 and KV tanks and they are heading our way. Our own aircraft are not able to contain them and, in the condition we're in, we could very well be entirely overwhelmed. I collect all the available crews as fast as I can and check out all the obtainable material, finally getting together five extra tanks to go with the ten already available. Fifteen tanks are all we have to halt, perhaps, a hundred enemy ones. After collecting all the available ammunition and fuel, we head for the frontline as fast as we can. Some light reconnaissance Pz.IIs are already scouting the area. 30 kilometers separate us from the enemy, and the road is slowing us down, because small forests and rocky areas have to be traversed in order to get there. We've been traveling for an hour when suddenly we see columns of smoke: the Russians have beaten us to it.

We seek out good positions on the high ground, as we want to take a look at the enemy through our binoculars. First we see four of our own reconnaissance vehicles. They inform us by radio about our positions in relation to the enemy's. Our reconnaissance tanks then have to hastily retreat and are speeding towards us, closely pursued by heavy enemy fire. Some distance away, shrouded in smoke and fog, we finally see the enemy looking for us.

We are well deployed, and are confident we can defeat them, but we are waiting for them to come within range at about two kilometers. I give orders and the gunner loads an armor-piercing shell. I hear the familiar sound of the breech opening and the shell being loaded, followed by the clang as the breech is closed and locked. I carefully select a target and fire. The vibration of the recoil is felt throughout the tank. The breech is opened once again and a jet of smoke is released,

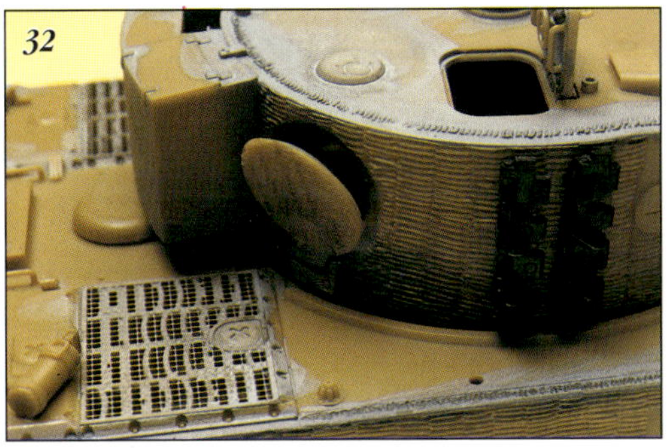

28. Remove all, and any mold lines.

29. Also, remove any mold flash.

30. Show Modeling photo-etch sheet number 007. Todo Modelismo grills could also be used.

31. There shouldn't be any difficulties applying any part of the photo-etched sheet.

32-33. The side hatch can be modeled in the open position by drilling it out and fitting a metal hinge.

34. Obviously the engine cover should remain loose, to allow it to be opened.

35. The turret roof was given some weld seams with the soldering iron. Putty will be added later.

36. The headlight is completed with a length of wire.

37. To position the handle of the cleaning tool, carve a housing for it and add a few small dents.

38. The side fenders have been heated and then well dented and bent.

39. The rear fenders were detailed with some small plastic parts and photo-etched bolts.

40. All the spare link supports were given small scratch built wire handles.

What & How

Texturing Zimmerit with a small soldering iron.

This is, probably, the oldest method for texturing Zimmerit paste. It is really meant for making large or small-type of texture patterns. However, the best pattern is the one consisting of parallel lines. Some modelers are reluctant to try this because of working directly on the kit's plastic surface and realise that any errors could be fatal. That said, mistakes are pretty unlikely as the tool offers excellent control.

Basically, fix a length of wire to the knife blade of the low-power soldering iron (15 or 17 watts). Do not use a more powerful iron as it could melt the plastic. To do the texturing, first draw parallel vertical lines (3mm apart) on the vehicle. Sometimes, this can vary, it can be up to 4 mm on the turret and there are other exceptions. Once the vertical separations have been outlined, take up the soldering iron and start making the horizontal marks, beginning at the top and working down. Each line is made close to the previous one, almost touching it and sometimes even working slightly over it. Exert just moderate pressure on the surface as we are looking for a moderate effect. On some actual vehicles, it can be seen how the person with the rolling pin for texturing the paste, has either gone too far to one side or over some of the other rows. This can also be simulated while, at the same time, seeking to maintain parallel lines.

The soldering iron also works well on intricate areas such as the mantle, or for making the weld seams on the turret roof. Working in this scale gives a proportionate effect, which is rather convincing.

1. A 17watt soldering iron, a steel rule and a pencil, are our tools.

2. Draw parallel, vertical lines at 3mm intervals.

3. The lines will cover the entire 'Zimmerit' plastered area.

4. Work from left to right, working your way down, pressing lightly with the soldering iron.

5. The blade can even be used on the intricate details of the gun's mantle.

6. Weld seams can also be done.

7. The area where the exhausts and their covers are positioned was left clear.

8-9. Convey scratches and damaged areas by simply not touching them.

10. The vertical front armor is a separate part that is easily worked and then fixed on after.

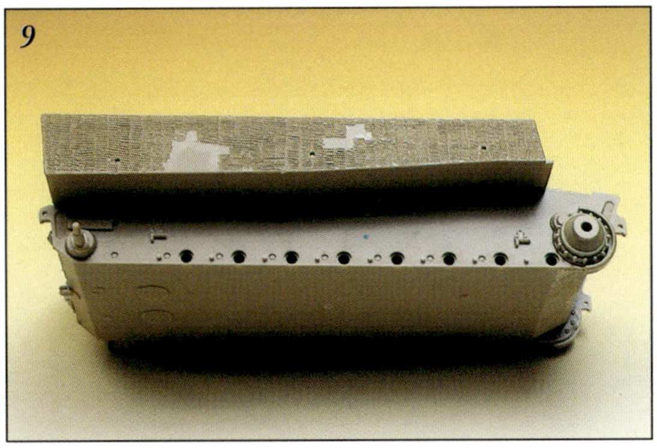

11-12. It is not absolutely necessary for the marks to be completely vertical. They can be displaced from left to right and even tilted slightly. Actual units appear in contemporary photos sporting just such inaccuracies.

Jagdpanther

We have been trying all day to cut the road leading to Arnhem This is being done to prevent any attempts at re-supply. We have received information that the supplies and heavy equipment are just two and a half kilometers from the town. The Jungwirth, our parachute brigade, is a heavily reduced force, with less than forty percent of its men remaining. Towards dusk, moving through the mud while hiding from enemy aircraft, I spot a company of tank hunters of the DLIX battalion, hurrying to join us. Their proximity gives us hope. In spite of the rain and the mud, the column is moving fast, even taking into account the weight of the machines and their guns. We hurriedly regroup and, as the first shadows begin to fall over the small forest, we kill the enemy with our knives, and hide very close to the road. We perceive the dull wartime headlights of an approaching truck convoy, spearheaded by a Sherman Firefly and a number of half-tracks filled with soldiers. The amazing thunderbolt that we see isn't from the sky but from the land, piercing the night's dark veil some three hundred meters away. The scream of the 88mm L-70 shell assaults our ears, and the Sherman becomes a fireball that continues to lumber forward, enveloped in an eerie inner glow. The brewing storm doesn't keep us waiting for long. Shells fired by the tank hunters hit the remaining vehicles in the column and, within minutes, everything is burning or explodes. Suddenly, the tanks approach at their top speed of 40km per hour, running over the burning remains to finish their job, destroying several transports and reconnaissance vehicles on the move.

The 'road of hell' will remain closed, blocking the way and making any further Allied advance impossible. The following day, September 25, was the start of Operation Berlin, that was, basically, the reactivation of the interrupted Market-Garden operation. The last vehicles to see action were the Jagdpanther.

ASSEMBLY

Considered the finest tank hunter of WWII, the Jagdpanther's performance was outstanding from 1944 onwards. It was a highly improved machine that inherited all the features of the original vehicle that spawned the Jagdpanther: The Panther. It was able to take advantage of all the enhancements introduced during 1943. Highly armored, some armored plates were 80mm thick and angled at some 35degrees, it was powered by a 700 hp Maybach motor that could drive its 46 tons to a top speed of 46 km per hour on surfaced roads, and 24 km per hour cross country. The 43/3 Pak L/71 gun could knock out any armored vehicle of the time within a 1.5 km range. Its biggest drawback was the absence of a rotating turret. The crew had to get used to aiming the gun by moving the whole vehicle. Final aiming adjustments were made with the gun's limited lateral movement. The Jagdpanther we propose to model is one of the first ones manufactured. The distinguishing features are: The shape of the mantle ring, and the one-piece gun barrel. The kit is from Revell, ref. 03006, with added detail from Todo Modelismo's No.5 kit for the grills, and Eduard's, ref. 35043, for the remainder of the vehicle. The gun barrel was replaced with another from the Jordi Rubio range, ref. 14, and its positioning in the mantle requires the use of two-part epoxy putty for it to be properly fixed.

1. Almost all books dealing with the Panther have sections on the Jagdpanther.
2. Epoxy putty on the surface of the Revell kit can convey the texture of Zimmerit paste.
3. The original Revell gun barrel is replaced for Jordi Rubio, ref. 14, one.
4. The air intake grille and ventilators are from a Todo Modelismo photo-etched sheet.

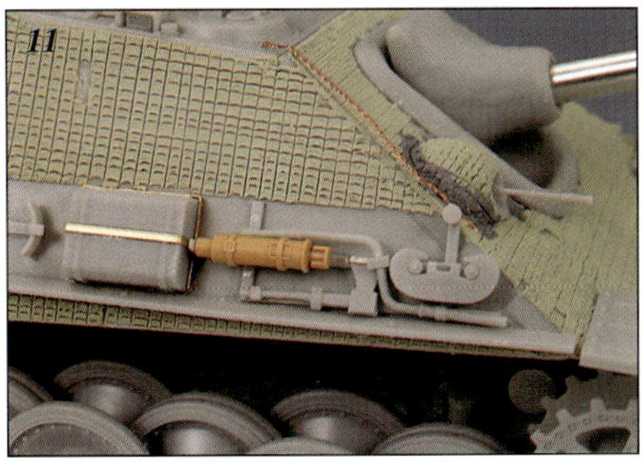

5-8. All other photo-etched parts are from the Eduard sheet No.35043.
9. This part that holds the gun's ramrod is the hardest to shape.
10. The Eduard parts for holding all the tools in place are absolutely essential.

11. A small chain can be placed here. The chain is designed to hold the machine gun's cover.

General assembly follows all the advice given on previous pages (including the photo-etched sheet). There is, however, a rather delicate part on the cylinder angle, holding the gun ramrod parts, that has to be bent in the middle (the photo-etched part comes flat). It is difficult because the part itself is so narrow and needs to be bent throughout its length. If it is not bent correctly, it will be rendered totally useless. The solution is to hold the part in a wide-jawed table vice and bend it slowly through 90 degrees with the help of a steel rule. Once all the photo etched parts are in position, we can concentrate on the small details, including handles, attachments (specially the ones that locate the spare track links). We will also have to prepare the tracks themselves, joining the links one-by-one. Group the linked lengths into four sections: The long sections for the upper and lower lengths, and the short ones to go round the traction and tension wheels. Do not fix them into place until after the painting is completed.

PAINTING AND DECORATING

Now is the time to bring the reader's attention to the chapter dealing with airbrush techniques used when applying German camouflage schemes, especially pattern number 12, which is the one chosen for this model. This scheme was inspired by a well-known contemporary photograph, showing a German soldier spraying the rear of a Jagdpanther. It consists of three colors, dark yellow, olive green, and brick brown, and will be painted primarily in acrylics, although enamels and oil paint will also be used.

Start with XF-60 as the base color and coat the entire model with it. Once that is done, add a few highlights with XF-57 to lighten all the horizontal surfaces. Also apply this color to the lateral and vertical surfaces that would be exposed to wear. By applying paint only on the required areas it will go some way to breaking up the monotony of the surfaces. This will help to give the vehicle more of a three-dimensional appearance. This can be accentuated even further by applying some XF-49 in the crevices and other sunken areas. In affect, this is the first shading coat. The procedure, in short, is; base color, followed a lighter shade of the same, then some shadows in a darker hue. Allow your personal taste to guide you into making heavier or lighter use of the contrasts. The final result will, to a great degree, depend on it.

The next step is to work on the green areas with XF-58. Remember that it is best to outline the edges first, and then fill in the areas. The shape of the lines is similar to those on a tiger, the big cat,

12-14. Views of the model after the Zimmerit paste has been applied and with all the photo etched parts in place.
15. We require Tamiya airbrush acrylics for the base colors, enamels for dry brushing, and oil paint for doing paint washes and giving those subtle nuances.
16. XF-60 is used to coat the entire surface of the model.
17. General highlights on the upper parts, and some vertical lines were airbrushed with XF-57.
18. Shadows on crevices, dents, and other sunken areas were done with XF-49.
19-20. 'Drawing' the outline of the green blotches, ready to be filled in later, using Tamiya XF-57.
21-22. The general layout of the green camouflage blotches. Note that the shapes are reminiscent of the pattern of a tiger's fur.

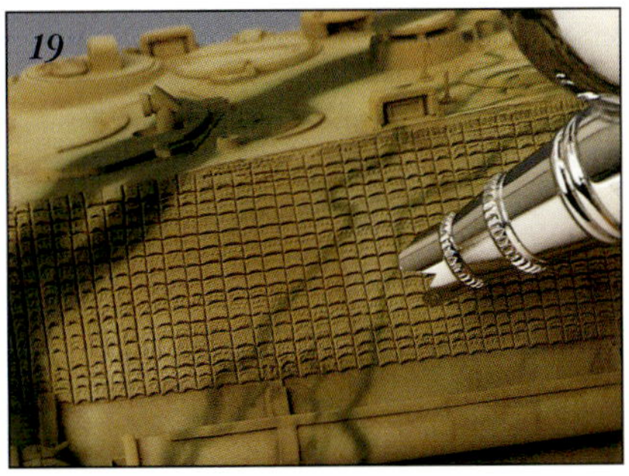

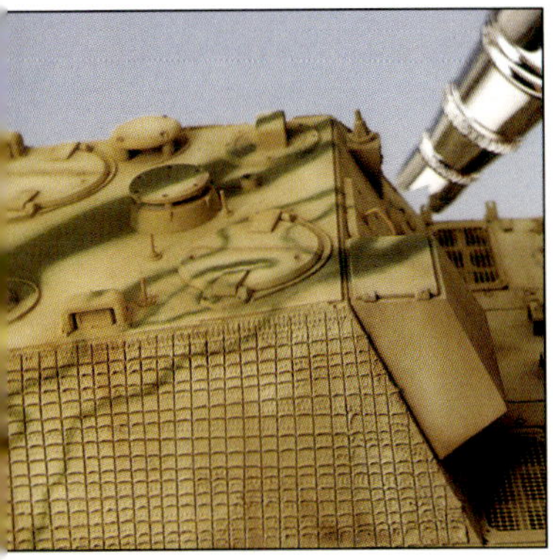

not the tank. Then, draw the outline of the green areas with XF-64. At this point, we can use the airbrush, working very close to the model's surface, using very little paint and low air pressure, in order to get lines of about half or one millimeter wide.

After that, work on the wheels and the profiling. Some modelers prefer to use the airbrush, but we have done this step using washes, blended paint, and dry brushing. For this use Model Color acrylics Nos. 984, 977, 917, and 876. Start with the darker colors and finish with the lighter ones, making sure that the lighter colors are undiluted. After weathering the wheels, dry brush Humbrol enamel No. 71 on all the bolts. Then, use some diluted black paint with a bit of brown to paint the rubber parts. If there is too much black paint, tone it down with some dry brushing.

Now is the time to profile the shapes and features of the kit with oil paint. This is a very important process and must be done carefully. First, apply highly diluted burnt-sand, thinned so that when the paint hits the surface it seeps into all the crevices and joints. This treatment should be applied over the whole model and also over all the surfaces including bolts, fastenings, etc... In short, go over everything that gives volume to the model to make it soar and stand out. You can also use some burnt sienna, green and sand paints applied to small areas and then blended in with the correct thinning agent. You must try and achieve a smooth chromatic effect and richness of color.

The next job is to dry brush with Humbrol enamels, using a single color for each color already on the tank (one enamel per camouflage color), and making sure that the colors match, and lightening the enamels very slightly with a little white paint. The enamels used are: 780 and 71, 113 and 71.

Now, go on to the paint peels, rust and all those little scratches that accumulate around areas like the exhausts. Rust on the exhausts is done with 872 and 911. Do not forget to diffuse some soot, using black, in each exhaust using the airbrush, and give a smooth black wash on the exhaust pipes. Paint peels are first outlined with black paint and then filled in with a rust brown paint, 981 on the old ones and 865 on the more recent ones.

The cross on each side should not be a decal. Instead, it should be painted on with the help of an adhesive mask. Draw the cross on a piece of masking tape, cut out the cross and stick the mask in the correct position and airbrush the white paint. Once the white cross has been done, repeat the process for the inner black part.

Doing the tracks is a much quicker process. Begin by airbrushing them with Tamiya XF-10, and then dry brush over that with Model Color 988 and 977, concentrating particularly on the sides. The inner edge of the tracks can be dirtied on those areas where the wheels make contact, while the outer side can be dry brushed with XF-56. This color must be applied to those areas in contact with the ground and end up with a 'friction polished' look. After everything has thoroughly dried, glue the tracks in position with super glue, taking care to identify each particular section before doing so. The antenna can be made from a piece of heat stretched sprue, painted black. This would be the finishing touch. However, give the model a last good look and airbrush a few sand colors to dirty it a little more, or enhance the 'dusty effect' with some pastel powder applied with a cotton swab. If, that is, from your point of view it needs it.

23. The green blotches need to be outlined with a 1mm thick line of XF-64.
24. The wheels are detailed and dirtied with Model Color acrylics Nos.984, 977, and 917.
25. The rubber parts are painted with a mixture of black and 876.
26. Oil colors used to convey all the subtle nuances: Burnt sienna, dark green, burnt sand, and natural sienna.
27. Burnt sand oil washes are used to shade some areas.
28. Humbrol enamel 80 plus some 71 and white, is dry brushed onto the green areas.
29. Humbrol enamel 71 and white is dry brushed on the dark yellow areas.
30. Intensify the highlighting on some areas by adding more white paint to the mixture.

31-32. Small dry brush touches to make the edges stand out.
33. Small paint peels and scratches made with black, filled with rust paint, and 98.

34. Preparing the adhesive mask for painting the German cross.
35. Tracing each of the two colored areas that make up the cross.
36. Cutting out the inner, and then the outer part of the cross.
37. Do the white area first.
38. Now place the mask corresponding to the inner, black part of the cross and apply black paint.
39. On lifting the mask, there should be a perfect cross beneath, even though the Zimmerit is rough.
40. Track sections and loose links to be correctly positioned later.

41. Tamiya's XF-10 is used for the base color.
42. On the outer edge of the track, dry brush some 977 and 917.

43. Loose links are also individually painted and glued in position.

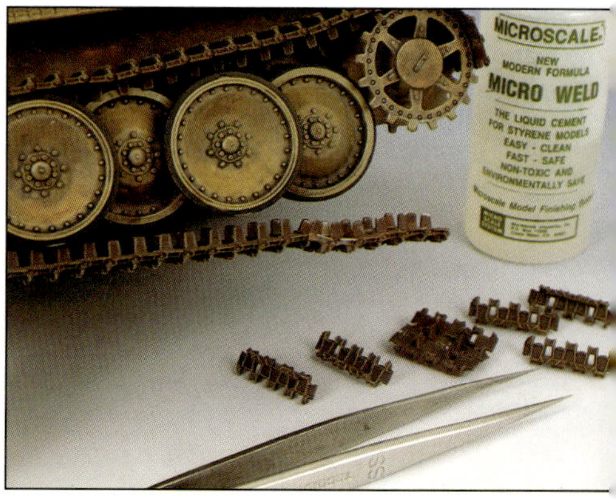

What & How

Zimmerit from epoxy putty

Some experienced modelers feel that this is the best and most realistic method of making Zimmerit, simply because it is pretty much the way it was done back in the Forties. This method, however, has one large drawback, the two-part putty is really difficult to make into the proper scale thickness. Quite often the end result is out of scale and, therefore, ugly. The lack of proper tools also helped to make this the worst method. Sometimes rectangular blades were used, and even sharp screwdrivers. All this made the process exceptionally slow and a good result isn't always guaranteed. That said, if the result is not right, remove the putty and start again.

A number of years ago, Tamiya came to the rescue with a new two part epoxy putty, the large one being the putty material, and the smaller one the catalyst. Squeeze out a line of equal length from both tubes. The putty tube, being the largest, will produce the thicker line while the catalyst tube will produce enough to activate the putty. Tamiya also supplies special knives, made to different dimensions and shapes for working the putty.

Once you mixed enough of the putty, spread it evenly over model's surface. Try to leave a thin layer that will slightly harden, and then use the appropriate tool that gives a realistic Zimmerit texture. The good thing about putty is that it can be worked into a horizontal line texture and also the one with small squares. When making the square pattern, first use the special tool for making square marks, and then use a triangular blade or scalpel for tracing the horizontal and vertical lines. Adhesive masking tape can be used for marking out the exact areas for the Zimmerit. Once the Zimmerit has been molded and has dried, carefully remove the tape, and you should have the defined area.

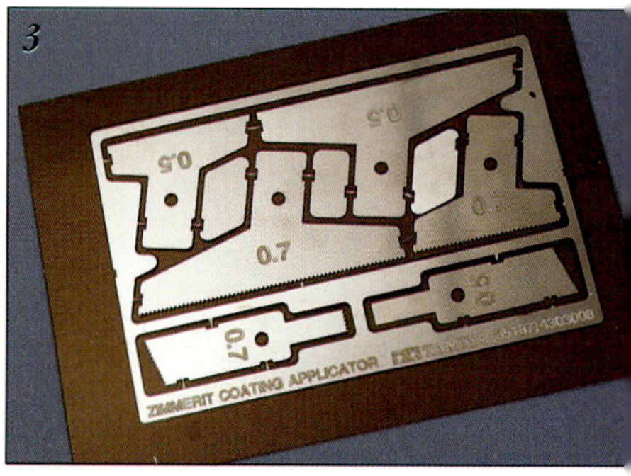

1. Tamiya products used for making the Zimmerit paste texture.

2. The large tube contains the putty material, and the smaller one contains the catalyst.

3. Photo-etched blades used for texturing the putty.

4. The mixture is prepared by squeezing a line of the same length out of both tubes. Note that they are not of equal thickness.

5. Mix them well, until you get a homogeneous mixture.

6. Spread a thin layer with a metal spatula.

7. A vertically applied dot pattern.

8. With the help of a scalpel or triangular knife, make the square pattern on the dotted surface.

9. When making the straight-line pattern, use the same tool but plow the entire surface of the putty.

10. By selecting a different knife, you can make wider or narrower patterns.

11. Example of a toolbox placed on the rear of a Jagdpanther.

12-13. Once the surface has been dotted, trace the horizontal and vertical lines.

14. Following the tank in the photo, position the masking tape that determines the area that needs the Zimmerit.

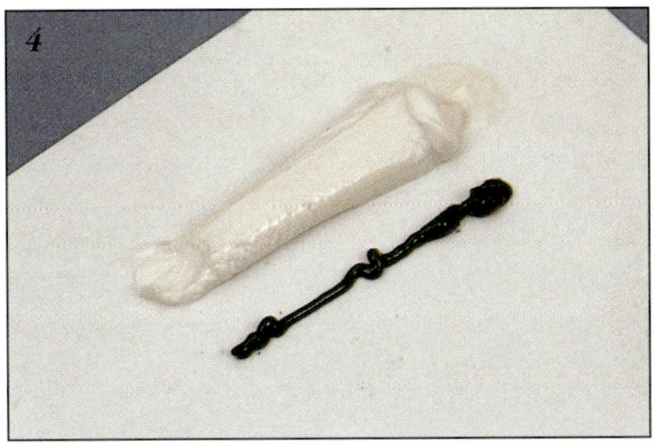

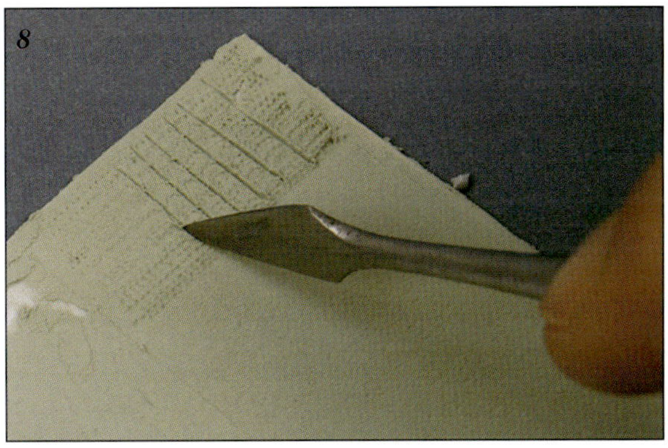

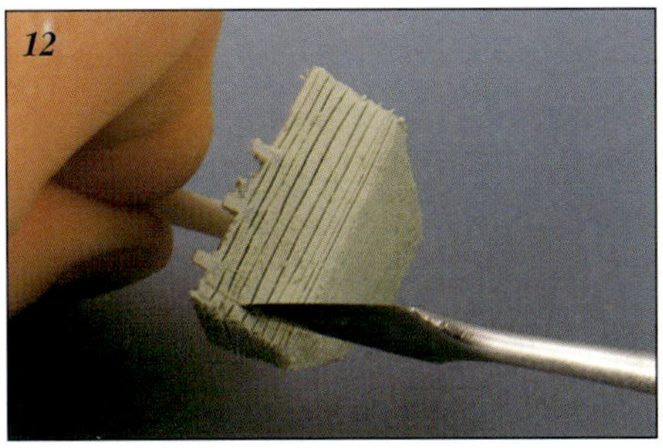

15. The first Zimmerit areas in the lower area of the chassis.

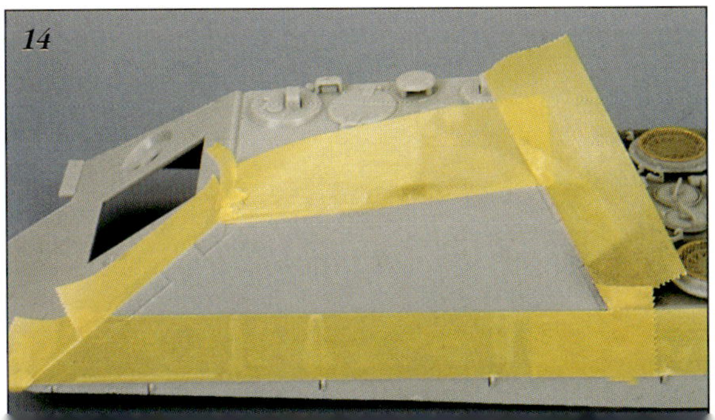

16

17

18

19

19-20. The rear carries some irregular squares in the pattern and some peels showing the surface beneath.

21. The entire vehicle sporting the chosen pattern.

16. Putty is carefully spread over the area. Do it with a flat, rigid tool or a spatula.

17. Pattern with medium squares on a Jagdpanther.

18. The pattern with the smallest squares was widely used on the Jagdpanther and Stug III's.

21

Foreword

The number of available resin kits on the market for modifying existing kits is truly overwhelming. This leaves little room for custom modifications even though many modelers get intense satisfaction from doing their own scratch built conversions. This not only gives the modeler the chance to show off his skills but is also a way of saving money. Superdetailing is also a pretty interesting pastime as well. It was not so long ago that the modeler had to make masses of scratch built parts out of Plasticard, wire, putty, and any other material to hand. Nowadays, with so many precision photo-etched parts available, much of the time consuming work is already done. That said, a perfect end result must still be obtained by using a pair of skillful hands. Moreover, what if you require a cylindrical part? Photoetched parts mostly do not exist for this shape, for example, the photo-etched platform grill on the Marder III. It really doesn't fill the bill and, to make it look right, it must be reworked with the addition of wire. Often, then, the wanted photo-etched part either doesn't exist, or, if it does, it isn't correct. When this happens, we must revert to the old-but still time honored way of scratch building the part ourselves. To do this, we can always count on the inestimable assistance of Evergreen products and others, which can be used for making all sorts of parts.

Sdkfz. 252

A Tamiya Sdkfz.250/3 Greif, ref. 35113, will be needed for this conversion. The first job is to cut off the rear as shown in the small line drawing. Making the necessary pieces is pretty simple, and if you want to leave the rear door and hatches open, you will have to bulk them up with 0.15mm Plasticard edging to make them stand out.

Once this has been done, carry on doing the detailing in the interior. We will also have to open up the engine ventilation louvres.

After gluing together the two halves of the chassis, continue work on the general details. Here, we must be a little careful as the kit, despite its overall quality, still has a few errors.

Start by sandpapering the front armor plate, replacing the lower part for another, scratch built part. The fit of the engine access hatches is much too loose and they should be remade.

The vision slots supplied with the kit are completely wrong, so it is best to mold six more out of the discarded rear end. Use four of these for the longer front slots and, directly below, position the openable detailed armored-glass windows.

The fenders should be flattened on the front, and adjusted to fit the chassis with two Plasticard strips. On the rear strips it is advisable to remove the ejector pin marks that are left during the manufacturing process and fill the holes. The long drop-like section can also be removed, but this is optional. The box for the exhaust muffler requires some steel strips wrapped round it, along with some rivets to hold it in position. On the opposite side, the toolbox needs a little rebuilding plus the necessary locks and chains made of braided wire.

The traction wheels require two fixing bolts per rubber shoe, placed on the steel strips, making a total of 24 bolts per wheel.

The transmission/suspension parts should be thinned down as much as possible, because they are much too thick. The smallest parts can be made out of leftover photo-etch material.

The drag hooks are also made of leftover photo-etch material. The plates for mounting the hooks should also be made of this material.

Using a mixture of putty and fine sand applied with a coarse haired brush, simulate dried mud on the lower areas.

The headlights must be positioned as low as possible. Replace the headlight covers with scratch built Plasticard ones surrounded by wire. The slot can be made with the heated tip of a screwdriver.

The small hooks (8) on the upper part of the chassis are cut in two groups on a plate. Make the plate from four pieces of 0.3mm Plasticard glued together. The plates on which they are welded are from four hexagonal-shaped

1. Even if you can't read German, the plans and the pictures are extremely useful.

2. Following the enclosed plan, cut the kit to make the conversion. Use 0.15mm Plasticard for building the new structure. Use 1mm Plasticard to strengthen the interior of the new structure.

3. The engine access doors are made of Plasticard and fitted with some photoetch hinges..

4. The curved fender part is also made of Plasticard.

5. The box containing the exhaust silencer was completed with a couple of steel strips and some rivets.

6. The engine ventilation louvres were opened with a knife, and then recovered with a new photo etched grill.

7. Detail, showing the door's locking system. It was made from a metal rod, plastic and a metal handle.

photo-etched hinges. File off the rivets on the hinges and cut them in half.

The reference rods (they delineate the corners when making manoeuvres, such as parking) on the front fenders can be made from two different sized hypodermic needles. On the inside of the needles, insert two "hairs" extracted from the inside of two line-drawing typographic pens (0.6). The remaining small parts are all made of Plasticard, copper wire etc... Remaining items, such as hinges and locks are from the Todo Modelismo photo-etch sheet No.1 for the Sdkfz. 232.

PAINTING

For the base color, airbrush Tamiya's XF-63. This can then be used for two separate highlight applications by adding varying amounts of white. Do this with vertical airbrush strokes and then, using XF-64, darken the vehicles surface. Once this is dry, repeat the process but, this time, use 416. This gives the first weathering. To get the subtlest results, use a fine paint jet and place the airbrush nozzle as close as possible to the model's surface.

Crosses, license plates and tactical symbols are Verlinden transfers, ref. 163. The division emblem is hand painted. Use sepia gray to blend in the transfers. Airbrush the lower areas of the vehicle with a coat of XF-10 and XF-52. The finishing touch is to dry brush 140 on all the edges. In some places, it is advisable to use a paper mask to avoid spoiling the adjacent areas. Highlight the track area with 72. This will give the impression of dried mud.

The tracks have oil paint ref. 339 as the base color, and the procedure to follow is identical to that on the previous vehicle except for the polished metal effect. This is because the tracks have rubber shoes that are pretty clean because of the water and snow.

Wear on the rear doors should be quite heavy due to the constant movement of the ammo boxes. Use gun metal as the base color for the paint peels and apply it with a fine brush. XF-16 will supply the polished metal effect that is partially covered with gray and brown (apply these with the airbrush). The gray and brown paint should allow the metal color to show through, varying in intensity and dependent on the time rust has been allowed to accumulate on the surface. Finally, give the model a coat of matt varnish to bring it all into a homogenous whole.

8

COLOR CHART

ENAMELS

Humbrol
- *33 mat black*
- *34 mat white*
- *53 gun metal*
- *62 mat leather*
- *72 mat khaki drill*
- *98 mat chocolate*
- *103 cream*
- *113 rust*
- *140 gull gray*

TAMIYA
- *XF-10 flat brown*
- *XF-16 flat aluminum*
- *XF-52 flat earth*
- *XF-63 German gray*

OIL PAINTS

Talens
- *339 English red*
- *409 burnt umber*
- *701 ivory black*

Mir
- *titanium white*
- *41 yellow ochre*

AIRBRUSH INKS

Talens
- *416 Sepia*

VARNISH

Marabu
- *mat varnish*

8. The tool handles are made from thick copper wire.

9. The toolboxes on the sides were rebuilt from Plasticard, photo-etched locks and copper wire chains.

10. View of the completed vehicle.

11. The tracks and wheels were hand painted, combining both washes and dry brushing.

12. The bottom has been brushed with a putty and fine sand mixture, in order to simulate mud build-up.

9

12

11

13

14

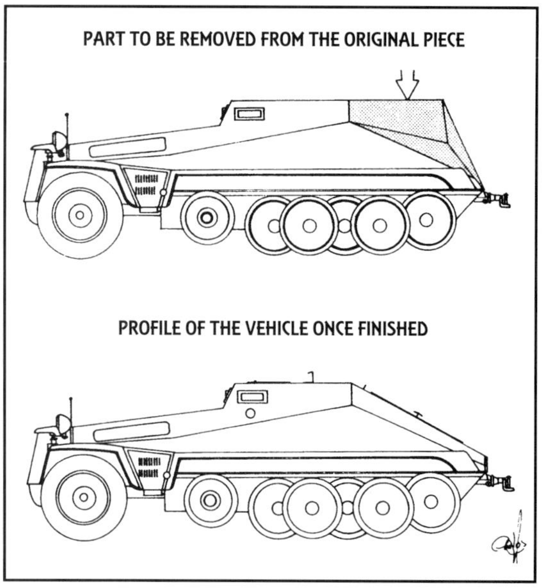

CONVERTING SDKFZ.252 (QUARTERING)

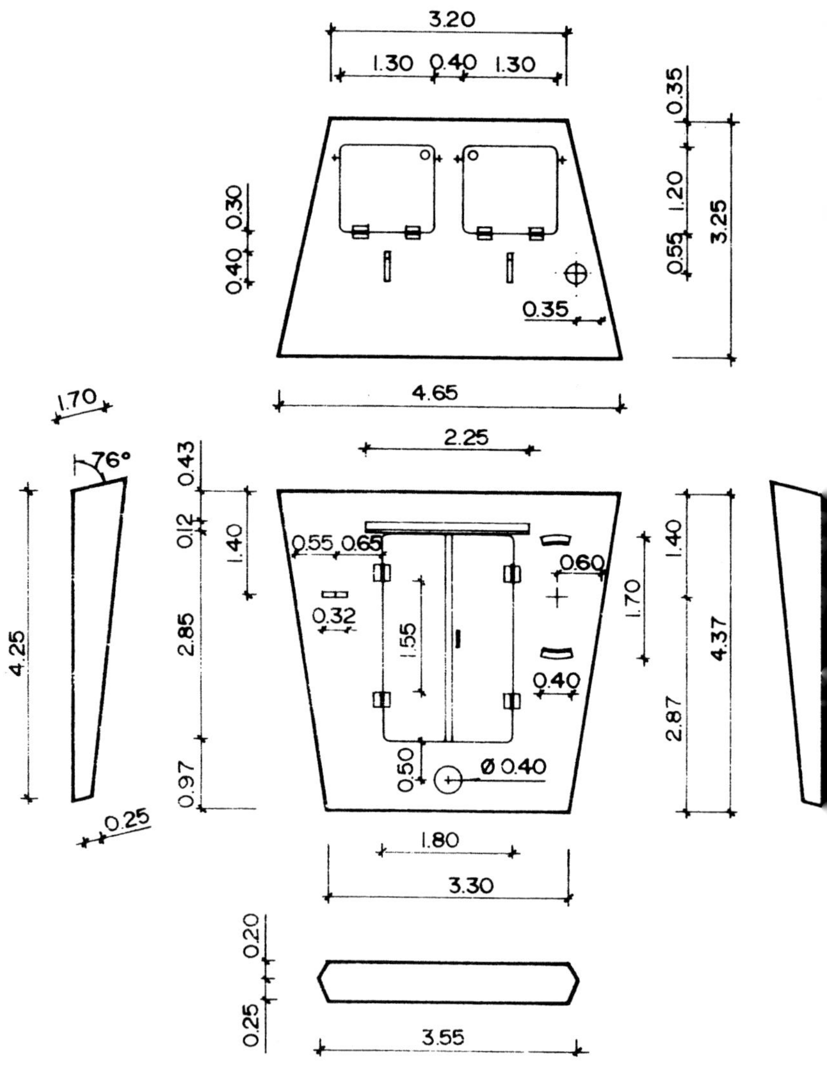

13. XF-63, lightened with white, was used as the base color. White was then used to apply two successive highlight applications. White also gives the impression of weathered paint.

14. Using XF-63 first, followed by 416 gives the first weathering.

15. Cover the track area in plastic. This will help us to hold the model without spoiling the paintjob.

16. Verlinden transfers are blended-in with a subtle airbrush application of 416.

15

16

17. The track area was airbrushed with some XF-52 and red brown, to make it look dirty.

18. Both the tracks and wheels have some fine table salt glued to them to simulate snow.

19. Be careful when painting the tools, otherwise you may spoil the adjacent areas.

20. The wooden block for the crank is made from balsa wood. It was painted using a combination of washes and dry brushing.

21. Paint peels are evident on the lower area of the rear door.

22. Wooden boxes and other added complementary items are visible in the interior.

23. The rear lights were painted red followed by a coat of gloss varnish.

24. Wheels were dry brushed with enamel No.72 and then given a few sienna-colored oil paint washes.

25. The locks are brass, and the chains rusty.

26. The division emblem was hand painted with a brand new No.1 brush.

Marder III Ausf. H

While the old Italeri kit (ref. 210) is quite obviously obsolete, by adding a fair amount of detailing we can make it into a decent representation of the Marder.

Start by laying down some photo-etched anti-slip flooring, Alhambra Models ref. 35005, in the interior. It has to be cut to fit. Also, glue some small steel strips, rivets and cables.

Use a metal pen tip and some parts from a slot racing car to make the transmission gear from the engine to the traction wheels.

Switch the position of the access hatch and the ammunition box on the plate that separates the fighting compartment and the engine.

The mounts for the armor plating covering the engine, and the ventilation grill supports are incorrect. Modify them with thin Plasticard.

Trim the fenders with a knife and then, using a heat source, give them a few dents. The plating on the front of the vehicle are supplied with the kit, but have been filed down as much as possible. The remaining plates were remade from thin Plasticard thus ensuring they are much more realistic and in scale.

Using the Todo Modelismo No. 2 sheet, take care of the numerous rivets and bolts that are missing along the hull, and also those between the traction wheels and the chassis. The gap in this area should be widened using a small 15mm Plasticard disc.

The upper area of the forward sights is then removed and the collapsible part rebuilt with telephone wire.

The machine gun barrel is a 1.5mm thick hypodermic needle, filed to shape with the help of a mini-drill. The sight was made from a 'U-shaped piece of metal strip with a small plastic block on both sides.

The gun support was detailed with needles. The clamps for the spare track links were made from leftover photo-etch material, completed with Todo Modelismo wingnuts.

The rear was completed with headlights and electric wiring. The luggage and tools were both scratch-built and made up from parts from the spares box.

The gun barrel cleaning rods were made from needles. The rear tray containing thin rods was made from copper wire and an Evergreen super structure to hold the copper rod assembly. Glue the perimeter part around the edge.

On the interior of the casement, place a fire extinguisher and four periscopes (made from four segments of Plastruct rod and then covered with thin Plasticard). Discard the other parts and scratch build them. The screens for the grenades are made by placing metal sheet around them, and then making the protective canvas from putty.
Glue 20 photo-etched hooks around the casement (Todo Modelismo issue No.1). These were originally used for fastening the canvas. Then glue 14 bolts onto the mantle. Change the position of the antenna, and build the upper railing and the awning sidebars.
Replace the gun with Tamiya's Pak 40, ref. 35047, and swap the gun barrel with a metal one.

PAINTING

Begin by painting the interior of the vehicle with Humbrol enamel 103. Then, while it is still wet, make some vertical brush strokes using white and 98. Once this is dry, make the shadows with 62 and 98 in all the crevices and corners.

The interior of the casement should be panzer gray, shadowing all the corners with black washes and dry brushing highlighting with white mixed with panzer gray.
The exterior of the vehicle was airbrushed white and then all the different nuances were achieved by applying different shades of gray, airbrushed on selected areas. Once all the different shades have been done, apply another coat of transparent white. That just about completes the airbrush work.
Now, it is time to work with paintbrushes. Start by applying several oil paint washes, use Nos. 41 and 409, to the lower areas of the vehicle around the tracks. Later, make some paint peels using a fine brush and panzer gray, making sure that the scratches and paint peels are in all the likely places. Applying some subtle white washes on the gray areas will give some very interesting shades of gray, while also eliminating any possible disturbing color contrasts. Mixing black and white oil paint, will give a gray that is good for shading all the corners, but do it every subtly. Any over-painting can be removed with a turpentine soaked rag. Repeat the process, using oil paint Nos.41 and 409, on the track area. All the bolts and rivets will probably become obscured during this process so give them a brush of either 103 or white, depending on the area. Dirt can also be simulated where it drips down, by using enamel No. 40 but, once again, try not to overdo it. Complete the weathering effects by applying rust using a mixture of oils 339 and 409. These should be applied on areas previously treated with enamel No.113 and also where there has been no paint for a considerable period and not been subject to any rubbing that would result in a polished, worn metal effect.
On the other hand, those areas heavily used by the crew will have a polished metal look to them. This is simulated very well with a subtle application of XF-16. Make sure you don't overdo it, otherwise it will not look real.
Paint the tracks with enamel No. 113 and then highlight by adding red and yellow to the mixture, and shade with the addition of 98. All these colors are applied as quickly as possible before each one has a chance to dry so they blend together. Once dry, give the tracks a wash of No. 98 and black that will give them additional contrast. Where the metal would have a polished look, do it the same as before, with XF-16.

1. Information has been obtained from German, American and Japanese books.

2. The inner part of the sights was detailed with plastic strip. The upper part of both seats has two thick, copper wire sections.

3. The engine access door and the dividing wall were made from Plasticard. The door should be placed on the left hand side

4. The grenade compartment is also made from Plasticard. The anti-slip floor is an Alhambra product cut to measure.

5. The engine ventilation grill was replaced with a metal one positioned on plastic guides.

COLOR CHART

ACRYLICS

Vallejo Film Color
a-2 gray
a-3 gray
a-94 olive gray
a-95 black
c-42 cadmium red

Vallejo Model Color
951 white
967 olive green
976 buff
981 orange brown
985 hull resd
986 deck tan
987 medium gray

Vallejo liquid acrylic
812 turquoise
816 olive green
817 ochre
818 golden brown
820 mahogany
821 burnt umber

OIL PAINTS

Talens
409 burnt umber
701 ivory black

Mir
41 yellow ochre

Varnish

Marabu
satin varnish
Quilosa
ceramic varnish

6. The upper part of the sights was hollowed out with a knife and then a length of telephone was inserted.

7. An overview, where all the additional elements can be seen.

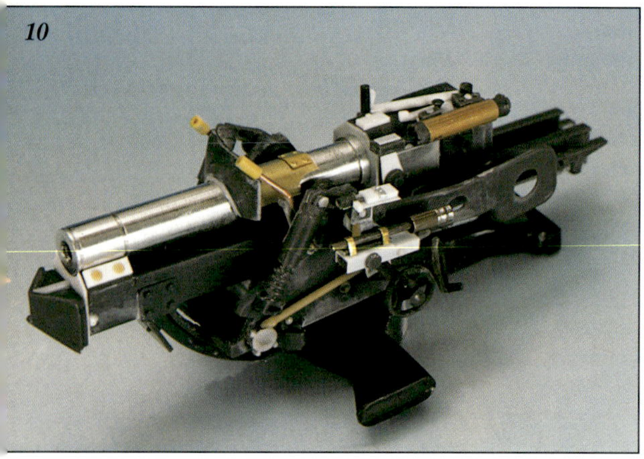

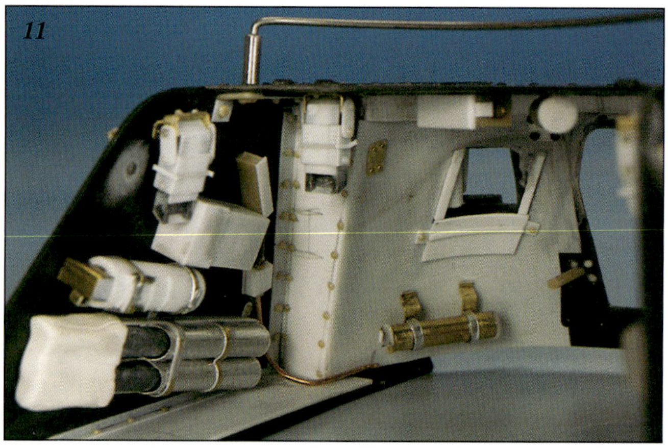

8. The gun is Tamiya's Pak 40. The barrel was replaced with one especially made. (See the plan on the following page.).

9. The gun mount was detailed with metal sheet, Plasticard, copper wire, etc…

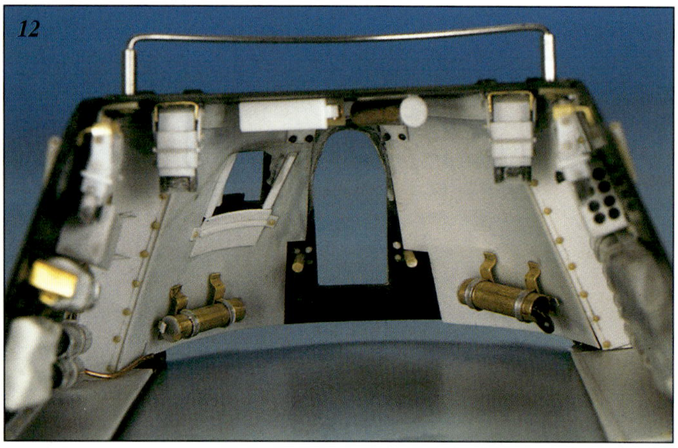

10. The sight and its mount were completely rebuilt from hypodermic needles and metal sheet.

11. The interior was replaced using thin Plasticard, metal sheet, and aluminum.

12. All four periscopes were made of plastic. Both cylinders are pen tips.

13. Gluing aluminum sheet onto the grenades will give us the necessary covers. The protective canvas on the grenades was made of molded putty.

14. The protective plate on the sight, and its guide was made of Plasticard.

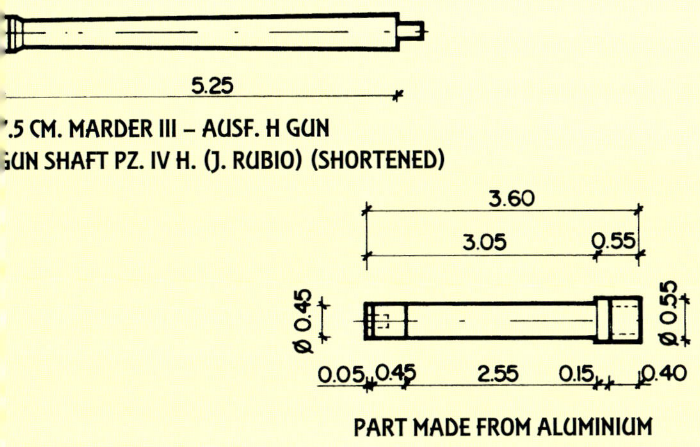

ENGINE VENTILATION

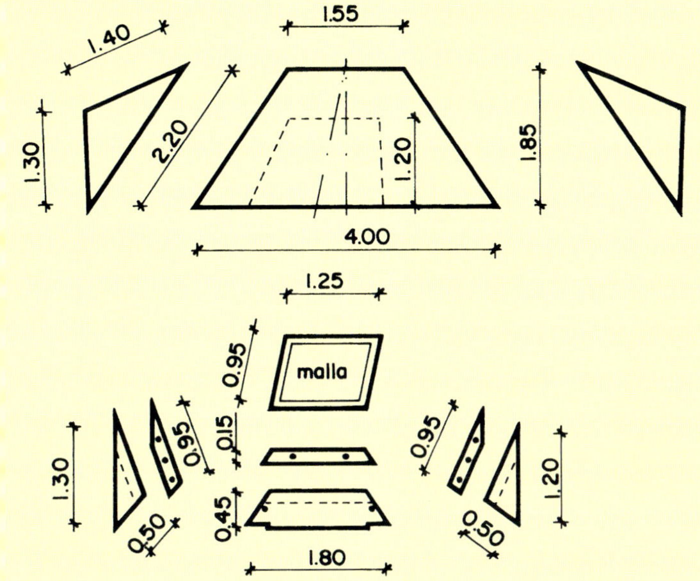

15. The mantle should have 14 bolts. Drill the appropriate number of holes and fill them with plastic rod.

16. The base for the antenna was also replaced. Note the nine small photo-etched fastenings on each side.

17. The elaborate interior goes a long way toward making the vehicle look realistic.

18. The gun mount was detailed with thin plastic strips. A number of pieces of sheet metal and photo-etched butterfly nuts made up the spare track link supports.

19. Overview of the front. The machine gun barrel is a hypodermic needle.

20. Fenders were trimmed to scale to make them look realistic.

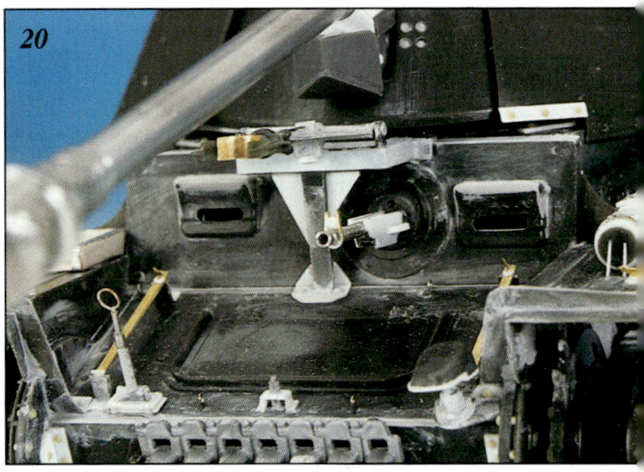

21. The fire extinguisher is a plastic rod detailed with metal straps.

22. The gun cleaning rods are made of 1.2mm hypodermic needles.

23. The canvas-wrapped load was modeled from putty and then fastened down with a photo-etched strap. The box was made from balsa wood.

24. The grill's plastic frame had to be made first, in order for it to hold the inserted rods that made up the grill itself. Super glue was used for this job.

25. Different plastic rods were used to make the exhaust silencer. The shovel was scratch built.

26. A number of circular handles, made from thin wire, were glued to the top of the engine cover.

27. Thin Plasticard was used to make the steel strips holding the fenders.

28. Plasticard toolbox with a photo-etched lock. The jerry can straps are thin metal strips.

29. The box on the vehicle is a means of identification (both this vehicle and the Panzer 38 used them). It was made from Plasticard, and each of the holes was drilled with a mini-drill.

30. The wooden block has a number of metal strips and a photo-etched butterfly nut.

31. Enamel No. 103 was used on the interior, along with white and 98. They were all used together so that they could be blended before they dried.

32. The anti-slip floor was given some washes of oil paint No. 409, and then dry brushed with some No. 53.

33. The gun mount was painted panzer gray. It should be given some washes and, finally, dry brushed.

34. The part of the mantle that protrudes should be painted white, getting as many tone variations as possible.

35. The exterior was airbrushed white with tone variations done with light gray.

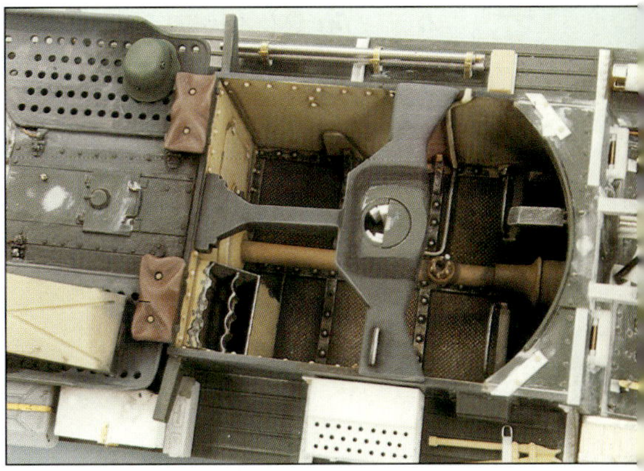

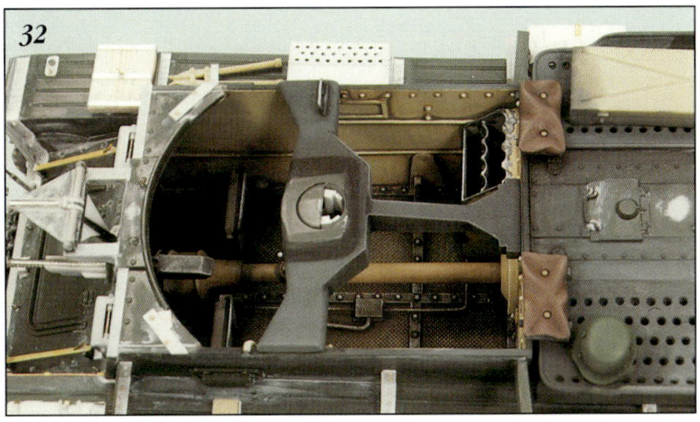

36. Subtle paint washes of Nos. 41 and 409 are applied around the track area. The edges of the wash marks can be smeared out with a clean, turpentine-soaked brush.

37. With a new No.1 brush make some panzer gray paint peels.

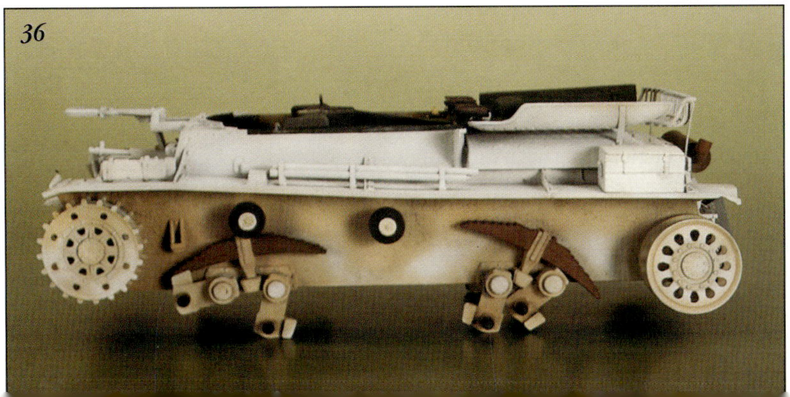

38

39

38. The winter paint scheme could be easily removed, so paint peels and scratches were extremely common and very obvious. Use turpentine-diluted white enamel on the paint peels to show different degrees of wear. Light gray paint is used to profile all the details.

39. Go back over the profiling, this time using a mixture of oils Nos.41 and 409.

40. Pure white is used to highlight the rivets. Some rust runs are carefully done using dirty gray and 113.

40

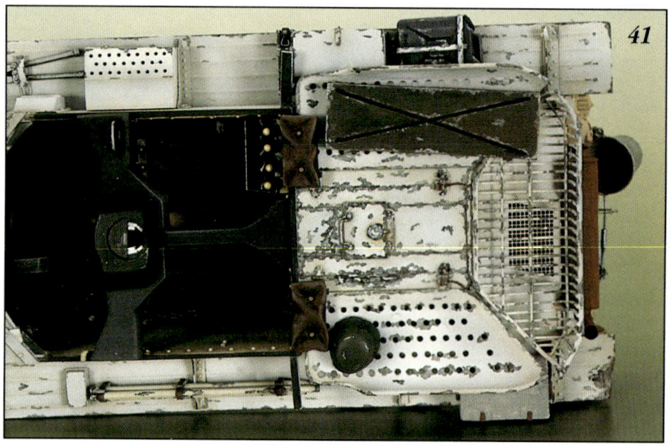
41

42

41. There is some heavy wear on those areas walked on by the crew.

42. Some subtle rust marks using burnt -sienna oil paint. XF-16 was used on the areas to give a polished, worn metal effect.

43. On the casement is seen the process of conveying vertical rust and dirt marks. This part is shown here ready to be worked on.

44. Enamel 140 was applied vertically beneath each rivet. Excess pigment can be removed with a turpentine-soaked brush.

45. Oil paints 409 and burnt sienna are used to simulate rusty areas.

43

44

45

46

47

48

49

46. Carry out a similar step-by-step process for the wheels. Shown here is a wheel with subtle gray and brown overtones.

47. Panzer gray paint peels, note that the scratches follow the natural "movement" of the wheel.

48. Subtle nuances made over the peels with white paint.

49. Highlighting the rivets with 103.

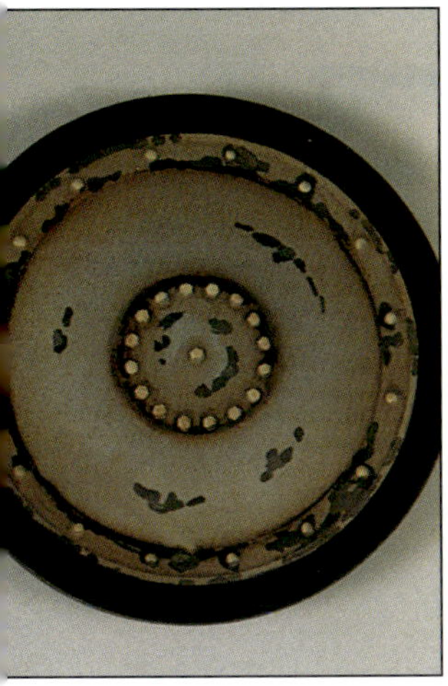

51

50. Rust marks done with 339 and burnt sienna.

51. The interior of the casemate was hand painted with panzer gray. Black paint is used to profile all the details, and white added to the panzer gray for dry brushing the prominent features.

52. The protective canvas was done in olive gray paint and gold paint.

53. The rubber links are fixed with super glue. Toothpicks help to give the links their distinctive droop.

54. Colorful complements for the model.

52

53

54

55. View of the completed model.

56. Use enamel 113 as the base color for the tracks. Before it can dry, "melt" 98 and orange onto the tracks.

57. After the tracks have dried, apply a wash of a mixture of 98 and black. Complete the job by dry brushing XF-16.

58. This picture clearly shows the ageing effect achieved by the application of rust and dirt. Both elements build up a realistic appearance.

59. The ammo box, jerry can, and all other complementary items break up the monotony of a white vehicle.

60. The cross is a Verlinden transfer. Paint the insides of the viewing slots black.

61. The wooden block for the crank was painted with oil washes of 409. Afterwards, it was dry brushed with enamel 103.

62. The pack wrapped in camouflage canvas was painted with the following acrylics: Pastel green for the base, olive green and red-brown for the camouflage blotches.

63. The wood texture of the barrel was done with the help of a fine brush and golden-brown paint over a dark brown base.

64. The exhaust's base color was 113. Before it dries, "melt" some orange, green and black onto it.

65. A Russian weapon (PPSH 41) was placed on the grill. Its strap is made of a piece of sheet metal.

66. The figure should be glued before the casement.

67. The wear is both heavy and obvious on the rear of the vehicle.

Foreword

In spite of the wide availability of both resin and plastic kits, there are still a few vehicles that seem to have been forgotten, or are only available as old and, in many cases, outdated kits. This is the case with the German Sdkfz. 10 half-track that was released by Esci in 1/35 scale. There were two variations of the vehicle, one fitted with a 20mm anti-aircraft gun, the Sdkfz 10/4, or a light artillery transport. Later, Gunze Sangyo resumed manufacturing the kits, offering the same basic plastic kit, but also including the anti-aircraft version, improving the guns, and including photo-etched and metal parts. The most important innovation was the introduction of the Pak 38 50mm modified gun, although the vehicle itself was basically the same. As mentioned, the Gunze Sangyo offering included a photo-etched sheet for the semi-armored version, a new set of link-by-link tracks, and a more accurate white metal gun. However, the Gunze Sangyo version, although interesting, still lacks detail, the same as the Esci version. Some time later, Scale Model Accessories produced an ammunition towing vehicle version, which meant that the kit required a number of modifications. Having said all that, there is still enough available information about this vehicle to enable a modeler to carry out all the necessary improvement and detailing. Because a whole slew of modeling techniques were used on the kit, a considerable number of pages have been devoted to it.

Sdkfz 10 with 5cm gun.

When the Germans first engaged the Russian armored forces they soon discovered that the majority of the guns carried by their own AFVs and soft-skinned fighting vehicles, including the anti-tank units, were not powerful enough. In view of this, they decided to put guns on almost any vehicle able to carry them. In addition, as soon as the 50 mm Pak 38's arrived at the front, they were adapted to gain mobility.

The Sdkfz 10 half-track was readily available and, so, was widely used for the purpose. The new gun could, under favorable conditions, destroy a Russian T-34. It could even damage the KVs if fired from the optimum range and when loaded with tungsten-cored ammunition.

However, a major drawback soon became apparent: The crews were badly unprotected and, at times, even a fragmentation grenade could put a vehicle out of action. The first measure taken was to lightly armor the vehicles, enough to protect the engine and driver, while the gun crew had to take refuge behind the gun shield. This makeshift device had to suffice from 1941 to the close of 1942.

THE KIT

The photo-etched parts, gun and tracks are fine. However, on this old kit it is necessary to improve the mudguards, all the indicators, transmission system, and the traction system for the tracks. It is also necessary to rebuild the interior, including the floor, seats, toolbox, hood and its fastenings, indicators, headlights, locks, small chains, fastenings, handles, etc. Although, admittedly, there are many small parts, the amount of work involved adds a high degree of satisfaction when the model is completed.

ASSEMBLY

First, remove the mudguards and replace them with the Todo Modelismo No.8 photo-etched parts. Some commuters are added and a handle on the right hand side. All these small parts are relatively easy to make with Plasticard, copper wire or any other material that comes to mind.

Cleaning and test fitting the chassis parts is quite a long job, because the parts have a lot of flash, and don't fit very well. The fit problems will demand some putty for filling any gaps between the joins. After around 45 minutes, we can sand all puttied areas, and also thin those areas that are too thick.

Using a new knife blade, thin the fenders, and make a few dents on them if you wish. Dents are easily made by first gently heating the area, then pressing with a brush handle. Sometimes, it is necessary to sand the dents a little, eliminating any surface irregularities.

Continue with the interior detailing by putting down anti-slip floor sections. These must be carefully cut to size. All cables and other systems, pedals, levers, etc., have to be scratch built from leftover photo-etched material, copper wire, etc. Such small parts will have to be glued with the help of a pair of curved-tip tweezers.

Some parts of the vehicle will require bolts and rivets. These are easily made following the procedures described in the appropriate section of 'What is it? How is it done?' Each traction wheel requires 24 bolt heads, so cover the

1. A few important reference works used for fine detailing during the making of this model.

2. Front panel, highly detailed with photo-etched parts.

3. Filler is used in some quantity to fill the many gaps and holes.

4. Covering the sides with Plasticard, and sanding off the unwanted edges.

5. Trimming the fenders with a knife.

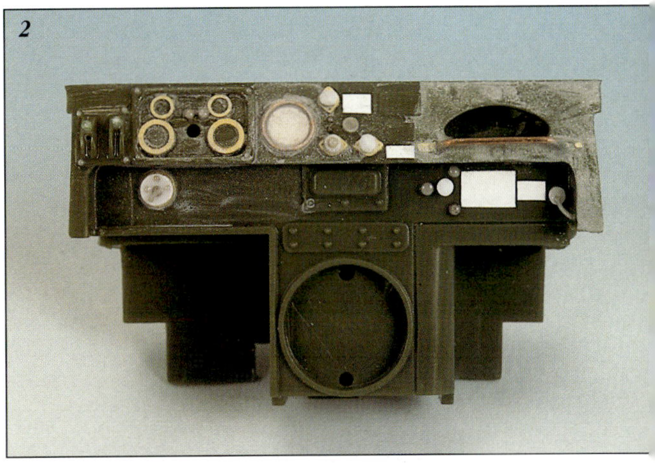

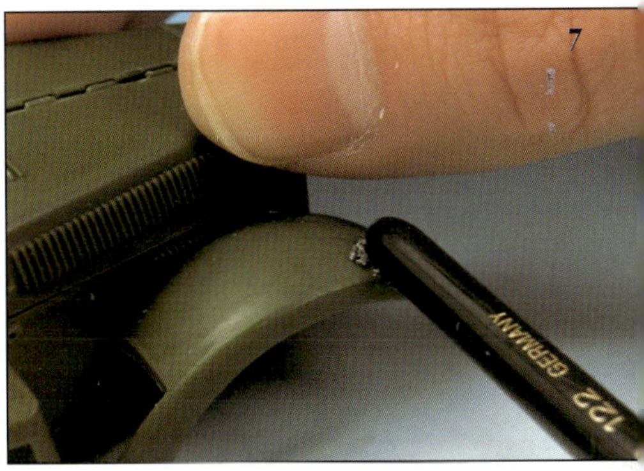

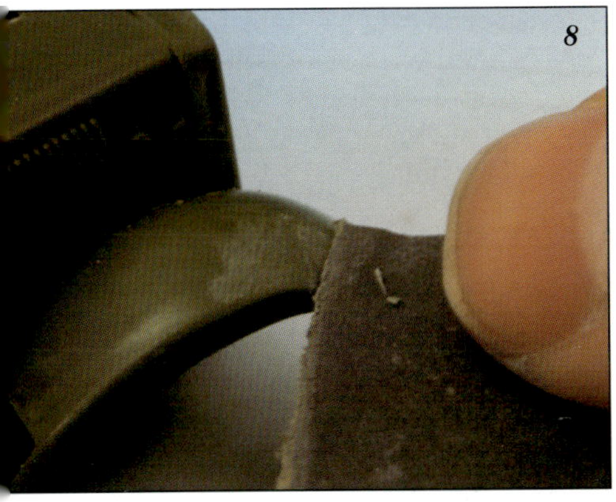

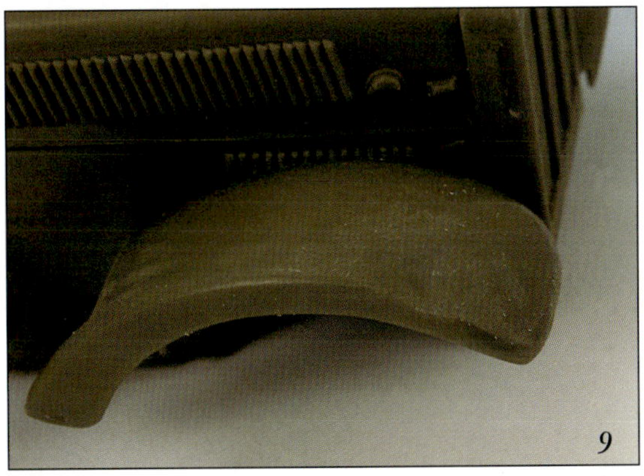

6. Dents made using a heat source.

7. Molding the heated surface with the back of a brush.

8-9. Sanding the dent. The final result should be moderate.

correct spot with liquid glue and then, with the tip of a knife, place a bolt head.

The toolbox on the right hand side needs a small chain made from fine, multi-strand copper wire, flattened with a hammer, and a small photo-etched lock. The box lid was scratch built from Plasticard, because the original part doesn't fit properly. Following the same procedure, make another exhaust cover on the left hand side. The hood locks also need to be remade from small plastic squares and pieces of heat-stretched plastic.

The rear seats need a backrest, so once the seat parts have been prepared, glue on a support strap made from thin sheet metal. This should be glued with super glue and held in place with your fingers while it sets. The backrest itself is molded from any two-part putty, placed on the metal base and eased into position with the help of a water-soaked brush.

By far, the most complex part to make is the folded hood on top of the spare wheel. First, make the bars by cutting four pieces of plastic rod (each 76mm long) and a fifth one of 66mm (cut in half). Both ends of the bars should be flattened with the help of pliers, and then bent to shape. Before gluing any of the bars, first mold the thin metal sheet that is used for the canvas part of the hood.

On each end of the flattened part of the rod, glue two metal strips, making sure that at least 6mm overlaps the end. Then, position a section of thin metal sheet, folded to look like the beginning of the canvas hood. Then, glue this first piece, and proceed to make it look like canvas using two-part putty.

The proceeding rods all need to be covered with metal sheet before setting them in place, folding the tin sheet, just like the folds of real canvas. The inner folds are simulated with putty. The final rod needs a slightly larger piece of metal sheet to cover it, recreating all the natural creases on its surface with the help of a brush handle. Finally, make the small metal strips for fastening the hood to the frame.

The kit includes additional photo-etched armor plates of wonderful quality. The plates shielding the radiator must be carefully lined up, because there are no guide marks. If you don't watch what you are doing, they can end up out of line.

Now it's time to put all the tools and complements in place, minding all pertinent locks and supports. The supports can be made on tin sheet, marking them with a pencil, and cutting them with a knife. Then they can be bent to shape with small curved tip pliers, and glued down with super glue. The mallet was made from scratch, while all other tools were sourced from other kits. All the handles were changed for 88mm thick plastic rod.

The gun is made of white metal with an aluminum barrel that, taken together, is a pretty acceptable piece. Assembling this gun is simple. The levers are a little oversize, and should be substituted for smaller ones from another kit.

The last scratch built element is the rearview mirror. The mirror is a small round plastic piece and a needle (ones used for pinning down butterflies). The mirror should be glued in place after the painting has been done.

10. *Details of levers and handles, all made from copper wire, Plasticard, and other metal parts.*

12. *The cover and base of the hood's fastenings were made of Plasticard , a scratch built copper chain, and a Todo Modelismo photo-etched lock.*

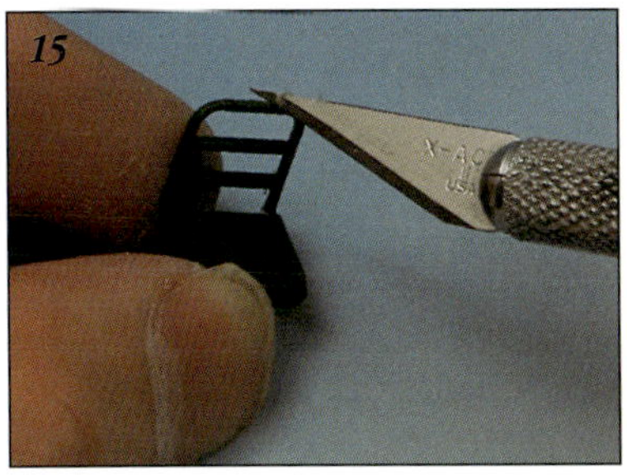

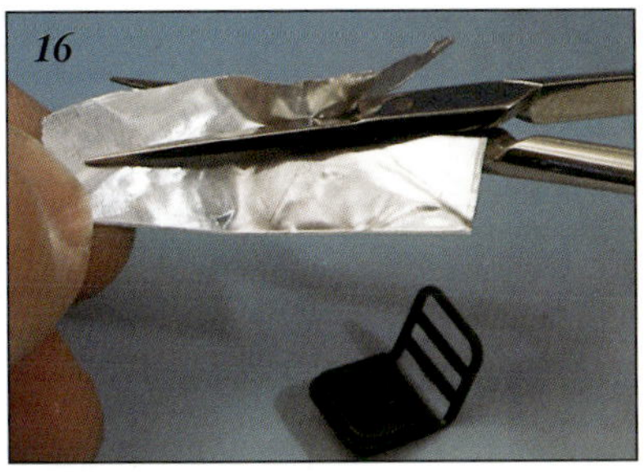

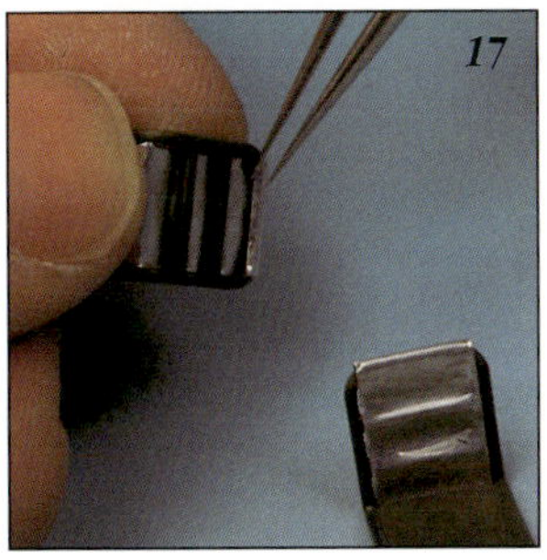

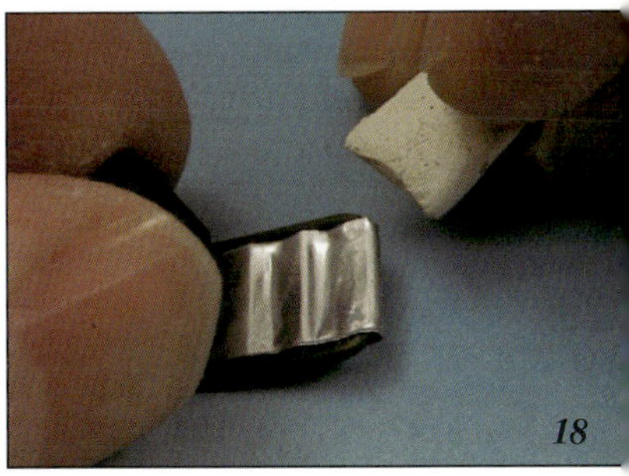

13. *Repeat the same procedure on the other side.*

14. *The hood strap made from plastic strip.*

15. *Polishing the surface of all the round parts.*

16. *Cutting metal sheet for the seat backs.*

17. *Adjusting, then fixing the part. Super glue should be used for this.*

18. *Milliput was used for molding the seatback.*

19. *Finish it off with a wet brush.*

20. *Use a blade to make the seats look used.*

PAINTING

Use the airbrush to apply the base color that should look weathered. To achieve this, I used a mixture of 59% XF-50, 30% XF-63, and 20% XF-18. Adding white to this mixture will give us our first highlights.

The camouflage blotches are XF-13 that is remarkably similar to the Luftwaffe green applied to army vehicles during 1941-42. Use a pressure of 0.5 kg and keep the airbrush nozzle as close as possible to the vehicle, making curved intersecting lines.

After letting the paint dry for two days, we'll be ready for the oil treatment. The oils on the palette are: ochre, and sienna tones, white, green, and Prussian blue. Applying the paint is not general but done on small areas, one at a time. First, brush some turpentine onto an area. Then, with a small brush, apply small amounts of oil paint (in this case blue) and carefully smear it to get a bluish overtone. Repeat the process with all the different colors, smearing, or rather 'melting' them with a turpentine-soaked flat tip brush. This process is carefully repeated over the whole of the vehicle's unworked areas.

On the floor of the interior, paint a burnt shade oil wash. Returning to the airbrush, prepare a highly diluted mixture of black, matt brown and German gray and spray it on the model's prominent features. This mixture will profile the details and enhance all the model's features.

There are, however, some areas that are quite small and profiling them must be done by hand. The enhancing work is now almost done.

Detail enhancing can be complemented with a light dry brushing of light gray paint on all the edges of the model. This will result in a highlighting effect.

The worn, polished metal floors are easily simulated by dry brushing a combination of aluminum, and gray metal paint.

Red-brown, black, and dark gray paint is used to convey rust marks on the lower areas of the vehicle, on some edges, and some parts of the interior. Apply the mixture with a fine brush. Next, tone down this mixture, and return to the inside of each rust mark. Some rust marks will display a polished worn metal effect, on the vehicle's interior for example. These are made with the mixture described earlier. The interior also requires some mud and sand from the crews' boots. These can be added by subtle airbrushing sand colors where they would appear. Make chipped paint areas on the wooden surfaces with brown paint.

Finally, apply a subtle matt varnish coat over the whole model. The indicators, and other glass parts on the mudguards should be gloss varnished by hand.

Next, airbrush the tracks with Tamiya XF-10 for a base color followed by a dry brushing of khaki. Give all the rubber parts a wash of black and khaki. The track's 'hook links' should also be highlighted with polished metal.

A final, very fine, overall coat of dirt, using Tamiya XF-52, can be airbrushed.

21. Plastic rods, cut to measure, and bent with the help of a heat source. They will make up the supports for the folding hood.

22. The canvas is tin sheet wrapped onto each plastic rod.

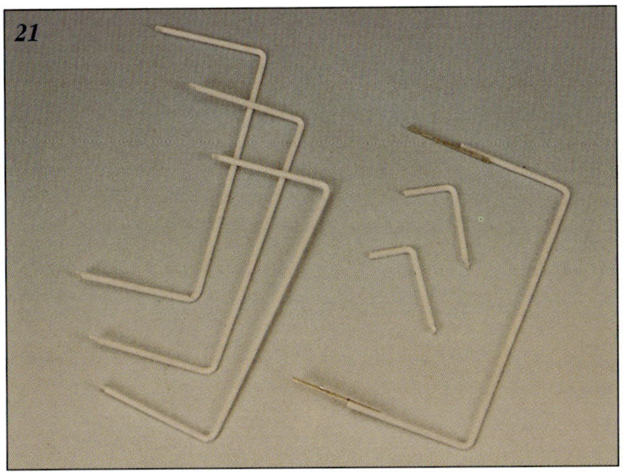

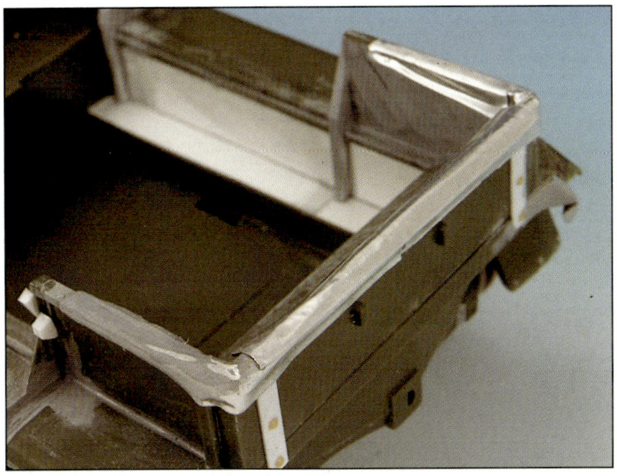

23. Piece of 'canvas' placed onto the plastic rod, and then placed on top of the previous rod.

24. There should be enough metal sheet for simulating the canvas' natural folds.

25. A pyrogravure can be used for molding the folds.

26. The two parts are glued together with putty. Try to make it look like realistic canvas.

27. The remaining rods with the 'canvas segments'.

28. The completed ensemble of rods and 'tin' canvas.

29. The folds are simulated with putty. Metal sheet partially covers the putty.

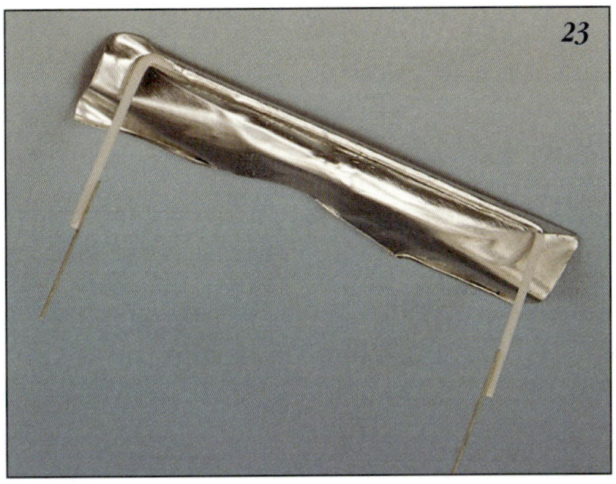

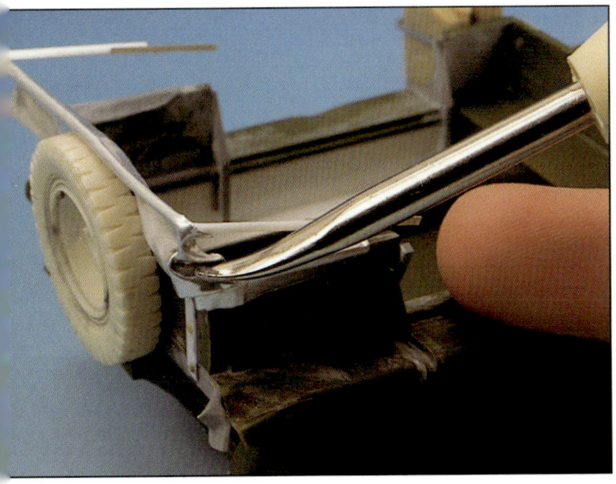

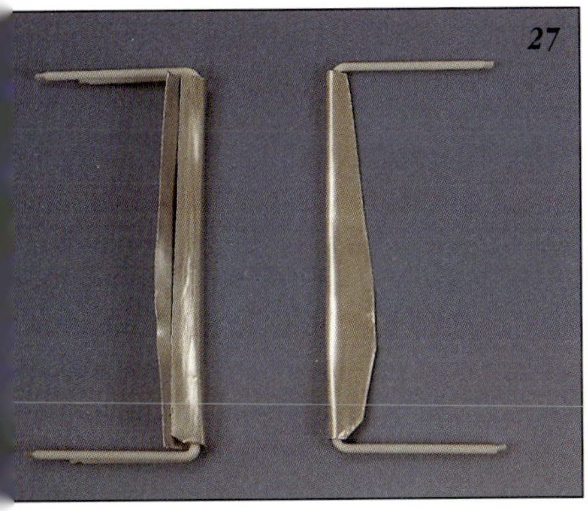

31. A new layer of metal sheeting is placed on top of the wet putty. Natural creases were made before setting the sheet.

32. Positioning the armor photo-etched parts

33. Making a metal strip to hold some tools.

34. Once piece has been cut, bend it into shape with pliers.

35. The part is placed on top of the fender.

36. The mallet's fastening.

37. Scratch built mallet positioned in its fastening.

30. More putty is used to unify the ensemble.

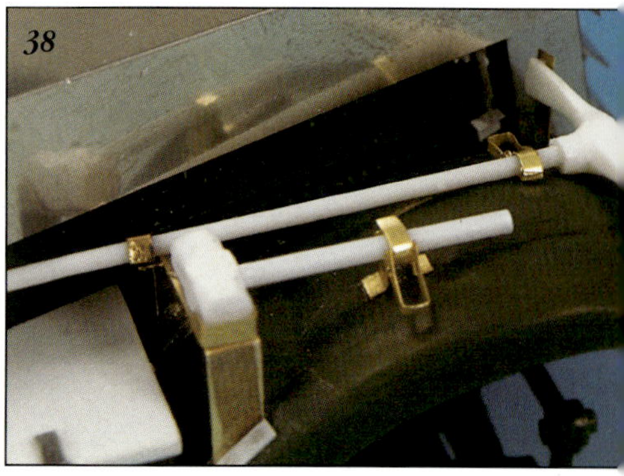

38. The small tool fastenings are pieces of photo-etched material.

39. The gun ensemble was primed with a highly diluted coat of putty.

40. The mudguard ensemble is also primed with putty.

41. Complex area of gear shifts, levers, etc.

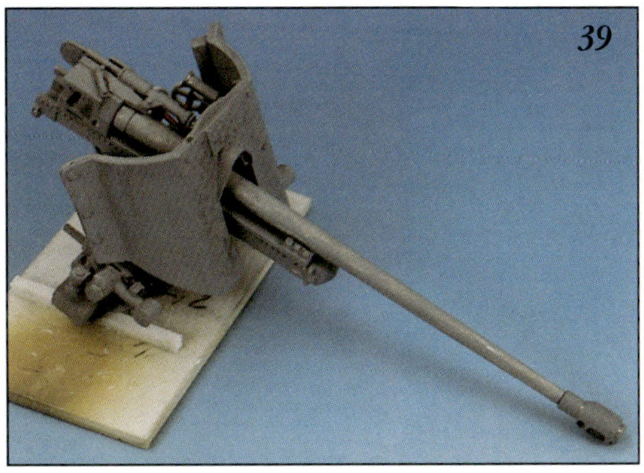

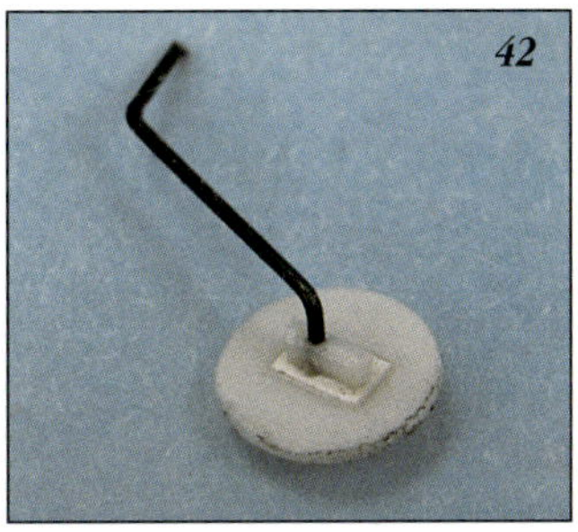

42. Rearview mirror made from a small plastic disc and an entomologists pin.

43-45. Different views of the completed model without the gun.

46-49. Completed model with its spare wheel, molded from another kit.

A

B

D

A. Dry brushed Khaki will give the highlights on the wheels.

B. A green jerry can breaks up the monotonous general gray paint scheme.

C

E

C. All straps are painted leather brown, and all the buckles are aluminum.

D. The butt lock is painted silver.

E. The horseshoe has been given a burnt-sand oil wash to make it look rusty.

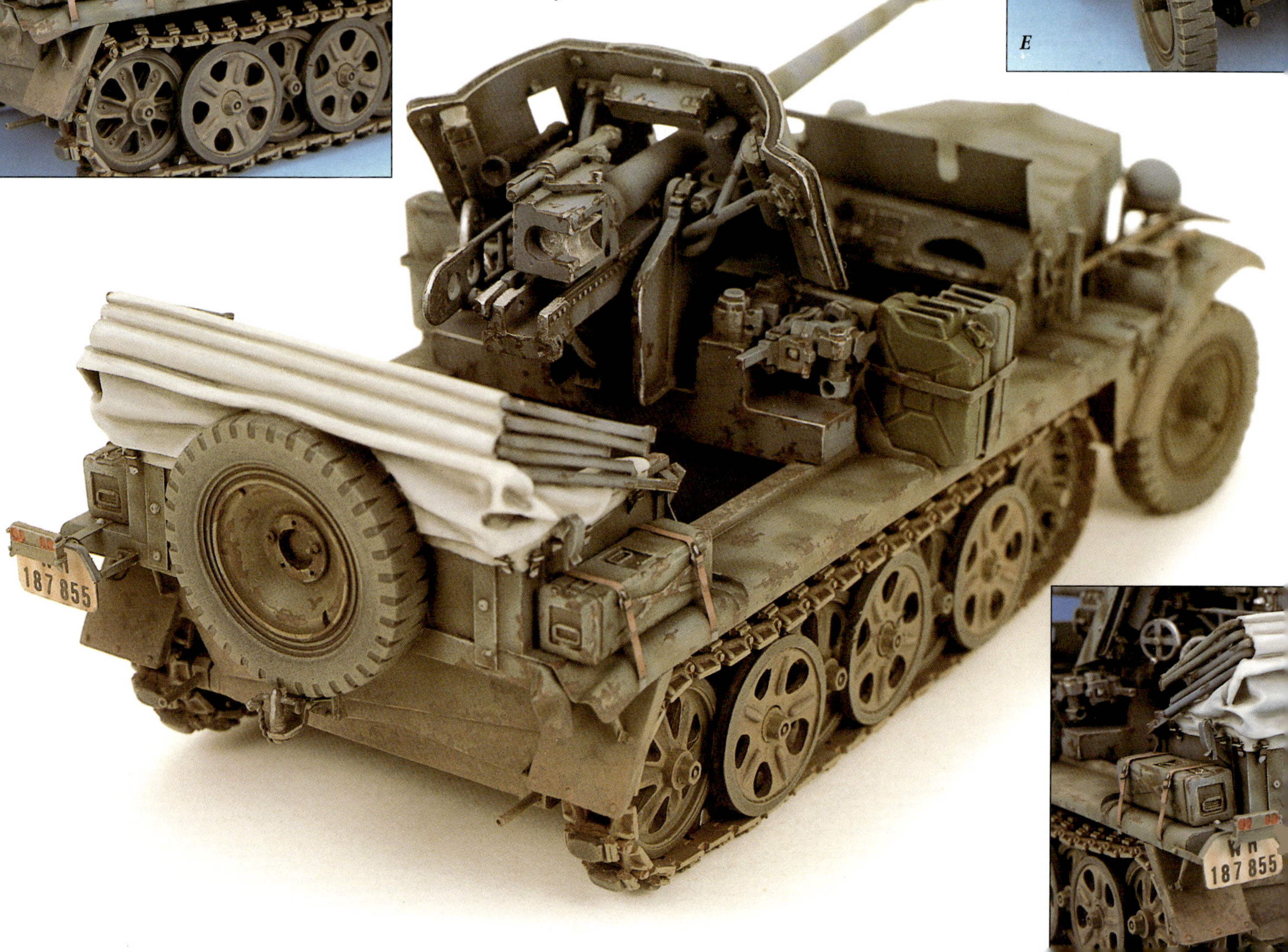

G

F

H

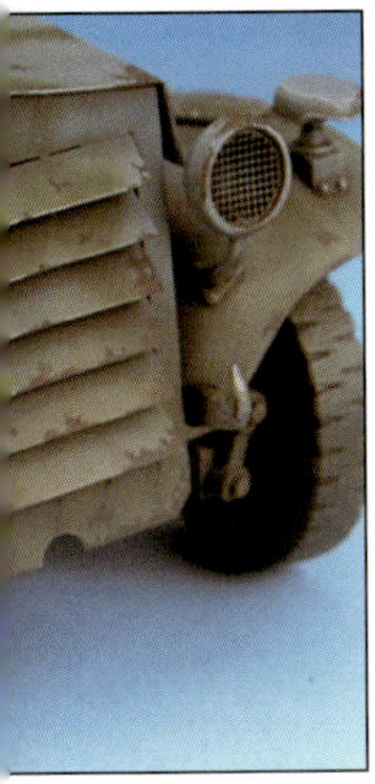

F. The gun's operating wheels have been highlighted with aluminum to convey wear

G. The metal part of the shovel was dry brushed.

H. The base color of the canvas is XF-57, clear gray, and white.

I. Adding white or black paint to the previous mixture for the necessary highlights and shadows..

J. On the mantle can be seen the results of dry brushing.

J

I

50. When dealing with thin parts where paint can easily chip, it is best to work on a foam rubber base.

51. The airbrushed base color is a mixture of Campaign blue, German gray, and medium blue.

52. For the first highlights, add a little white to the previous mixture.

47

48

49

50

51

52

53. This view gives a clear idea of the effect.

53

54. Highly diluted Japanese green will do for airbrushing the camouflage scheme.

55. Camouflage scheme of intertwining green lines.

56. Overview of the scheme.

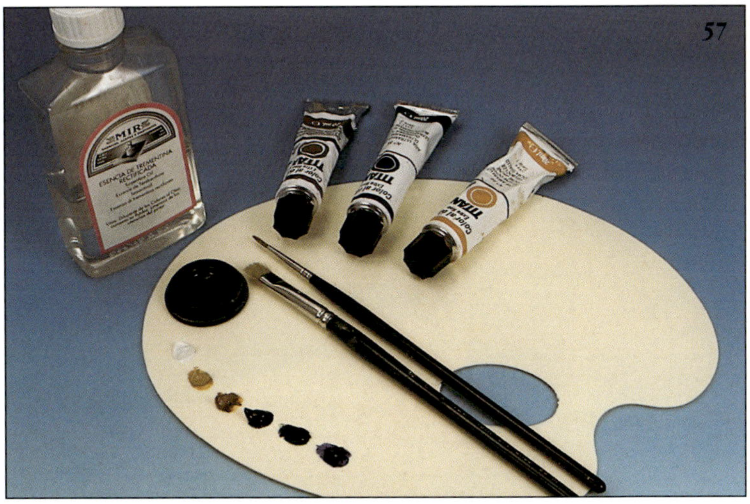

57. The oil treatment calls for the following materials: A No.4 flat tipped brush, a No.2 round tip brush, oil paint, and turpentine.

58. Work on small areas, one area at a time. First, spread some turpentine onto the chosen area.

59. Lay down small amounts of Prussian blue oil paint.

60. Using the flat tip brush, soaked on turpentine, smear the paint just enough to leave a subtle transparent coat.

61. Over the same, still wet area, apply the different oil colors.

62. Use the large brush and blend the colors into each other.

63. If a specific color is judged to be insufficient, repeat the process.

64. Repeat the process over all the different areas of the model.

65. Vertical brush strokes will create the right 'falling dirt' effect.

66. The vehicle's has been given a burnt sand oil paint wash.

67. Oil 'effects' should be quite subtle. Only the slightest transparent veil should be visible.

68. Overview, displaying the effect of the oil paint.

69. Mixing black, brown and gray paint in a 10% diluted mixture, airbrush some shadows on all the joints and crevices.

70. Airbrush work is very neat and clean.

71. The airbrush can't be used everywhere. In this case use a small fine brush instead.

72. Once everything is dry, dry brush some light gray on all the prominent edges.

73. The dry brush technique give highlights that will make all the small rivets, bolts, etc., stand out.

74. The dry brushed highlights on the vehicles interior is done with a mixture of aluminum and gray metal.

75. Combining red-brown, black and gray paint to make all the rust marks.

76. Adding a little orange paint to the previous mixture will give a highlight mixture for the inner part of the rust marks.

77. Burnt sienna oil paint is used in applying a subtle transparent 'veil' on all the rust marks.

78. Rusty paint peels are evident on all the areas subject to wear.

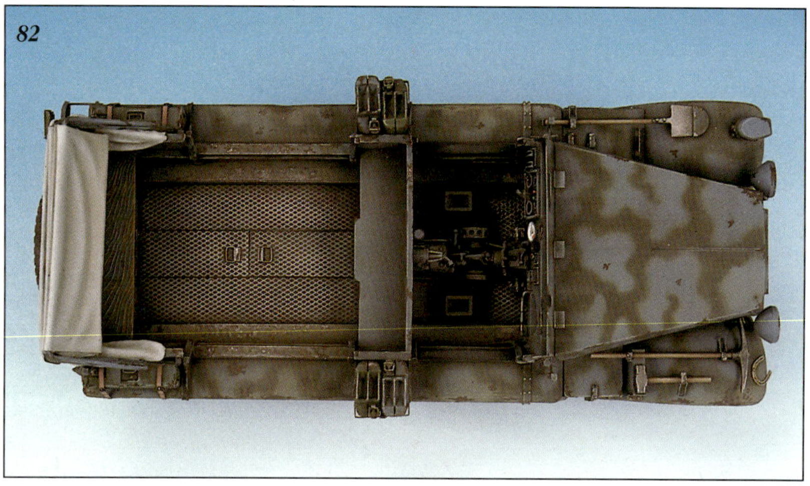

85. The intricate interior stands out, thanks to the paint washes and the dry brush technique.

79. Using the same dry brush mixture as that employed on the interior of the vehicle, go back to all the edges showing rusty paint peels on them.

80. Airbrushing a sand color on the interior will give realistic dirt accumulations.

81. Scratched paint on the wooden surfaces can be done with medium brown, highlighted with gold-brown.

82. This mixture is also used on the handles of all the tools.

83. Glass can be conveyed by using gloss varnish.

84. Such small areas must be worked with a new No.1 brush.

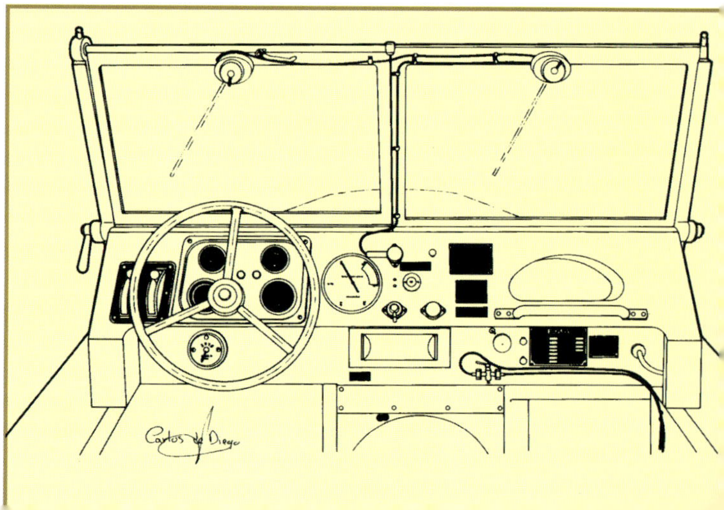

86

87

86. Heavy details will invariably stand out more after a good paintjob.

87. Tamiya's XF-10 paint was used as base color for the tracks.

88. Khaki paint will help simulate small dust particles sticking to the tracks.

89. Give the rubber parts a wash of khaki and black paint.

88

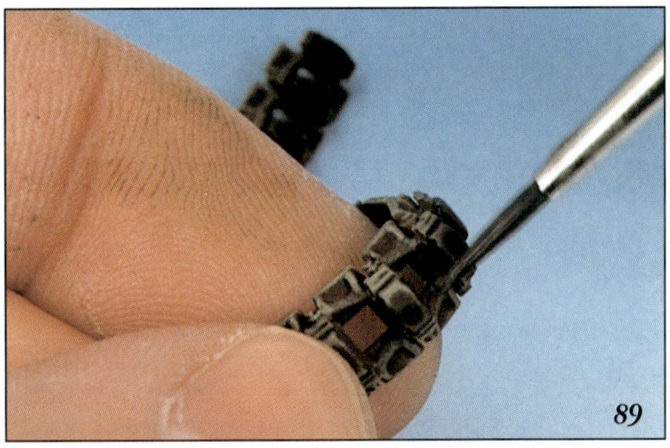
89

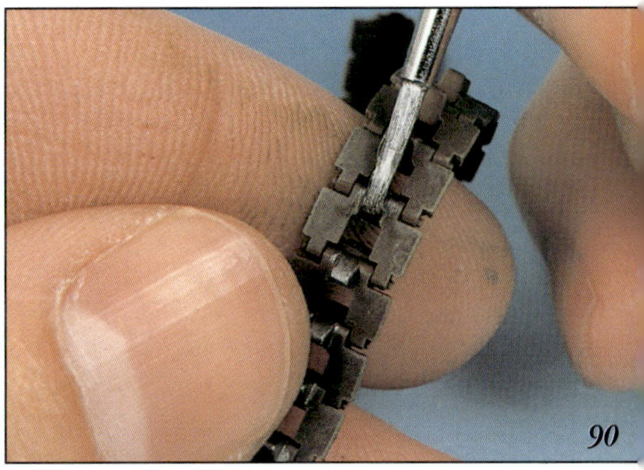
90

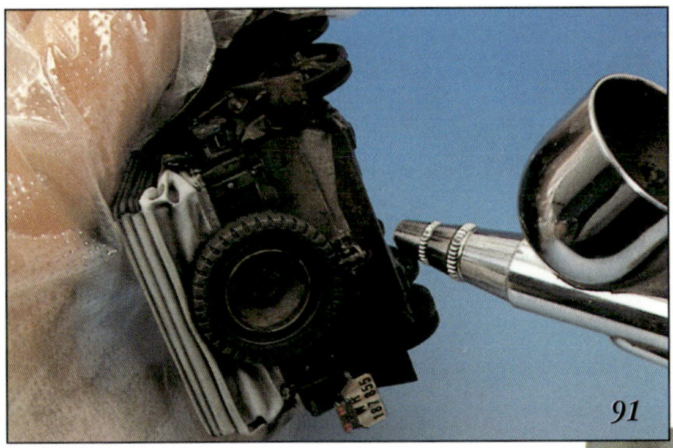
91

90. The hook link part of the track should be dry brushed with a light metallic paint.

91. The lower areas of the vehicle have been given a matt sand airbrush wash, which will make it look appropriately muddy.

What & How

Bolts and rivets

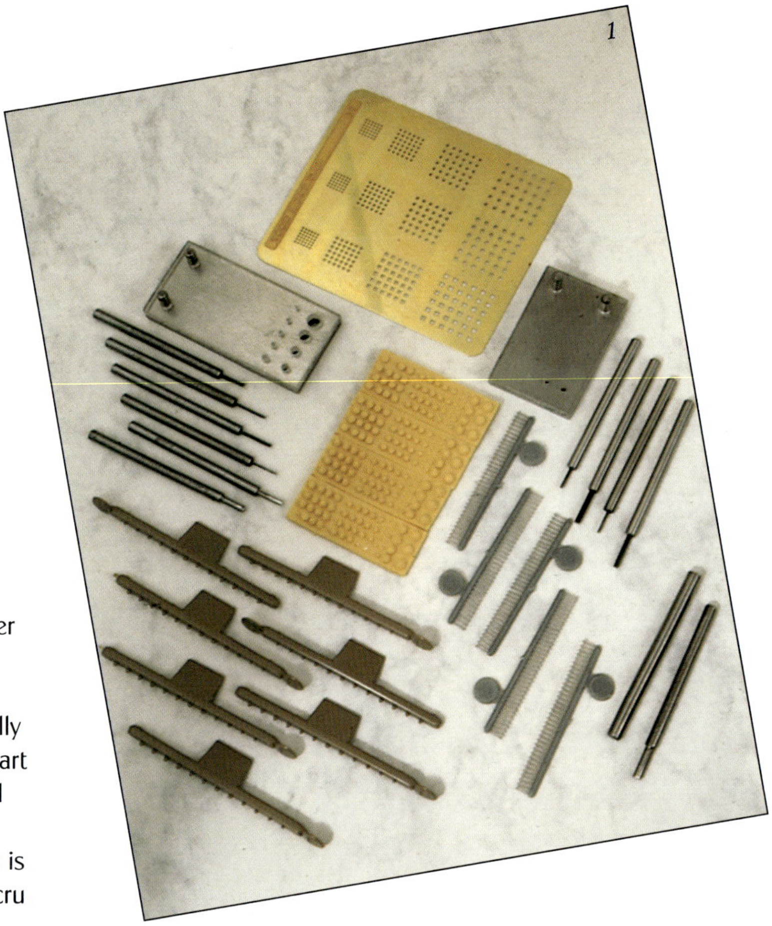

When assembling model kits, we can encounter problems relating to bolts and riv ets. Plastic kits frequently lack both items, simply because they were left out during the design stage, either deliberately or otherwise. Resin kits quite often exhibit the same lack of detail, once again either left off or, quite often, knocked off during molding. Regardless of the reason, the careful model er will never allow these missing details to go unno ticed. There are several ways to replace missing bolts and rivets. They can be done with a hole punch, obtained from a photo etched sheet, sourced from old kits, or simply bought from your favourite hobby shop. The plastic and resin parts should be fixed with super glue, especially if they are going to be mounted on either resin or metal. However, there are some glues that will 'melt' plastic to resin.

When cutting bolts with a knife, it must be done carefully so that the angle is correct otherwise you will have to start all over again. Damaged bolts can be easily spotted and must be discarded.

When time comes to glue rivets and, especially, bolts, it is essential to make sure they are completely flat. This is cru cial, because small bolts have a tendency to sit on one side rather than flat. If they have been cut slightly off, they can sit quite crooked.

If you cannot trust your own pulse, you can fix these parts using gloss varnish and a brush. Once you've positioned the rivet/bolt with the help of your brush, fix it with a tiny drop of liquid super glue.

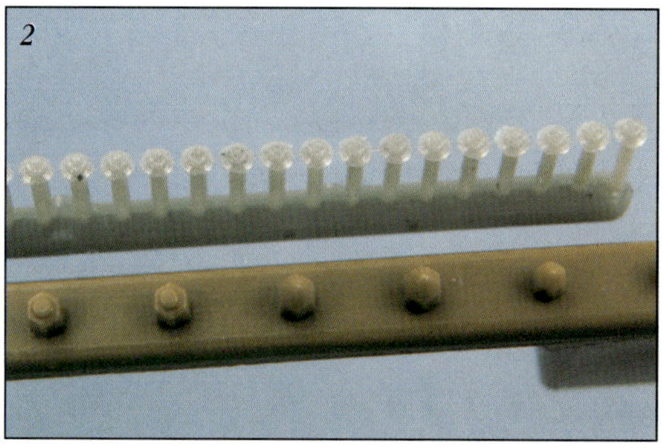

1. Different tools for making bolts and rivets from either plastic or resin.

2. Plastic and resin bolts are found on a support piece.

3. Carefully melt a piece of leftover plastic but DO NOT let it catch fire.

4

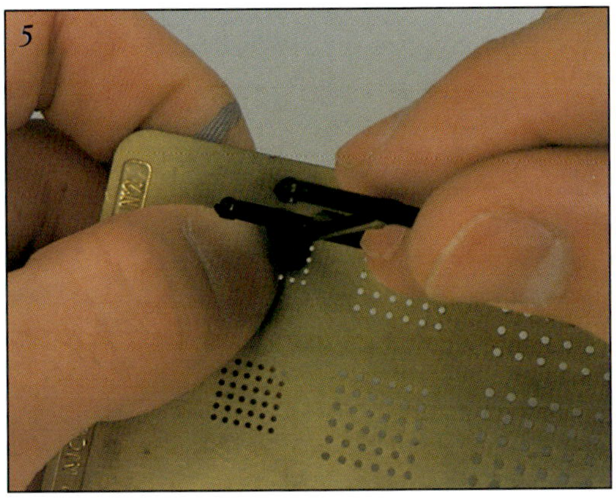

5

4. Now press the soft plastic against the photo-etched sheet, thereby obtaining a number of useful copies.

5. By repeating the process, we can obtain all the parts we want.

6. The rivets are clearly marked on the end of the plastic.

7. Carefully remove the parts, ensuring that they drop onto a piece of paper.

8-9. Here are some examples of the use of rivets.

10. Resin bolts are carefully removed with a new knife blade.

11. Bolts and rivets can also be sourced from old or broken parts on other kits.

12. Old and outdated model kits can be a source of spare bolts.

6

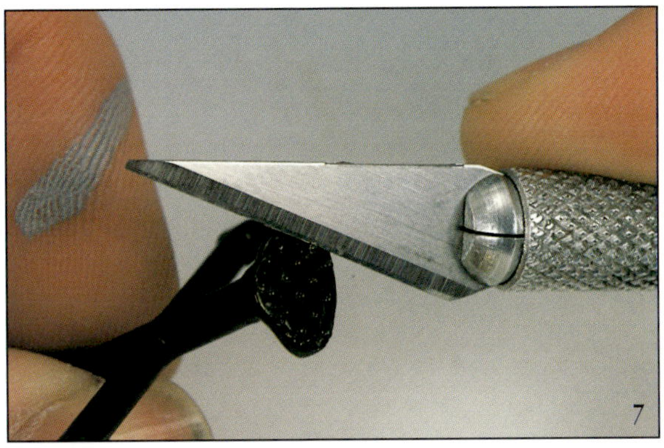

7

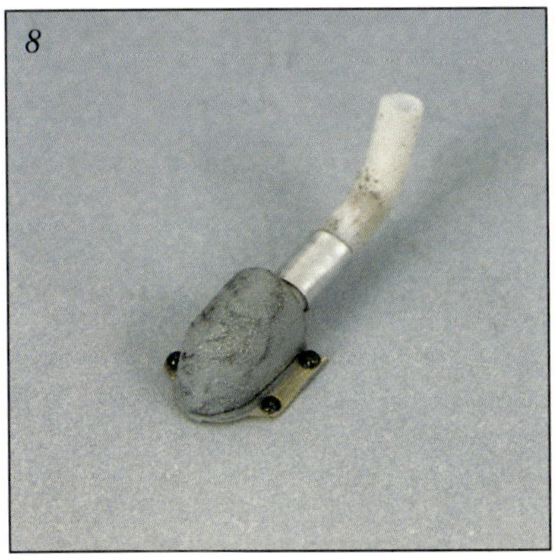

8

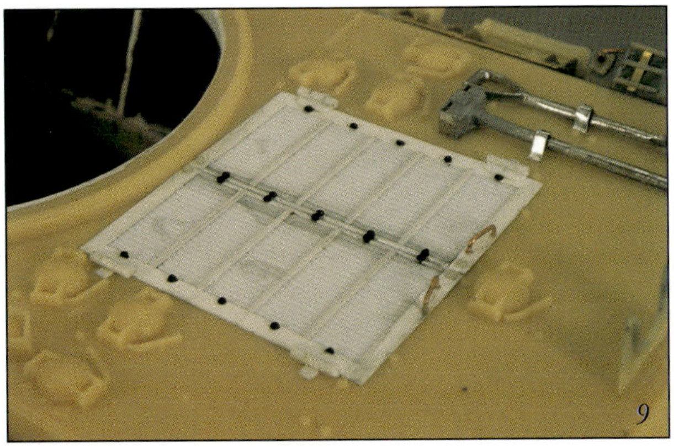

9

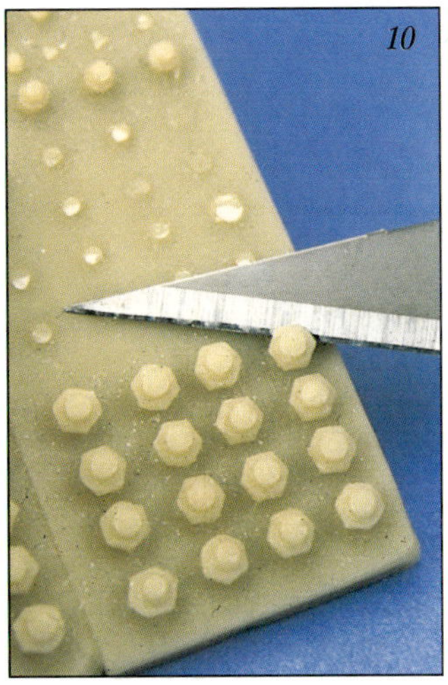

10

11

12

13. Special hole punching tools.

14. A sheet of Plasticard is inserted. A punch of the desired diameter is then used on the sheet. Just tap the punch with a hammer and, hey presto, a part is made.

15. Special punch for making different kinds of rivet.

16. The hammer hits the punch.

17. Apart from Plasticard, you can also use acetate, sheet metal or other materials.

18. When gluing plastic bolts or rivets onto plastic, first apply some liquid glue onto the area.

19. Place the part on a blade tip, and set it in position.

20. Once in position, it is recommended to apply more glue to the part, to make sure it stays in place.

21. View of a few newly placed rivets.

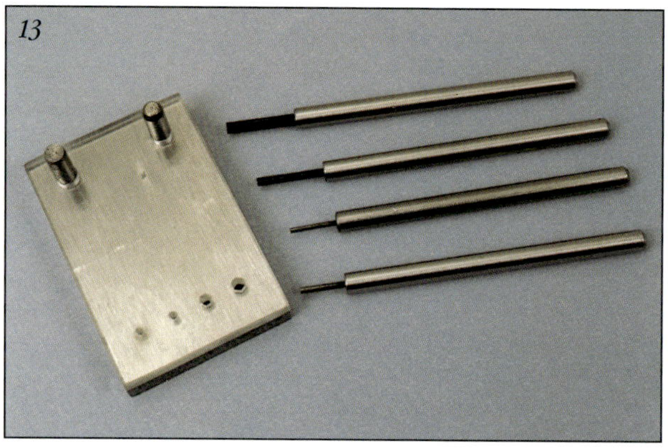

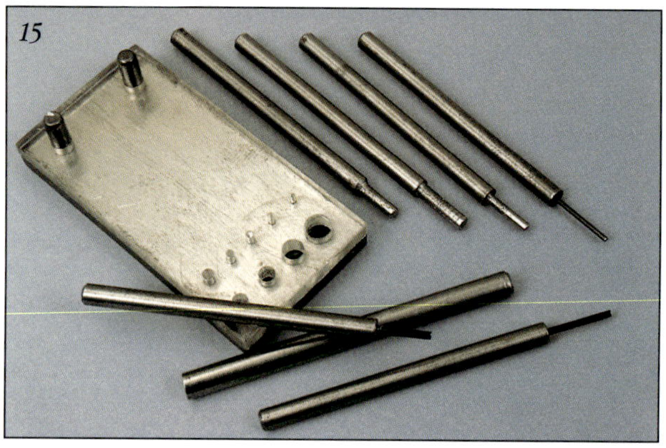

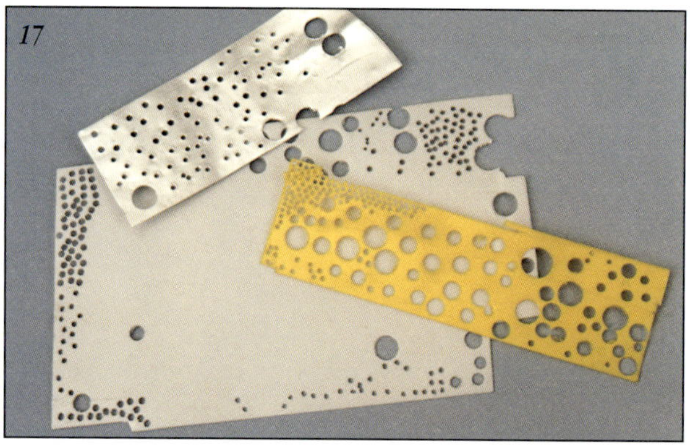

Foreword

Sooner or later, a beginner will attempt to model a damaged or destroyed vehicle. Few, however, are truly successful attempts, as most of the time it is done in a hurry and carelessly. Usually, they give the vehicle a few dents here and there, along with some other damage. Believe it or not, it is harder to model a damaged/destroyed vehicle than it is to make an undamaged one. When important items of a machine are either damaged or even totally missing (hatches, locks, etc) then, quite often, other usually hidden internal elements become visible, and the appearance of each of these elements must be carefully researched and reproduced. Nowadays, some kits include the necessary parts for making a damaged/destroyed vehicle. That said, it's best not to take things for granted, so, sharpen your modeling skills because, in this chapter, you are going to need them. After doing your homework, you'll discover that there are lots of parts (especially wiring and other small, and sometimes large components) that simply aren't there. It is these components that usually need to be scratch-built.
We have chosen two vehicles with which to illustrate this type of work: a German Pz. IV, and a Soviet T-34. The Soviet tank was modeled to portray an altogether different, little known version, representative of the period. One strange detail will be the painted turret that stands out from an, otherwise unpainted vehicle. The unpainted surfaces have a quite rusty having been left for well over a month. The study of rust development is quite educational.

T-34. 1941

During the 'Great Patriotic War' (as the Soviets used to call WWII), there were three grave crises. These were the sieges of the three principal cities, Stalingrad, Moscow, and Leningrad. While all three cities eventually held out, it was at the most enormous cost, both human and material. The need for armored vehicles became so desperate, that vehicles often went into battle with the absolute minimum of anti-rust primer on them. Sometimes, they didn't even have that, or just the turret but not the chassis was painted, or vice versa. A version with just the turret painted was chosen as our subject, mainly because it fitted in with a diorama portraying the siege of Leningrad.

The T-34 version to be modeled is the intermediate one, manufactured from 1940-1942. A comprehensive conversion is necessary for both the Tamiya and the Italeri-Zvezda products, even if some details of each kit are better than the other. If the Italeri kit is chosen, it is supplied with the Kirin turret, although both kit versions still require a lot of work in order to accurately portray a turret such as found in Leningrad during the period. The turret requires additional protection and a reinforced mantle, in place of the rounded one. For the engine bay, an MB kit, containing die cast and photo-etched parts, is required. There is another kit by Verlinden, but it contains less parts.

The vehicle portrayed has been knocked out by after being hit by a 50mm anti-tank projectile. The shell's impact was on the rear left side of the vehicle, destroying its chain drive.

The required items for this job include, Italeri's T-34/76 M-1943 ref. 282, Kirin's Appliqué Armor Turret T-34/42 ref. 28501, Jordi Rubio's Soviet Tank-Gun 76,2mm ref. TG-07, Todo Modelismo photoetch sheet No.5, and MB Models Engine Kit ref. 1035.

By following a few simple steps, the 1943 Soviet T-34 can be converted into a 1941 version.

Let us start with the Kirin turret, which is a copy of Tamiya's 1942 T-34 turret, with additional armor plating on the sides.

If this turret is carefully compared to contemporary photos of an actual turret, it can easily be seen that it isn't correct and that it must be modified slightly. First, remove the front armor plating and replace them with 0.25mm thick Plasticard. The welding seams on the plates are done following the procedure as reviewed on Page 45. The Tamiya version requires exactly the same modifications.

Once the aluminum gun barrel and the three rings have been fixed in position, trim the hatch's fastenings with a knife. The vehicle fastenings are solid blocks and are, therefore, incorrect. The rear access hatch should also be removed.

Once the turret has been done, assemble the chassis and wheels. The forward tension wheels should be moved forward slightly. The rear should be modified by removing the high part of the armor plate, and replace it with some Evergreen plastic rod, making sure it is bent like the ones on the actual 1940-41 tanks. The main body of the vehicle is where

1

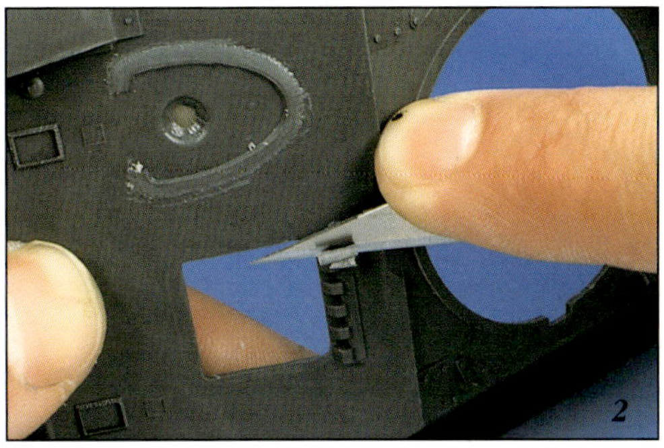

2

1. Research material used.

2. Armed with a knife and sandpaper, remove all the details on the front.

3. Carefully remove the front fenders.

4. The finer cuts (vertical fenders) are done with a knife.

5. The weld seams are carefully made with a knifepoint on a low voltage soldering iron.

3

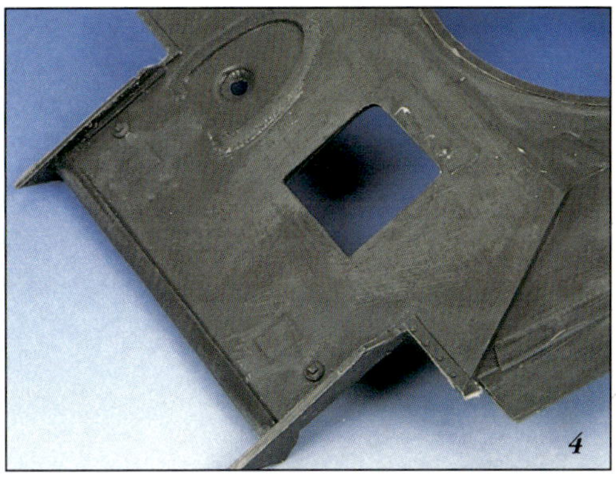

4

5

6

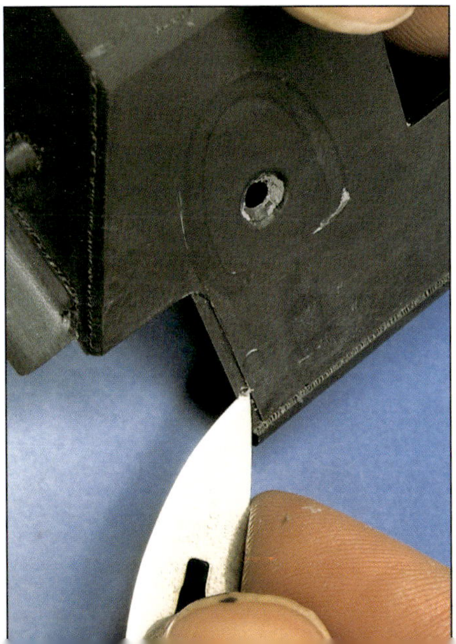

6. A scriber is used to mark the joins between the armor plating.

7. View of the continuous line.

8. Use a knife to trim the lower plate.

7

the majority of the modification must be made. Begin at the rear, adjusting it to conform to the above mentioned curved part. Similarly, cut a square hole for the rear access hatch. This allows access to the chain drive. As we want to see tits interior, hollow out the area and match it to the upper hatch and ventilation grill.
The front and rear fenders should be removed completely, carving the fitting lines, where the side and front armor plates meet, onto the plastic surface.
Move the machine gun position, placing it slightly to the rear and, in consequence, slightly higher. As a result, the forward part must be rebuilt, adding some bolts.
The driver's hatch must be scratch built. The detailed plans for doing this are included in the text.
The textured area of the fenders must be carved with a knife. After applying heat, a few dents can be made in this area.
Now, position the towing cable moorings. These were a distinguishing feature of the last units made during 1941. The small plates for these moorings must be scratch built from Plasticard. The headlights were sourced from another kit.
All the moorings and fastenings, on both sides of the tank, were also scratch built using copper wire and sheet metal.
Finally, detailing the rear! Position the photo-etched grills from the Todo Modelismo No.5 photo-etch sheet, and insert the engine into its bay.

PAINTING

The vehicle chosen for portrayal is one of many that took part in the heroic defense of Leningrad against the Nazis. While the city remained in contact with the rest of the country, many armored vehicles manufactured in the factories were immediately sent to fighting units across the country. A few units, however, remained in the city to defend it against the invader. When these tanks left the factories, they were quite frequently unpainted. This is why we are dealing with a tank that only has the turret, and subsequently left to rust for several weeks after being knocked out. The unprotected steel surface reveals, therefore, the devastating effects of rust.

The Engine

Airbrush the engine and gearbox with a mixture of silver and iron gray acrylic. Then, do the shading with a mixture of black and brown, dry brush the highlights with gray metallic.

The Chassis

The 'rust' is a mixture of 40% red-brown, 40% yellow-green, and 20% matt red. Highlights are then done after adding matt yellow to the mixture. Next, use red-brown and orange to give the model more chromatic richness.
Once the acrylic paint is totally dry, give the vehicle an oil treatment as described on Page 56. The colors to be used are ochre, Neapolitan yellow, dark burnt-sand, burnt sienna, and light green.
Later, with the airbrush, give it some coats of red brown, dark yellow and orange paint. After that, do the profiling using a mixture of black and brown paint. The final dry brushing is with a mixture of orange and yellow zinc. Dry brush the tracks and surrounding area with a creamy khaki color to simulate mud.

Turret

The turret's base color is a 50:50 mixture of dark green and olive drab paint. Highlight with matt green and dark yellow.
The oil treatment and profiling work is the same as that done on the remainder of the tank. Dry brush with light olive and pale ochre gray, with orange for the rusty areas. The whole model can now be given a coat of matt varnish.

9. Extra texturing between the plates is made with the soldering iron and knifepoint.

10. The rear plates are carefully removed. The two halves of the chassis are assembled temporarily.

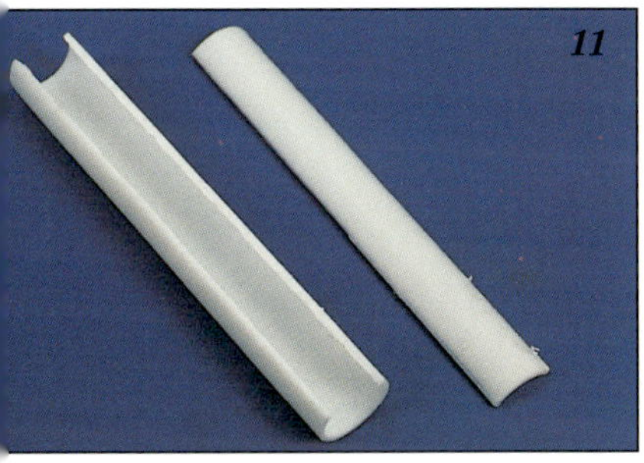

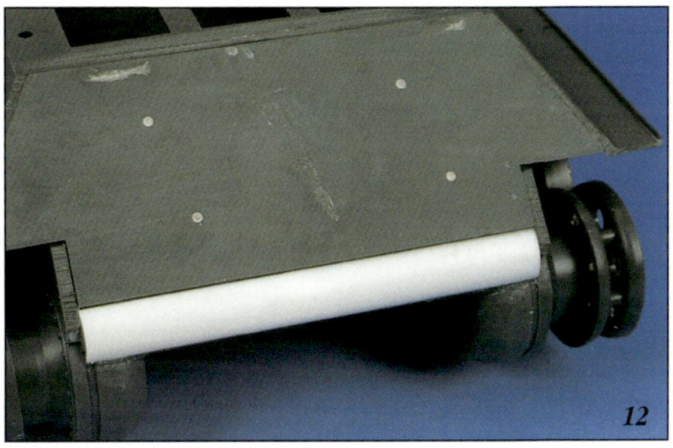

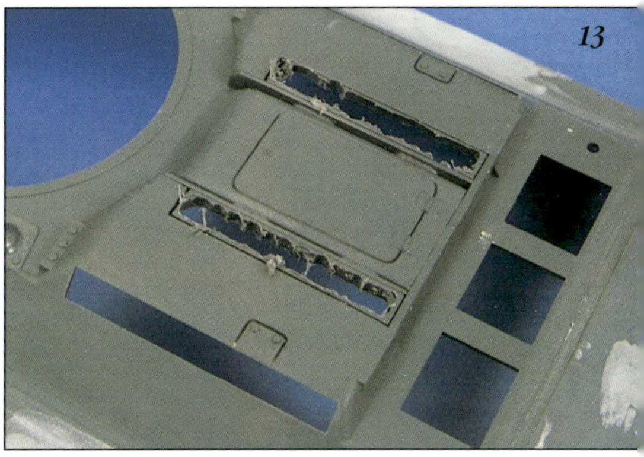

11. A plastic tube is used to make the curved part on the rear.

12. Once you're sure the part fits, glue it in position.

13. A number of holes are drilled in the upper part in order to hollow out the necessary areas.

14. The smooth finish was achieved with a knife.

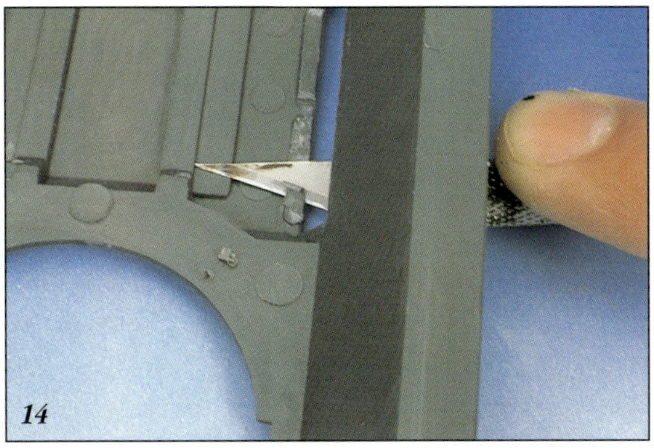

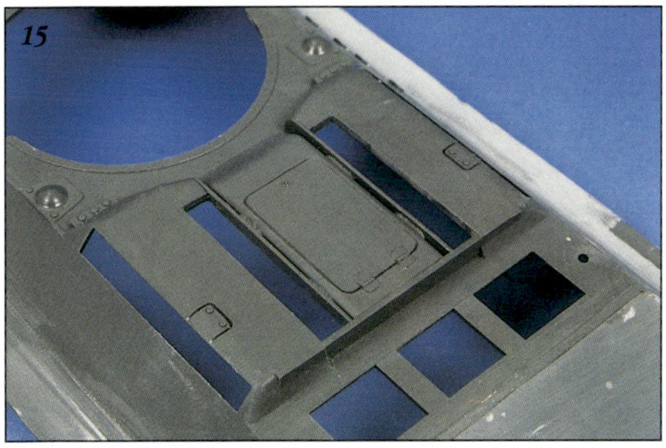

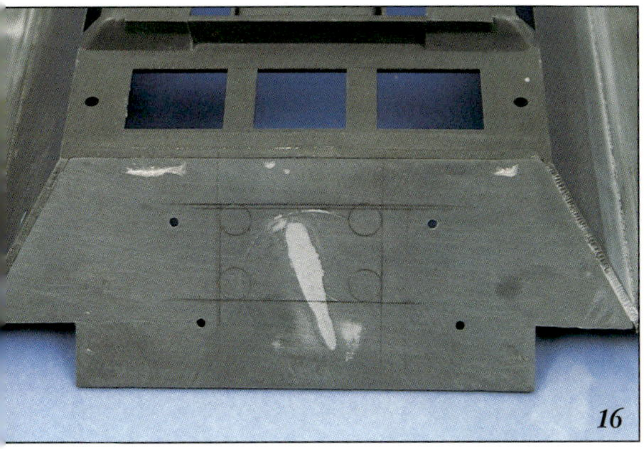

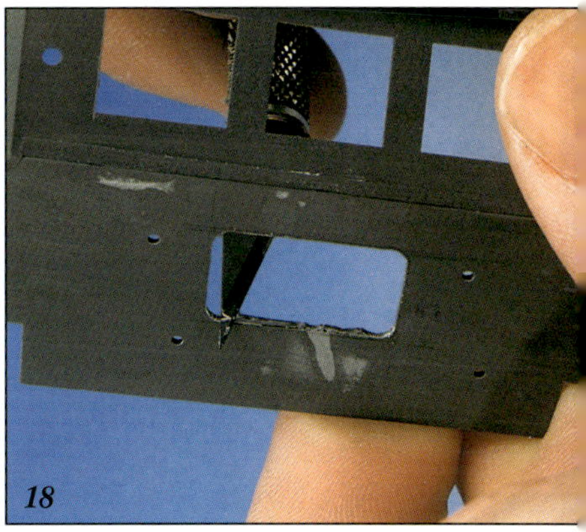

15. The final result is certainly clean enough.

16. Pencil marks indicate the position of the access hatch.

17. First, drill four holes. Then use a mousetail file to connect the drilled holes and empty the hatch.

18. A knife and sandpaper will give us clean edges.

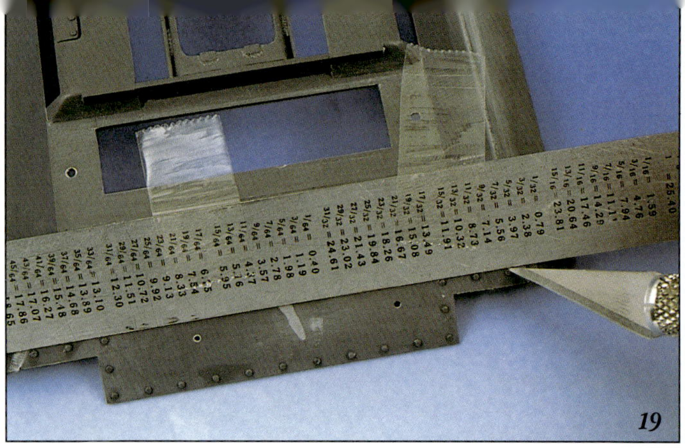

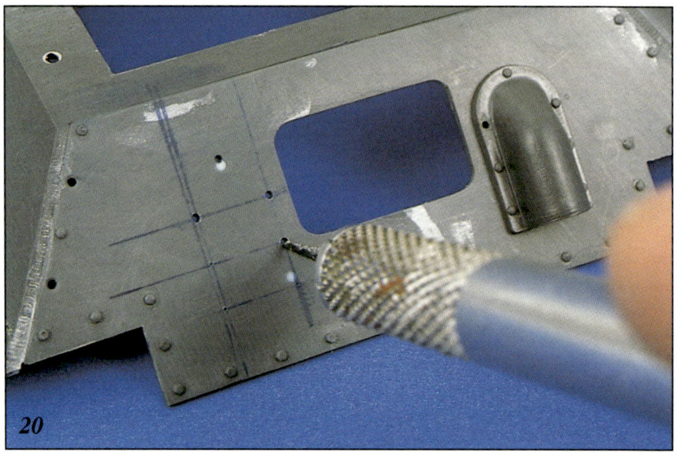

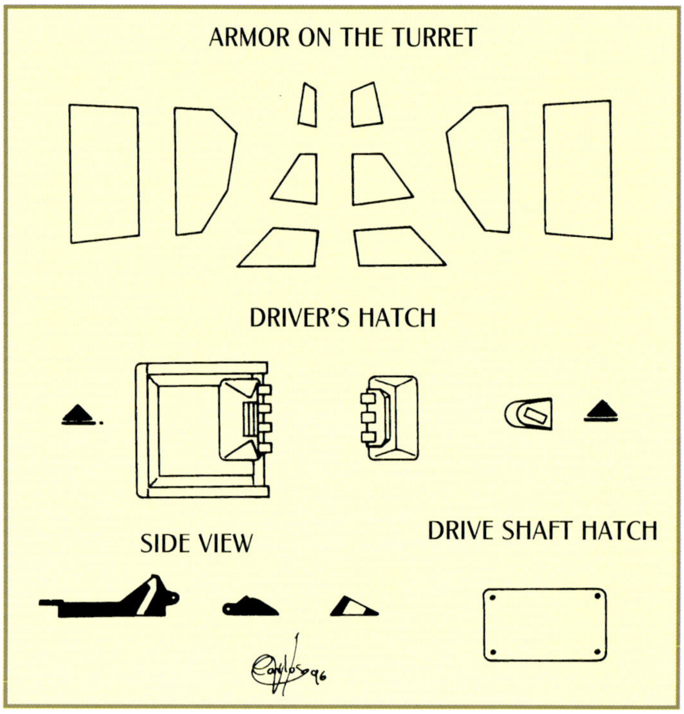

19. Now glue on the sprockets that were previously removed to allow work on the rear. A steel rule will come in handy.

20. Even though the Impact blew off the left exhaust shield, the mounting bolt holes must still be drilled.

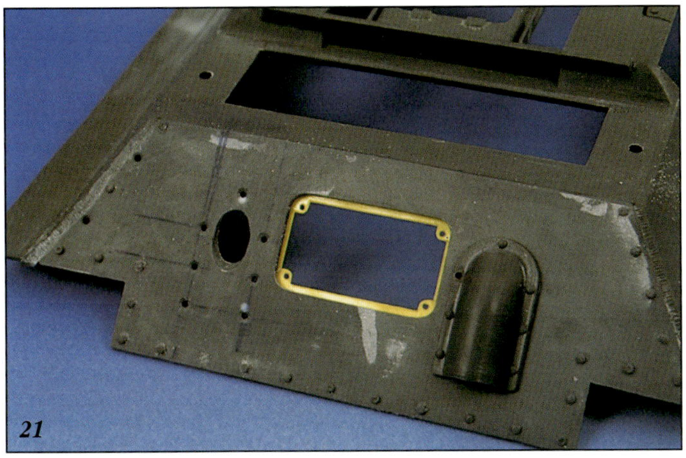
21

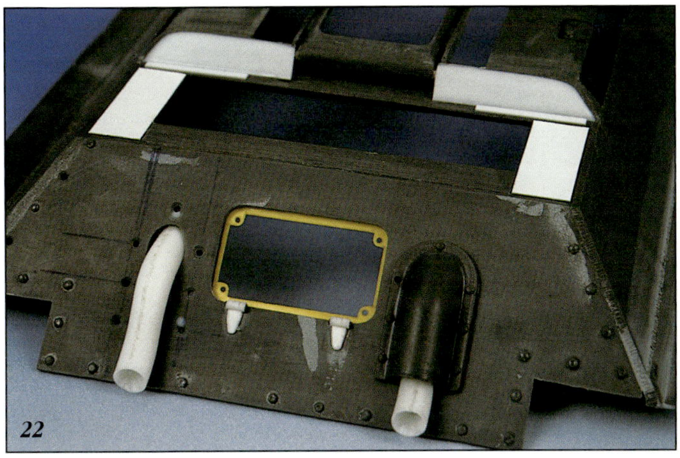
22

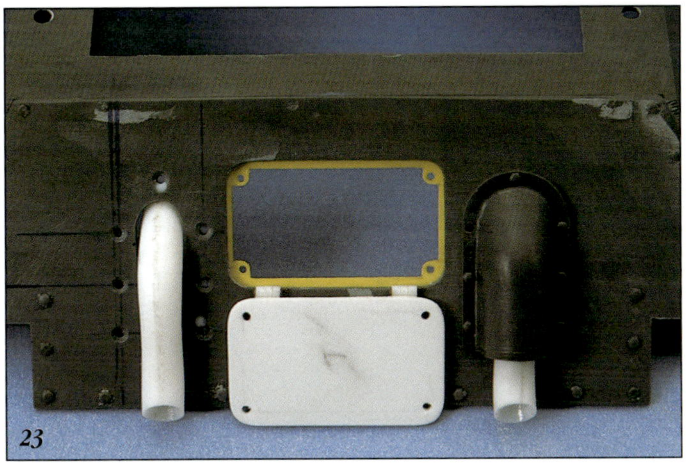
23

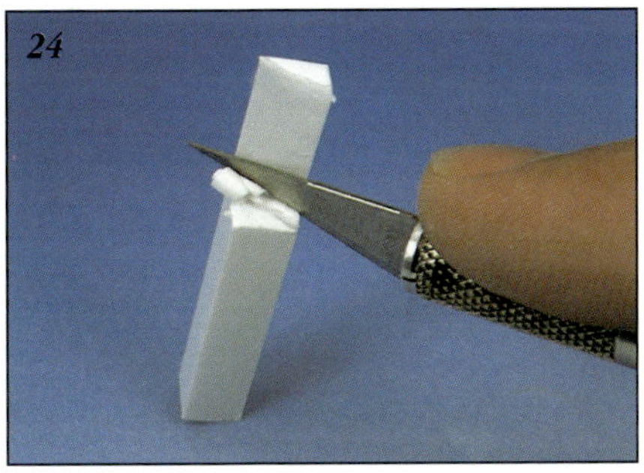
24

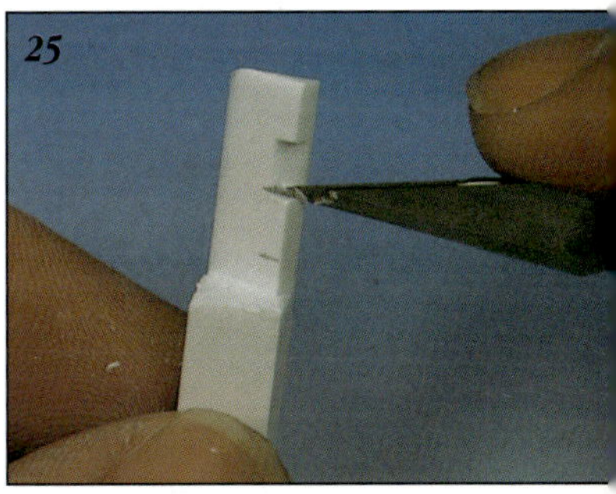
25

26

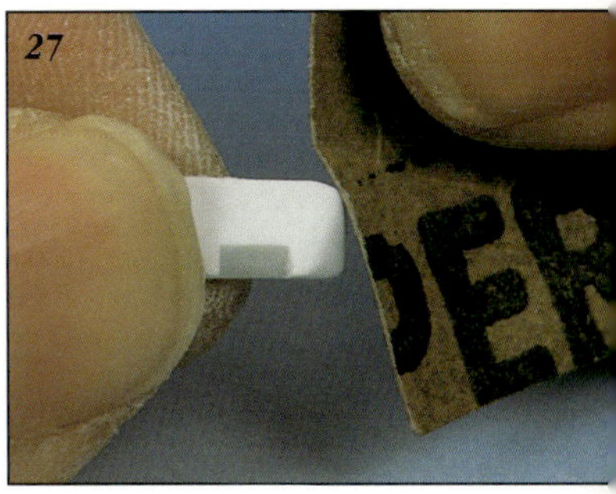
27

28

21. Use a piece of acetate to make the thin frame that carries the four bolts for the hatch.

22. Plasticard was used to make the base for the upper hatch.

23. The exhausts are bent plastic tubes, the hatch is 1mm thick Plasticard

24. Carve the base of the driver's periscope from a piece of square plastic rod.

25. To get sharp, clean edges use a new knife blade.

26. The sides are carefully removed

27. The edges are sanded smoothed.

28. The completed part

29. The driver's hatch is completely scratch-built.

30. Here is the completed part. The periscopes were sourced from another kit.

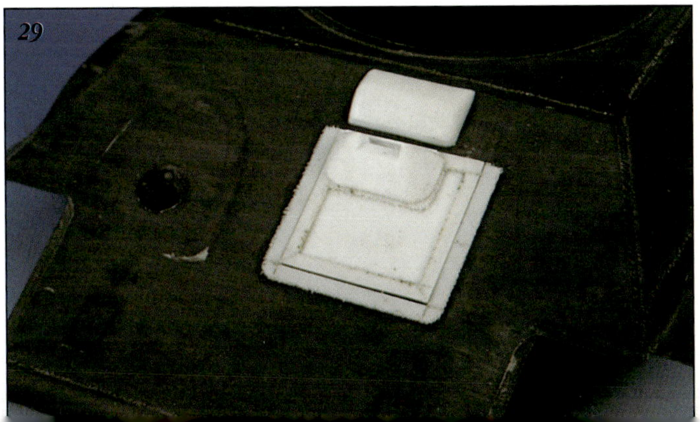
29

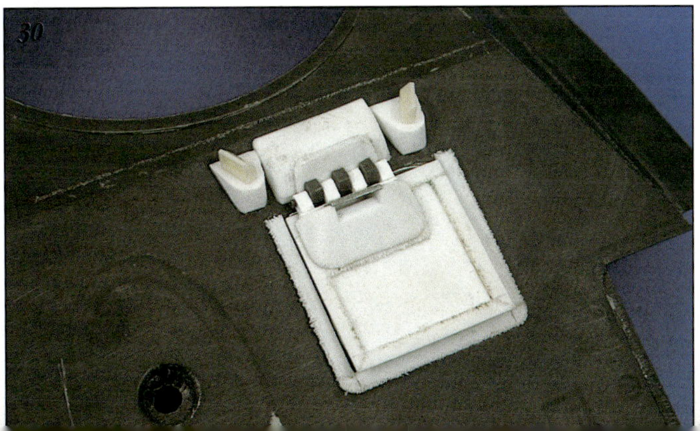
30

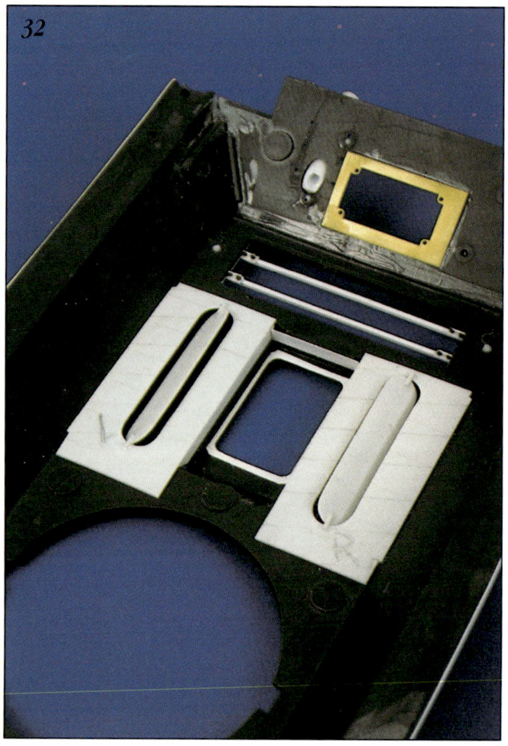

31. The front is completed with two headlights, the towing cable fastenings, and the machine gun's base.

32. Inside the chassis, place 0.20mm thick Plasticard plates.

33. Place the photo etched grills on the exterior. You must also make the hinges for the large grill. This large grill will not be placed on the vehicle, but beside it as though it had been blown off.

34. The grill's support was hollowed out, and a thin metal mesh placed in it.

35. The mesh's frame was made from acetate.

36. The drive shaft, originally designed for Tamiya's T-34 kit, doesn't fit properly so it must be lightly sanded until it fits.

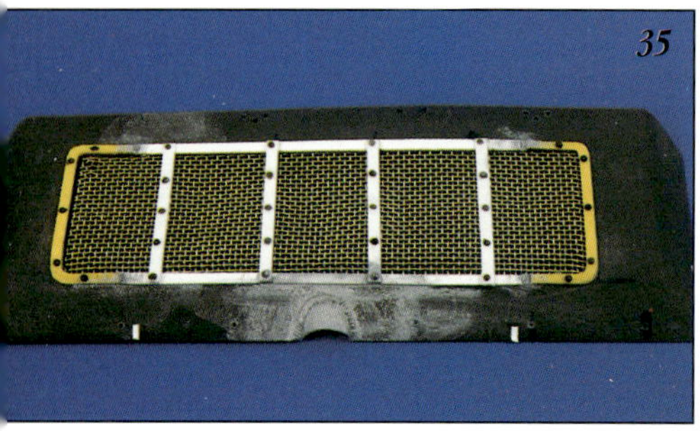

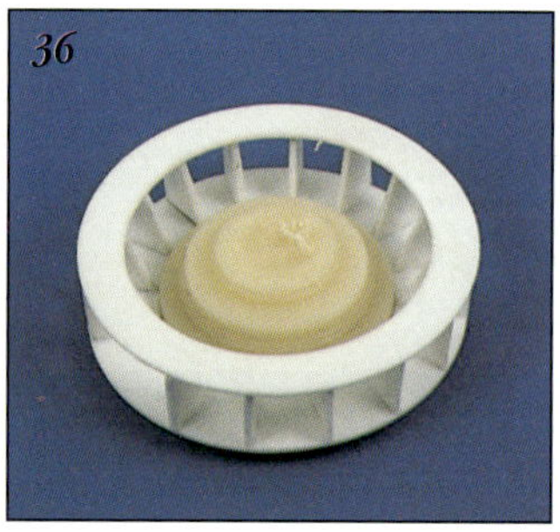

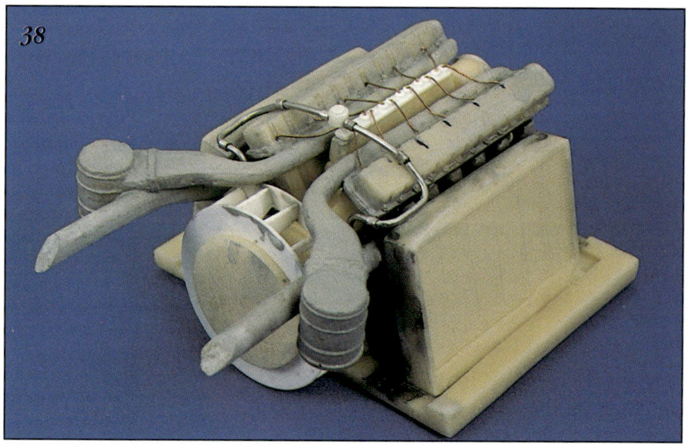

37. The ventilator was carefully detailed with 0.2mm thick Plasticard.

38. The assembled engine complete with all its detailing, copper wire, metal, etc.

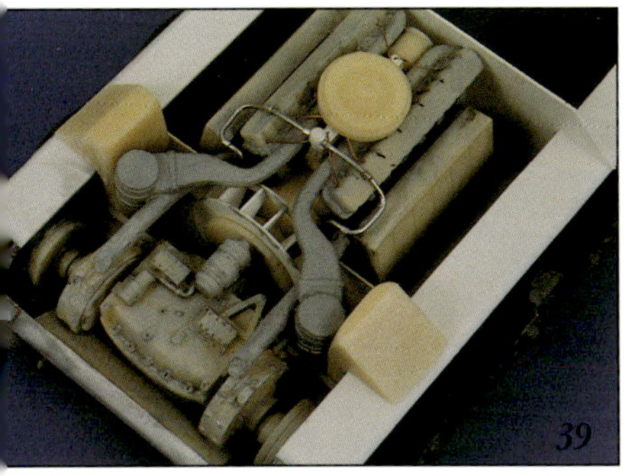

39. *The ensemble is ready for painting. The remains loose for ease of painting*

40. *The base color is applied with an airbrush. The base color is various proportions of silver and iron gray paint, depending on the areas to be painted.*

41. *The rust is red-brown paint, and detail profiling is a mixture of brown and black paint.*

42. *The engine should be quite dirty. Metal gray paint should be discreetly dry brushed.*

43. *This picture shows the intricate copper wire system.*

44. *Varying the proportion of base color and the intensity of the profiling mixture, will make each component stand out.*

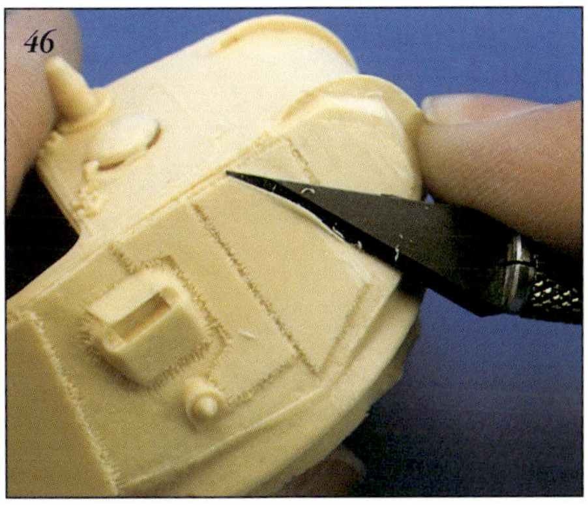

45. *Finally, apply some black grease stains using a fine brush.*

46. *The turret's front armor plating is not correct, and should be removed.*

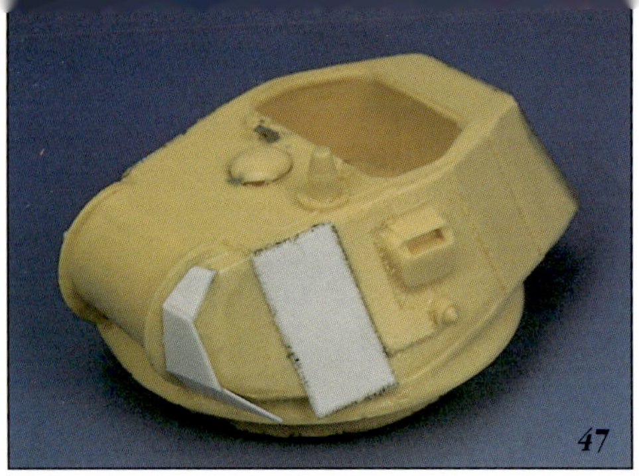

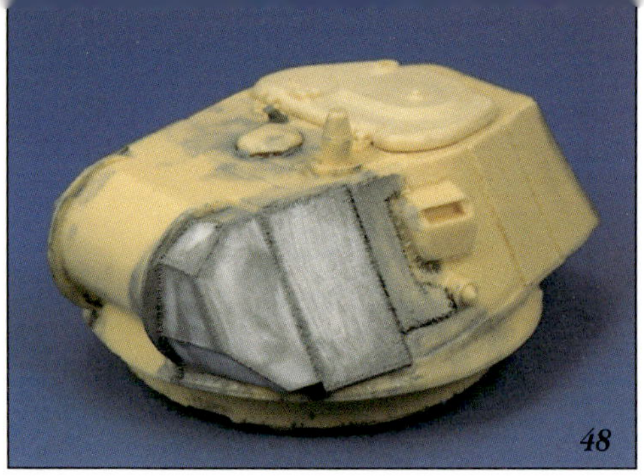

47. Following the plans (included in the text) cut new plates from 0.25mm thick Plasticard.

48. After making the weld seams, use diluted putty to insure a perfect fit between the plates.

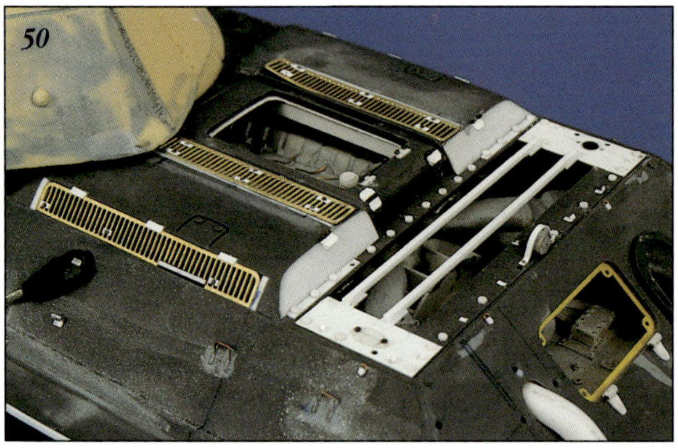

49. The turret is completed with the addition of an aluminum gun barrel and the three rings on the roof.

50. The upper and lower parts of the tank can now be glued together.

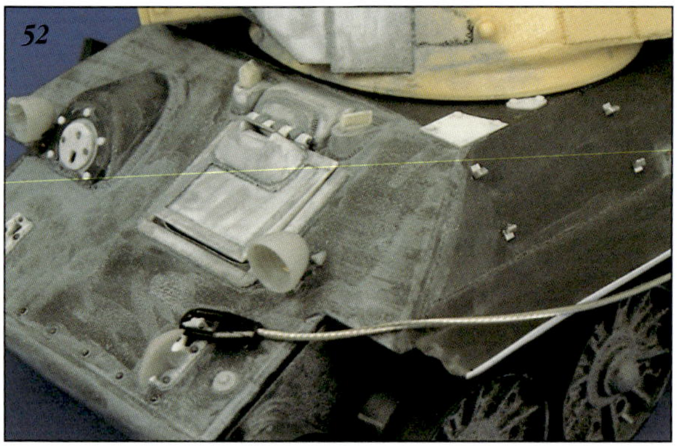

51. This is the area where most of the scratch-built parts are used.

52. Thin metal sheet is used to make all side fastenings on the vehicle.

53. Finished and ready to paint.

54. The base color is a mixture of red-brown, matt red and green-yellow paint.

55. All the different tonal variations are achieved with the use of oil paints.

56. While we are busy profiling, we can make the vertical rust marks using black and brown paint.

57. The paint for the turret is both dark-green and olive drab.

58. This picture shows the effects of the weathering and profiling that have been done.

59. On the edges of the additional armor plating, dry brushing some orange paint to help convey the rust marks.

60. The turret and body during the first phase of the painting process.

61. During the second phase, the effects of wear on an abandoned vehicle can be appreciated.

62. During the final phase the subtle profiling and dry brushing effects can be seen.

63. The headlight reflectors were made from thin metal sheet, and then punched with the hole-punch.

64. Cracks on the headlamp reflectors are done with paint (dark gray and brown) and a fine brush.

65. Small drills will simulate different size impacts on the vehicle's surface. The edges of the most recent hits have a 'polished metal' surround.

66. The dried mud on the lower areas was made with a mixture of fine sand and putty. Dry brushed cream and khaki paint complete the effect.

67. The exhausts have a 'burnt rust' look.

68. The engine's ventilation areas are darker than the rest of the tank.

69. Profiling and dry brushing make all the small parts stand out enhancing the model's outline.

70. The completed model.

Destroyed Panzer IV

When it was decided to make a diorama portraying a war ravaged urban area featuring an armored vehicle and several Russian soldier figures, we chose a Panzer IV from among the incredibly wide range of tanks on offer. This tank appeared particularly suitable because of its relatively small size, its thin armor plating that made it eminently suitable for displaying battle damage. The vehicle, although obsolete by 1945, was still widely used during the period where all resources became of immense value to a dwindling, ill-equipped army.

From a modeling viewpoint, damage can only be fully exploited if the vehicle has been left in this state for at least a month, preferably two. The elapsed time allows rust to settle, and appear in its own right.

At some point, most modelers has been tempted by the idea of including a destroyed vehicle in a diorama, and quite often ended up doing it. That said, quite often, the vehicle becomes a secondary element in the diorama, and the destroyed vehicle is an outdated model retouched for the occasion. This means that the final result portrays exactly that, a destroyed vehicle that stands out from the diorama because of its lack of quality, manifested by the item used, in most cases an old kit or model. As you will see, by starting out with a new kit, complete with aftermarket photo etched and resin parts, the result will transform the diorama.

However, a well-built model isn't everything. Careful study of the effects of an explosion and how to re-create it using paint is a key factor for getting our model to convey to the viewer the information and feelings that we want to achieve. This can be, perhaps, the most difficult part for the modeler who may end up becoming discouraged by the lack of information. In this study, we intend to present the main guidelines for making such vehicles, even if there is little information to go on. That said, the situation is changing, and the available information is growing steadily. Good photographic analysis assists us in making damage look believable.

ANATOMY OF AN IMPACT

The tank, a Pz. IV G with a sand-colored camouflage scheme, received a direct, close range hit from a 100mm shell fired by a Soviet SU-100 tank destroyer. The direction of the impact caused further damage to the structure of the German tank. It entered to one side of the front, causing the vehicles own ammunition, stored directly behind the driver's position, to detonate. The ensuing explosion was the primary cause of the vehicle's present condition. The vehicle's crew was killed instantly, due to the anti-tank projectile exploding inside the vehicle, causing more damage to the interior than to the exterior. The shattering internal explosion almost destroyed the tank's chassis's frame, and lifted the turret from its position. All hatches were either blown open or, simply, blown away. Those blown open were the turret's left side hatch, and the ones on the front of the vehicle, adjacent to the gearbox.

The front portion of the left track area was also torn off, while immediately following the initial explosion, fire destroyed most of the interior, reducing everything to ash and leaving it charcoal black. Once the fire had burnt itself out, the burnt areas became rusty almost overnight, while the less burnt areas remained smoke blackened. Many of the tank's accessories, including the fenders, were blown off and completely disappeared. Now the vehicle's colors vary in tone, ashes from the burnt paintwork and other fire-consumed objects, cover the tank.

CONCLUSION

Using logic, it is reasonably simple to follow the effects of the damage and how it was caused. Of course, it is vital to know what actually knocked the tank out. Was it a landmine, a 37mm or a 88mm shell, a bomb dropped by a Stuka, a flame thrower, ...? However, in this instance, we do know that this particular vehicle was destroyed by a 100mm anti-tank shell.

The second thing to consider, damage wise, is the actual victim. There is no comparison between a Pz. IV hitting an anti-tank mine and the same thing happening to a Royal Tiger. We also have to determine the damage done, those areas totally destroyed, the areas that remain intact, the burnt areas, the smoked-blackened surfaces, and so forth.

We must also consider if further damage was caused as a consequence of a secondary factor. In this case, the secondary factor is clearly the detonation of the tank's own ammunition.

Finally, we shall consider the overall look of the destroyed tank, and the time elapsed since its destruction.

ASSEMBLY

We chose to base our destroyed tank model on an Italeri Pz. IV kit. The front section of the vehicle is the most difficult part, because part of the drive shaft has to be rebuilt. The Verlinden aftermarket kit of this item only offers the central block, the rest has to be built from the blueprints. In such cases, it is necessary to have an intimate knowledge of the tank itself, mainly because we have to be aware what could be destroyed, what could be burned, and what would escape unscathed. The fender supports also have to be scratch built from aluminum sheet, also the covers for the rear ventilation grille. The Todo Modelismo photo-etch sheet, or any other sheet dedicated to this vehicle, will be sufficient to afford the vehicle all the necessary details.

The front hook, front bogie, and the first return roller disappeared in the explosion, so holes must be drilled to indicate where they had been.

The turret also requires a number of modifications. The rear basket was trimmed and left open and a new lid was made from aluminum sheet and plastic. The lower part has two wooden strips riveted on. These were used to suppress any static created by friction with the antenna. They were completely consumed by the subsequent fire.

The right hatch and the access plate to the drive shaft on the burnt side were also been blown off, and photos of the period do not show that they were blown onto the turret.

The Jordi Rubio gun barrel is excellent, jutting out of the cylindrical mantle shield. The turret's interior was built in a, more or less, complete form.

The engine bay, damaged in the explosion, contains a Verlinden engine, with the remaining parts built from scratch or borrowed from other kits. Note the hanging rear fender, suspended from a single spring.

The turret rings and gears were made from plastic and wire.

PAINTING

The painting process also has to follow a number of logical steps. The first thing to do is paint the vehicle in its original sand color camouflage scheme, along with the corresponding washes and other effects. This is crucial, and is also the reason for choosing a simple camouflage scheme. A complicated one, when damaged, would look somewhat confusing, while also not looking very good after we've completed recreating the effects of the explosion.

If we were to recreate an explosion on a Royal Tiger sporting the 'ambrus' camouflage scheme during the Battle of the Bulge, the best solution would be to tone down the three camouflage colors with several sand or dirt colored washes. Then, when painting the burnt areas, we would have to rely heavily on Tamiya's transparent colors.

Anyway, be that as it may, once we have finished painting the least affected side, painting

the difficult, burn out effects can begin. It is advisable to plot, on a vehicle blueprint, the damage suffered by the structure (a photocopy of the kit's instruction sheet will suffice). These pencil sketches will help determine the damage on the model.

Once everything is clear, begin applying the lightest colors and those colors closest to the impact area (rust and orange colors). Airbrush Tamiya's red-brown along with a few transparent orange colors. Subtle applications of Humbrol No.62 will pretty much complete the work at this stage. The result should have a real orange look to it.

We can now begin using the whole spectrum of red colors. They are distributed around the orange areas and mainly covering those areas in shadow and better protected. It is also advisable to apply some irregular red marks onto the orange surfaces. The colors used are Tamiya's Hull Red and Humbrol Nos. 62 and 70, plus Tamiya's transparent red to finish it off.

The darkest reds are used to darken the most hidden areas, crevices, joints, rivets, etc... always using the airbrush.

General washes

At this point, apply an overall wash of Tamiya's transparent red-orange so that everything blends together into a homogenous whole. Don't worry if everything appears a little glossy, this is a good sign as scratches and paint peels will appear sharper at the end.

The next thing is to make the 'chemical paint peels', in other words, to get the irregular shapes that are formed when synthetic material is burnt on a metal surface, they look like paint peels on local areas. For this, use two Humbrol mixtures diluted with turpentine.

On the undamaged areas, apply a coat of the tank's original color. Then, with brown, paint some smaller paint peels on the outer areas. Finally, apply a final wash of highly diluted Tamiya transparent red and red-brown.

Paint peels

After allowing the previous paint step to completely dry (a matter of a few minutes), we can begin to apply the paint peels. The peels should have a 'photo negative' distribution, as opposed to those on an undamaged vehicle. All crevices and the more protected areas, apply scraps of the original sand color that would be left on the predominantly rusty surface. On the area nearest the main impact, apply conventional paint peels ('photo positive' ones) with Humbrol No.62, following an imaginary radius of the circle caused by the impact, in a star shape.

SMOKE BLACKENED AREAS

On those areas that change from the base color to rust, airbrush some Humbrol matt black paint so that It appears smoke blackened. Use a hand-held mask on some areas for better definition. In order to get an aesthetic, although not quite a realistic effect, apply the black paint in a proportion of three to two. What we mean is, apply black paint twice per every three areas where the dominant color's orange. If one sees pictures of actual damaged vehicles, it is obvious that these proportions are incorrect. However, in this case, to make sure that our model looks realistic, we must use a little artistic license.

OTHER ELEMENTS

Now, we can apply all the other effects that contribute to making the model look as realistic as possible.

Following the explosion, mud, sand and rubble would have rained down on top of the tank. This is done with small textured bits of putty. Once dry, they can be painted with light colors, such as Tamiya's buff mixed with sand. This mixture will look like dried mud. Use Humbrol No. 29 for fresh mud.

Complete the job with black and white pastel chalk dust to simulate the 'ash' of burnt material. The pastel dust can be applied with the tip of a screwdriver on all the areas that need it. Pastel dust can be permanently fixed with tiny drops of clean turpentine. It is best to let it dry thoroughly, and not touch it too much, even when dry.

COLOR	ORIGIN	POSITION
1) Large orange areas	- Rust	- Close to the area of impact, and on prominent areas.
2) Red areas	- New rust	- On crevices, and surrounding the above areas.
3) Black rust	- Burnt rust	- Where permanent parts were rollers, etc.).
4) Camouflage	- Non-burnt paint	- On areas far from the flames.
5)Over burns	- Half burnt paint	- On protected areas, those areas just outside the flames.
6)Gray	- Chemical action	- Paint peels (all over the vehicle).
7)Smoked areas	- Charred areas	- On areas untouched by the flames. -

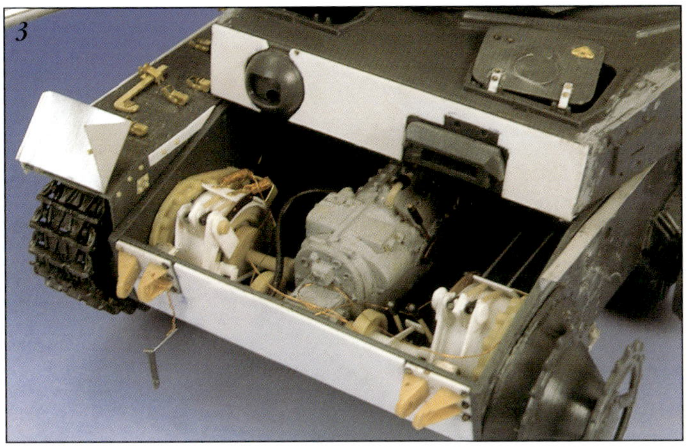

1. Reference material used for this tank.

2. The many scratch built areas are easily spotted, as they are a different color.

3. The chain drive system made from a Verlinden kit along with many scratch built Evergreen items.

4. Several hatches were blown off, leaving just some bolts and rivets, and a few hinges.

5. All additional armor plating on the front was made from Plasticard.

6. The interior of the hatches, fender supports, and turret ring, all require some detail work.

7. Surrounding the turret is a plastic ring, and the base of the hatch hinge was remodeled to look like it had been torn off.

1

15

14-15. *Some pieces made of wood and placed in the box have disappeared. Rust and burnt areas appear close to the ashes.*

2

3

1.Front area, showing the charred areas where the flames broke through.

2. The intense brown area attempts to simulate large areas of burnt paint caused by the extreme temperatures.

3. Some ash has found its way onto the top of the structure.

4. The rubber tires on the wheels have completely burnt away.

5. All those areas where the flames broke through have a very black surface.

6. Ash covering the horizontal areas of the fenders.

7-8. The engine appears burnt and blackened.

9. The heat intensity sustained by a given area. This will also determine the rust color.

10. Some areas have suffered the effects of fire less than others. These will look almost the same as the tank before its destruction.

4

5

6

11. Flames have broken out of the hatches so these, in turn, are blackened.

12. Burnt-off paint leaves whole areas bare. The gray paint shows through.

13. Washes and filters are used to simulate wear in all its different stages.

8. A new edge was put on the fenders, and the photo etched tool holders were put into position.

9. The original gun barrel was replaced with a metal one, its shielding was also blown off.

10. The ventilation areas with protective shields made from Plasticard.

11. The rubber tires on some wheels were totally burnt, so they should be filed off.

12. Verlinden's resin engine was used to rebuild this area.

13. The radiator and its cover has disappeared, the engine is visible beneath.

14. The toolbox lid should be removed, the sides trimmed, and a new Plasticard lid made.

15. Both the exhaust's silencer and the gas ventilation system were rebuilt.

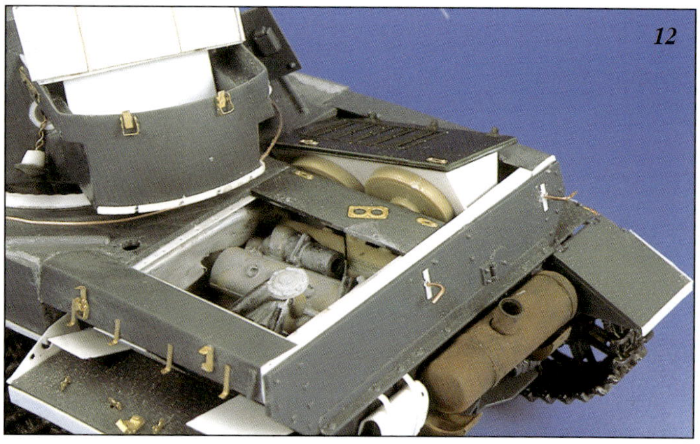

Foreword

Scratch building is simply making a model from blueprints of the particular vehicle. It is the most difficult accomplishment that a modeler can aspire to. It is, therefore, not a job for beginners. It requires the command of many tools and building materials in order to successfully hurdle the many problems that will, needless to say, arise. It is also necessary to have the ability to transform any type of material (metal, plastic, resin…) into whatever shape is required. It also calls for inventiveness, three-dimensional imaging, and a high degree of engineering skills in order to turn a drawing into a three dimensional object. Quite often, the necessary part can be sourced from the most common everyday object and we must have that extra ability of being able to spot it. While some of these skills are possessed by all good modelers, for a scratch builder it is necessary to possess them all. Straight and flat surfaces are usually easy to make, but the job gets harder and increasingly complex when curved shapes and other intricate forms are encountered. Fortunately, two-part epoxy putty comes in very handy for these types of structures and is an invaluable aide for all types of scratch building. When complex pieces are needed in great numbers, making molds is usually the best option. Everything I have mentioned contributes in some way in making scratch building much simpler.

Scratchbuilding

A few years ago, the purpose of this discipline was simple enough: To make vehicles that were unavailable commercially. Interesting vehicles, neglected by most kit manufacturers, could only be obtained by 'scratch building'. Not too long ago, scratch building also had a recycling side to it; commercial kits were scavenged to obtain some of the necessary components to build whatever you wished to do. Nowadays, demanding modelers work with scale blueprints, showing all the elements that go to make up a particular vehicle that is then constructed from Plasticard, plastic strips, cubes, and rods, along with sheet metal, wire, tubing, resin, molds, etc.

The industry, meanwhile, has taken a huge leap forward, and injected plastic parts along with resin ones, are on offer in a wide variety of shapes and sizes, sometimes offering large parts designed for a number of purposes. As can be imagined, scratch building is difficult and not many modelers have the talent necessary for it. It requires craftsmanship, experience, and a good dose of common sense when it comes to figuring out the different parts that must be made. The discipline would be even more difficult without the invaluable assistance of firms like Evergreen, which manufacture a wide variety of plastic elements in standard sizes.

Let us begin with scale blueprints, showing six different views of the vehicle, front and rear, both sides, and above and below. Photos from all conceivable angles are, indeed, most welcome, including close-up shots of even the most insignificant details. All this type of reference assist us in avoiding having to invent parts that might later prove to be incorrect. This happens, especially when making a rare vehicle. So, to sum up, excellent reference material is an absolute must.

Next, we have to go to the expense of acquiring all the manufactured materials: Large amounts of Plasticard and other plastic shapes, including U and V shaped pieces, rods and tubes, wire of different diameters, different types of filler, putty, etc. super and other liquid glue types. All these are crucial during the assembly.

Acquiring the necessary tools is also crucial. Essential tools include several kinds of saw, drawing instruments, a steel rule, calipers, a cutting compass, different bladed knives, riveters, hole punches, screws, a minidrill, drillbits, etcÉ

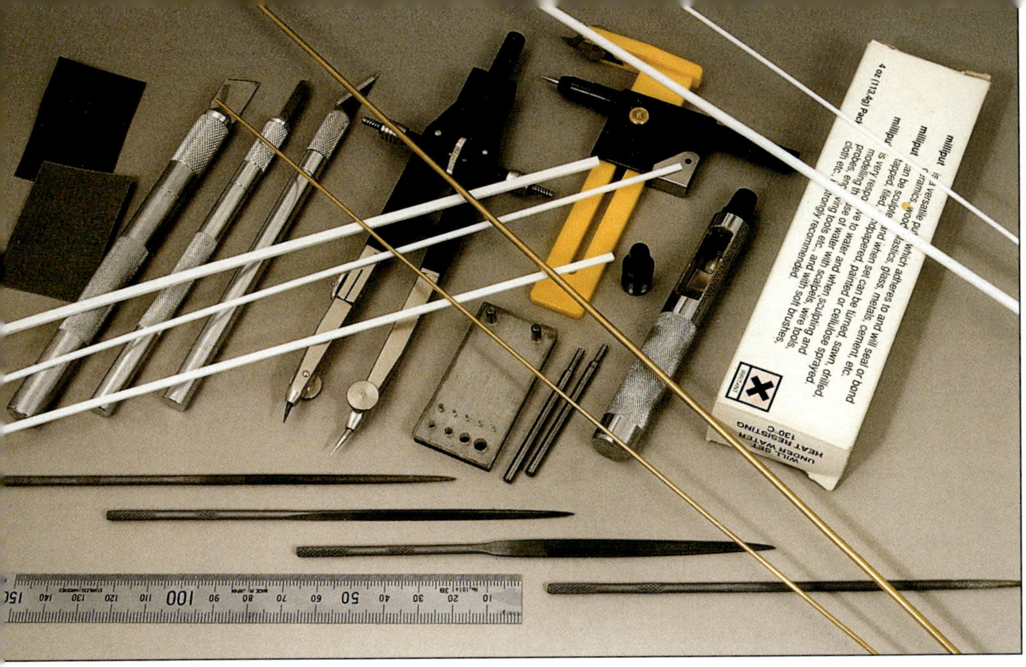

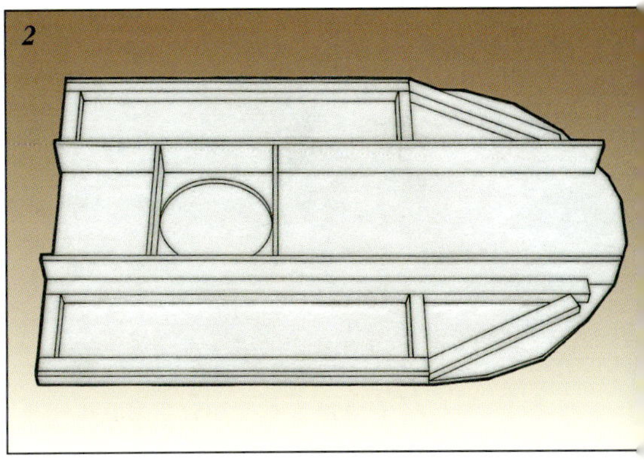

1. *Tools commonly used for scratch building.*

2. *Diagram showing the base structure for our model.*

3. *The second layer on the base. It gives a solid internal structure.*

4. *Undersides of the vehicle. The air cushion will be fixed here.*

5-6. *The entire structure is a 'skeleton' structure that was later covered with thin plastic sheet.*

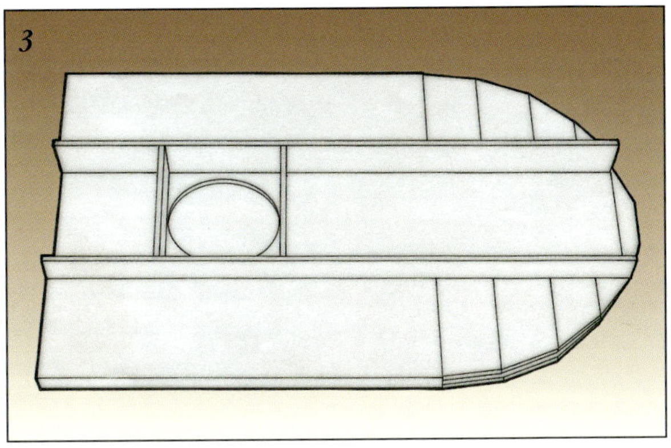

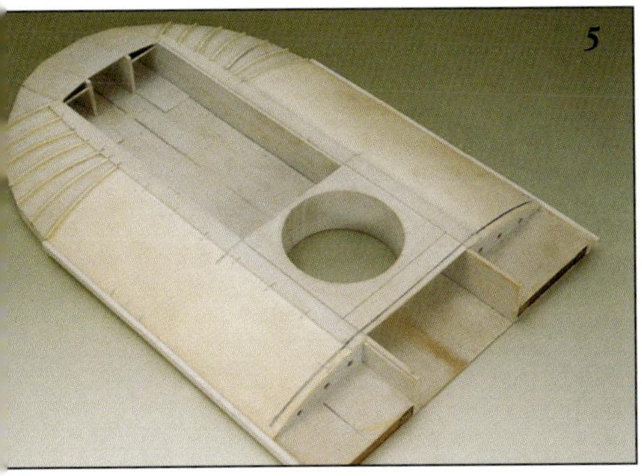

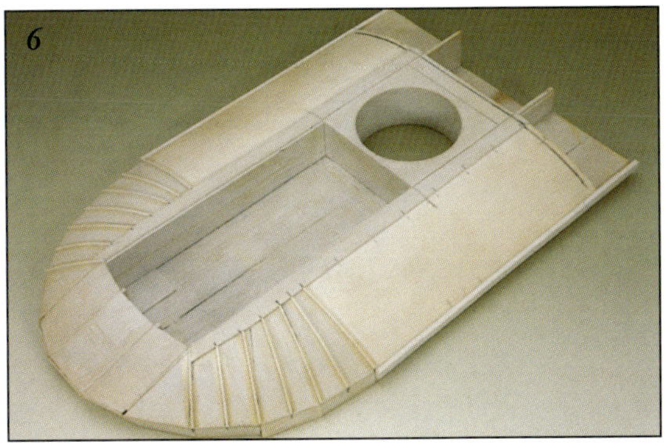

7. *Original and molded copy of a 'rib' on the 'skeleton structure'.*

8-9. *Up to here, most parts are flat with little volume and, therefore, pretty easy to build. Curved parts require finer adjustment, and the plastic will have to be slightly bent to shape.*

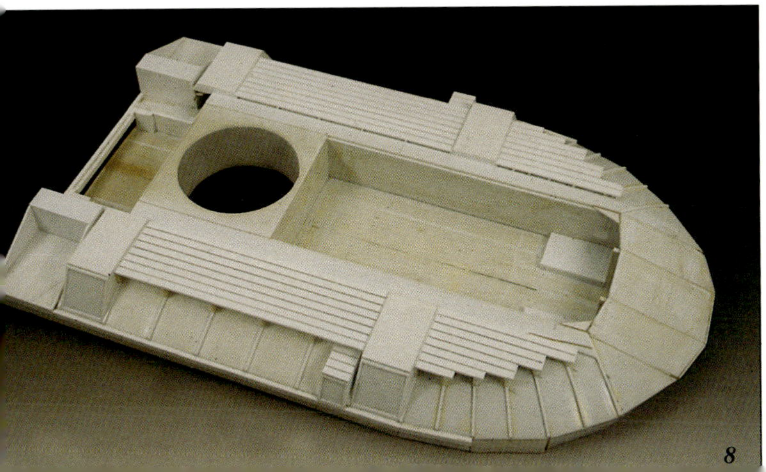

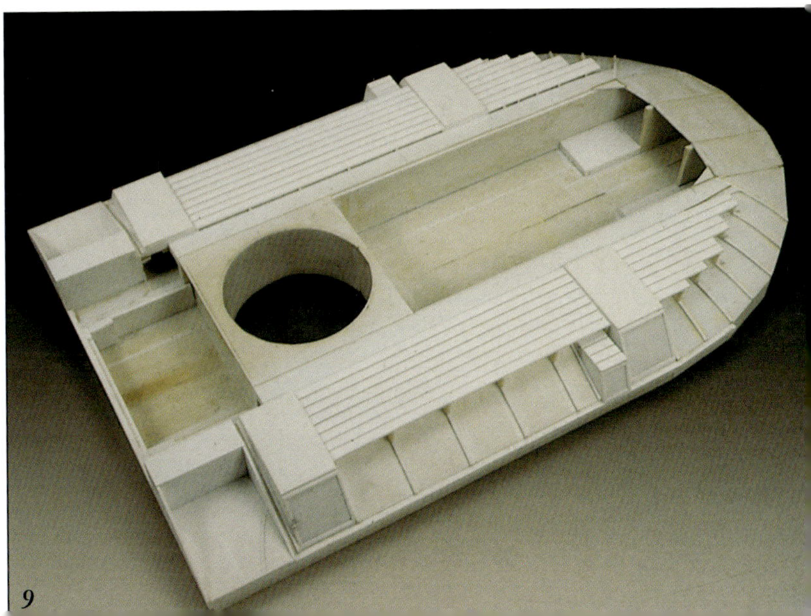

With the reference material handy, usually including different scale blueprints that will have to re-copied in the correct scale, 1/35 or 1/72, etc. A trick for obtaining working measurements is to divide a 1:1 scale measure by 35 (working in metric). Sometimes, the blueprint measurements don't tally with the actual vehicle measurements. This calls for re-adjustments, sometimes varying both height and depth to match our requirements. Draw the troublesome areas onto the blueprint itself in order to make the necessary adjustments on paper, which is always easier than adjusting the actual part with actual tools.

Before making the actual plastic parts, many modelers prefer to make a cutaway paper model to check the working measurements. Once this has been done and double-checked, only then take up the plastic sheet, ensuring that it is the correct scale thickness.

All models need a base from which to build either up or down. With the job in question, the blueprints show a dividing line between the air cushion and the remainder of the structure. This is the base we used. The air cushion base should be strong enough to hold the upper structure and must, therefore, be solidly built. After cutting it out of 1mm thick Plasticard and positioning the longitudinal ribs, they were strengthened with wooden strips fixed with epoxy glue. The strips have to be thick enough to give the part the required strength. This meant that another strip was glued next to the first one.

The elements forming the part have a similar structure to the sections of a tangerine or an orange, and should be measured and shaped in strict concordance with pictures of the actual part. This is a delicate process, because you have to get the curved effect, identical to the actual part on the craft. This is why an internal 'rib cage' will assist in shaping the curved areas. This cylindrical shape is then glued onto the upper area, forcing it into shape by the judicious use of superglue, thus adapting it to the rib structure.

The hull parts are fairly easy to make, as they have no curves, and are almost straight. The area holding the turbo fan is a rounded shape and is cut out using a cutting compass. On the bent area of the hull, there is an elaborate wooden platform made of Evergreen strip and fixed with

10. Many parts have to be tested on paper first, to get the correct measurements.

11. All the features are made from parts cut to measure to the correct shape.

12. The platform was made from a number of standard plastic strips, all from Evergreen.

13. The lateral pieces, that match the air cushion's 'Orange sections', are designed to strengthen the structure.

10

11

12

13

15

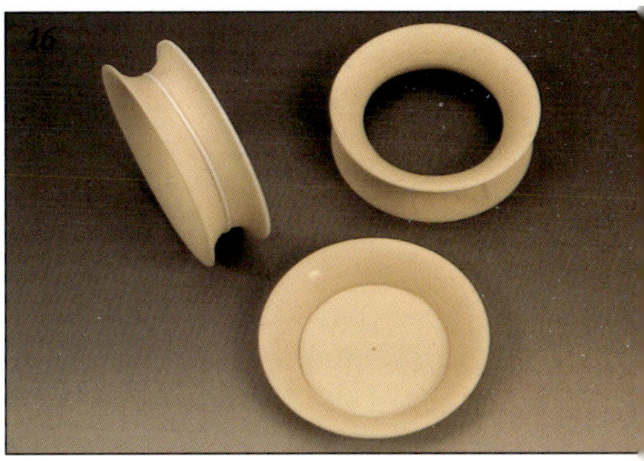
16

14. The air intake for the turbofan. This was made by gluing together several, progressively larger plastic rings. At first, the surface will look quite uneven.

15. After a tough filing and sanding job, the surface looks much more even. Filler is used to fill any gaps.

16. Copies were made from a mold. The base of both copies was removed, and then they were glued together. The result resembles a wheel.

17. Positioning on the corresponding area.

18. The rear is built up using all the necessary parts.

19. Round-edged boxes are built square and then snaded to the correct shape.

17

18

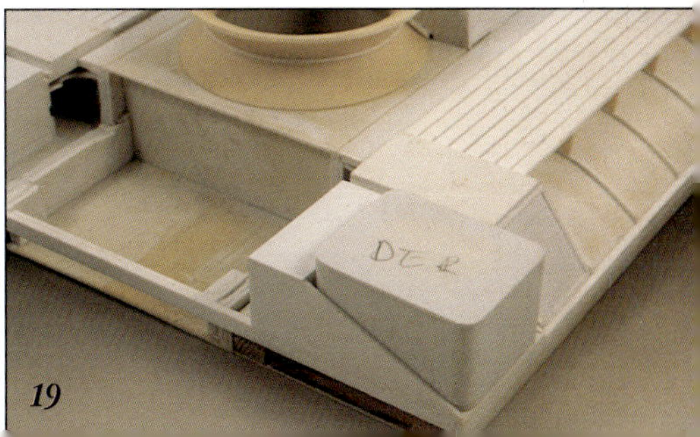
19

curved wedges. It is advisable to make one curved wedge, mold it, and make as many resin copies as required.
The remainder of the hull parts are made in the same way: different sized boxes, some straight elements with a few angles, sometimes on Evergreen square frames and made to different dimensions.
The turbofan air intake is a complex structure composed of several plastic rings made with a cutting compass, The diameter must be progressively increased, to achieve the conical shape, slightly open on the sides. Once the rings have been glued together, they must be sanded down to the necessary curved edge. A mini drill is required to polish the part well enough to conceal the ring structure making up the part. If a mistake is made with the mini-drill, fill the area with an epoxy filler, re-sand and polish.
When the part is ready, make a mold to obtain a copy. The new part is then glued to the old one at the base, the new part's base is removed, and the join between the parts filled and sanded. The resulting wheel-shaped part will be glued to the rear of the vehicle.
The turbofan is made from a number of pieces placed around the radius of the circle, a base and a cone. The cone can be taken from an aircraft kit, in this case one from a 1/48 Hercules kit. The part's base, with the shaft, isn't a problem. Just make the necessary curve on the ends to allow it to fit the sides, placing a small cartridge in the center on which the shaft rotates. The hardest parts to make are the beams for the fan, because they are mounted just above each other, and all placed at an angle. Carefully divide the fan's circumference, measure and cut the parts, and then glue them together. It is highly advisable to make a paper model before making the actual part.
The fan is powered by a couple of mini electric motors, each fitted with a wheel holding a band to transmit the power to the fan. You will need to induce some friction in order to slow the fan down, and the motors must be positioned vertically so that the drive band is in the right position. A wheel is fixed to the base of the fan onto which the drive band is fitted.
The cabin roof is arched. Therefore, carve one curved piece, make a mold, and make five pieces (5). The curved roof parts go from the turbofan to the cabin. That part of the roof adjacent to the turbofan has been carved from balsa wood. This was carved with the necessary curve, a small hole was then cut for the fan's drive band to pass through. If, during the assembly a part is damaged, epoxy putty will usually suffice to repair it.
Both the fan's shaft and mount are pretty difficult to make because you have to make a hole in the part to allow the shaft to pass through. Do this by holding the part in a table vise, a small tower drill is even better. Then select a drill bit slightly smaller than required, drill a hole in the center from one side, then turn it over and drill from the other side until both meet in the middle of the part. Then, using the correct diameter drill bit, make the final hole. Once this is done, pass the shaft through it, making sure that there's a drive band wheel on one end.
The part on top of the rotor is made pretty much like all the other parts, and resin copies of it can be easily made.
The propeller was from a 1/48 Skyraider kit, and can be used straight from the box, or make a resin copy.
On the turbofan's sides there is a moveable part made of Plasticard and some Evergreen strips. Complete the hull with some easily made rectangular parts. All the windows are square, except for the small ones on each side that have rounded sides set in a small frame. These can be made with a circle cutter and a knife. The cabin roof (0.5mm Plasticard) is given its rounded shape by placing it on a wooden cylinder and applying a heat source. Once it is the correct shape, glue it on top of the arches with super glue. The special curve on the front of the roof means that it must first be carved from balsa wood, or, as in this case, modeled from putty. Putty also permits us to adjust any imperfections and, once it has cured, it can be carved. Final finishing was done with wet and dry paper. Don't forget to make the pit for the twin machine guns that will be added later.
All the other engine details are constructed in much the same way as the other parts.
The radar is placed on top of a traditional support structure along with a special systems box. There is a small motor for turning the radar scanner mounted higher up the structure. The screen is made from an old PCE Monogram kit plus a few added details. (See what we mean...the spirit of recycling comes in useful!). The screen is glued to the top of a plastic cylinder, which will act as a handle when making molds of the part. The cylinder can then be removed from the copies. The radar itself is a pretty straightforward part that is reasonably easy to make. On the roof, and around it, there are several circular parts and rivets that were made with a hole punch.
Once the superstructure is complete, it is time to work on the air cushion, specifically on that area where it is fixed to the superstructure. The parts we now make must match up exactly with the upper structure, although they will be elongated vertically. The most difficult part is the bows with its shortened shape, which

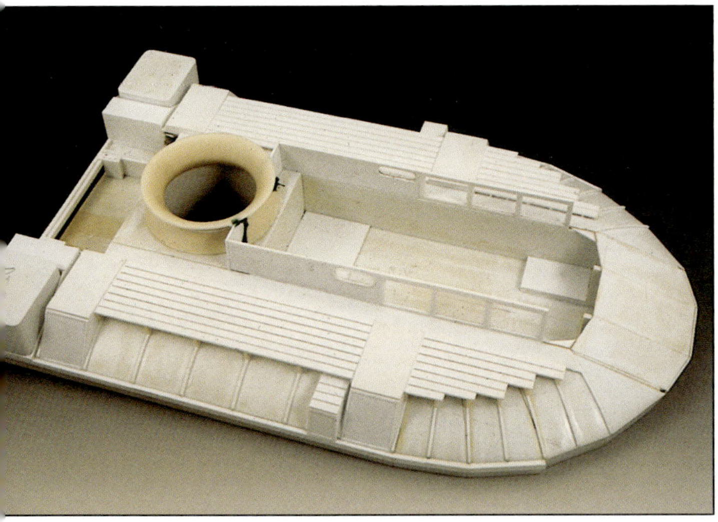

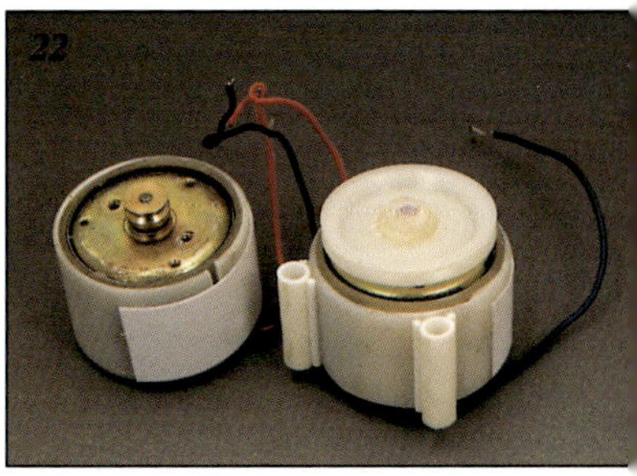

20. The walls are built, with an eye to the placing of the windows. Small windows are punched first, and are then enlarged.

21. The rotor is a very difficult piece to make because of its many beams. Take careful measurements before making the part.

22. Motors from a radio cassette are used to propel the fan and propeller.

23. The motor is positioned horizontally in order to power the propeller. It has a small wheel for transferring the power to a drive band.

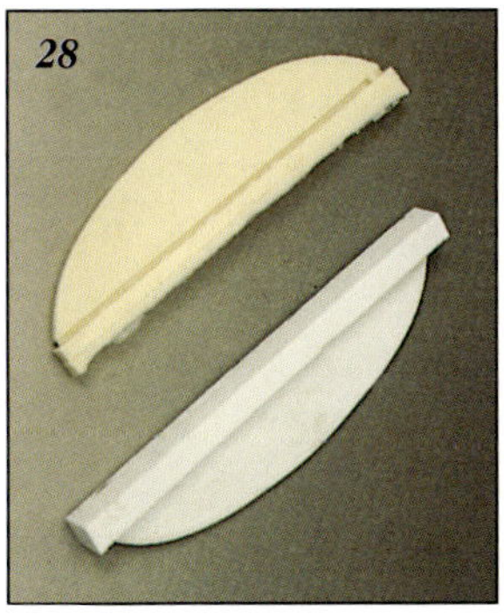

24. The motor for the rotor, positioned vertically to power the fan.

25. The window aperture is one. Divisions for each particular window were placed later.

26-27. The turbofan air intake joins with the balsa wood part surrounding it, continuing all the way with the roof.

28. Five arches (beams) are required to make the roof. This calls for a mold and resin copies.

29. The correct position of all five beams. Note how they match the window frames.

30. All parts in place up to this point.

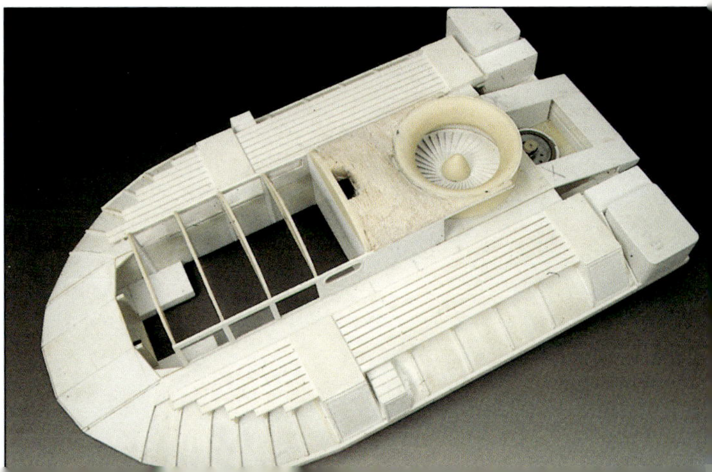

reduces the height of the air cushion.

The exhausts are shaped like an elbow. They are made from two Evergreen tubes (cut at an angle), glued, filled and sanded. A mold is then made and a resin copy obtained. The steering system is a rather strange set of parts, because they were obtained from an old 1/32 Sabre kit, and were originally parts of the rear flying surfaces. If you have them, it will save some carving! If you don't have them, they are easily scratch-built from Plasticard, trimmed to size, and given the correct aerodynamic cross-section using files and sandpaper. Copies are then made, and they are glued in position. Follow the same process for the horizontal stabilizers. Once you have all the parts, proceed with positioning them on the platform.

Next, is the air cushion. This can be difficult, because if it is not convincing, the result will look unrealistic. First, make a number of 'ribs' around the hull, caught between the bottom of the vehicle and a base (like the sole of a shoe!). The bows are curved and so should the front part of the cushion. This part is the difficult bit, so take your time and get it right. Once all ribs are in place, cover them with 0.5mm thick Plasticard, forced into shape using super glue. Begin by gluing the upper area, and then work down, forcing the card into the correct curved position. Troublesome areas on the air cushion can be dealt with later using epoxy filler, the same as was done with the roof.

The cylindrical weapons compartment, with a truncated part, was constructed of plastic circles and rings glued together. There should be a small opening at the bottom.

The twin machine gun mounts were made by copying examples on similar craft (patrol boats). The machine guns used are available from the Verlinden range of resin accessories.

The pilot and co-pilot seats are modeled from epoxy resin. Molds were obtained, and the copies glued to a Plasticard base. There's very little information available for the interior of the craft, and the crew seats were made with little detail. The seats themselves, however, pretty much follow the pattern of those in helicopters of the same era. No information was obtainable for the controls, so they were obtained by modifying the controls of a 1/32 scale, F-104. After adding all the small fine details such as antennas, hooks, wipers, etc, the model is ready for the next phase.... Painting.

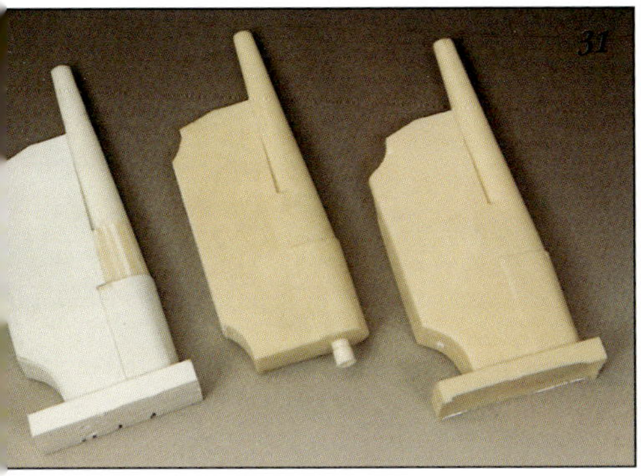

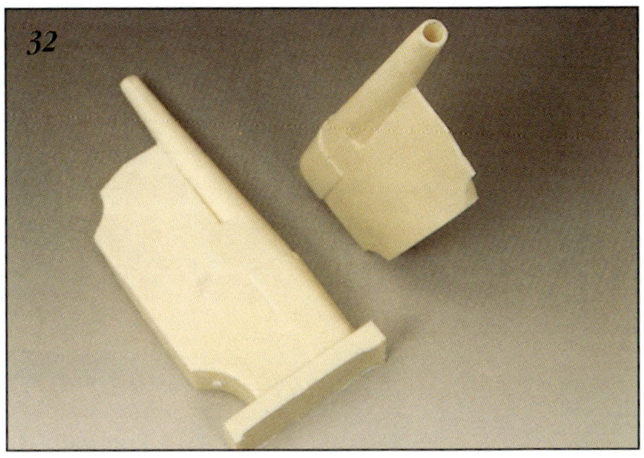

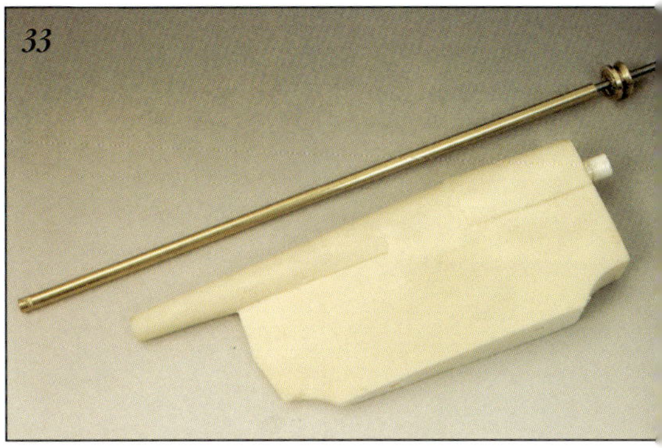

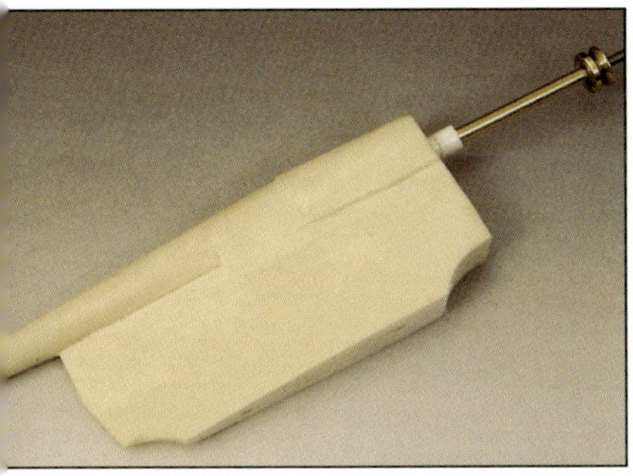

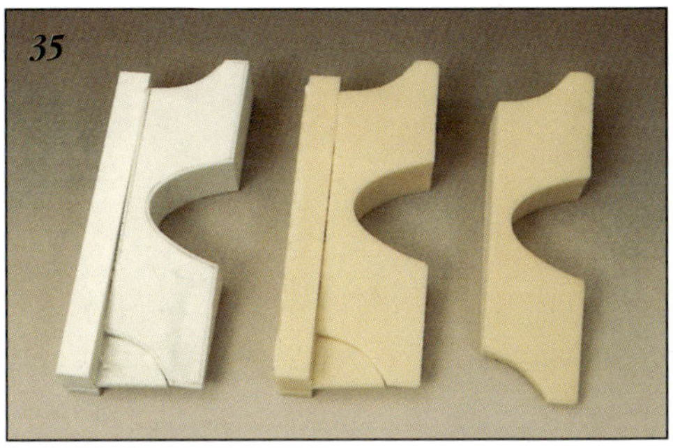

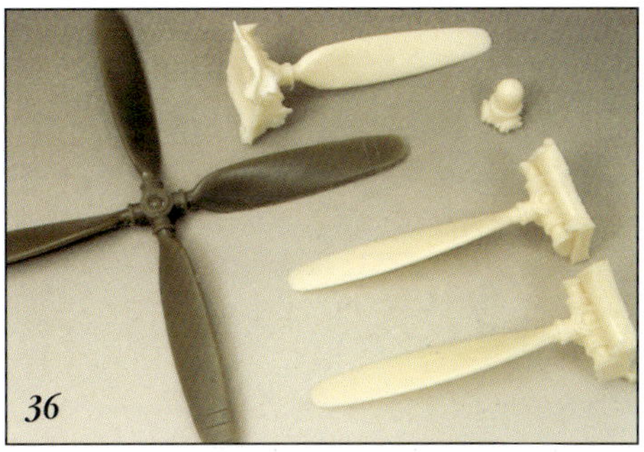

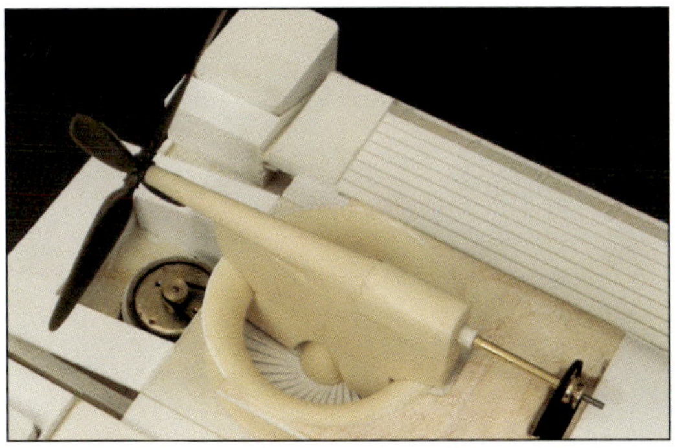

31. Propeller support made from Plasticard.

32. A mold is made from the original piece. Mold 'flash' is removed from the resin copy

33. A hole must be drilled in the part. It should be drilled from both sides until they meet.

34. The hole should allow a metal rod to pass through fitted with a small wheel on one end that will later carry the drive band.

35. The part holding the plastic rotor. A mold was made to get a resin copy.

36. Propeller from a 1/48 Skyraider. It can be used as is, or make a resin copy instead.

37. The full ensemble of rotor, support, and fan in the correct position.

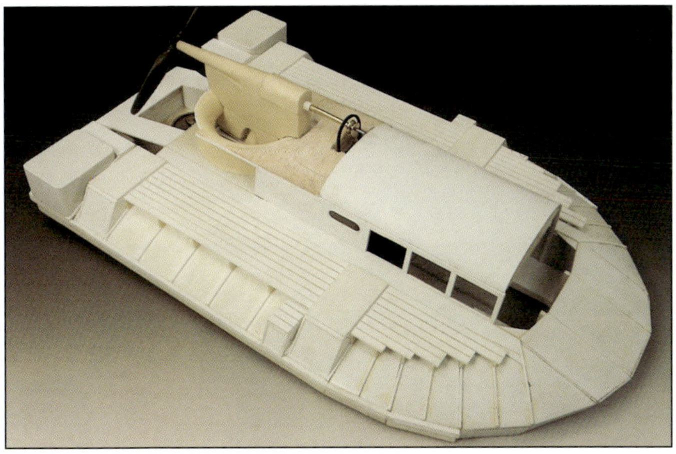

38. A thin, previously shaped Plasticard sheet will become the roof.

39. Position of the platform for the steering system.

40. Detail of the position of the turbofan air intake.

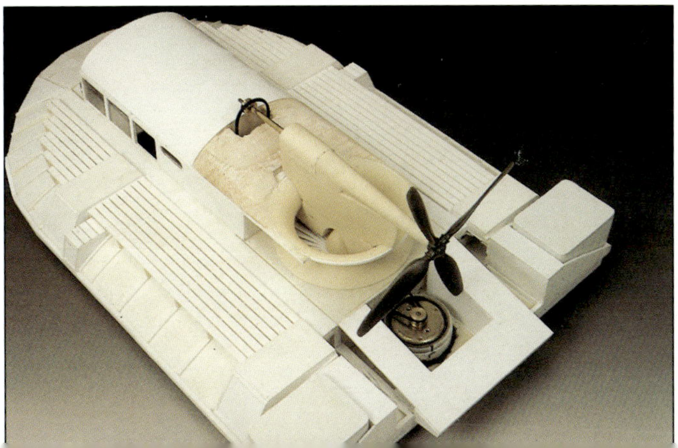

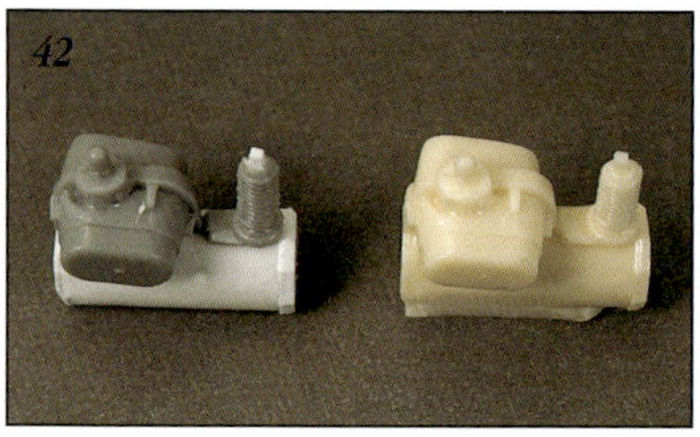

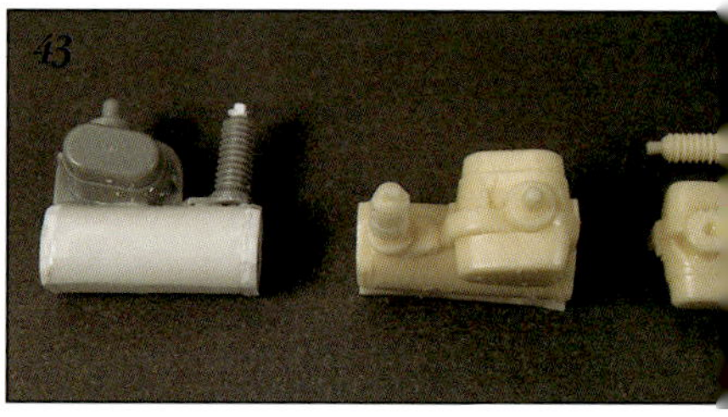

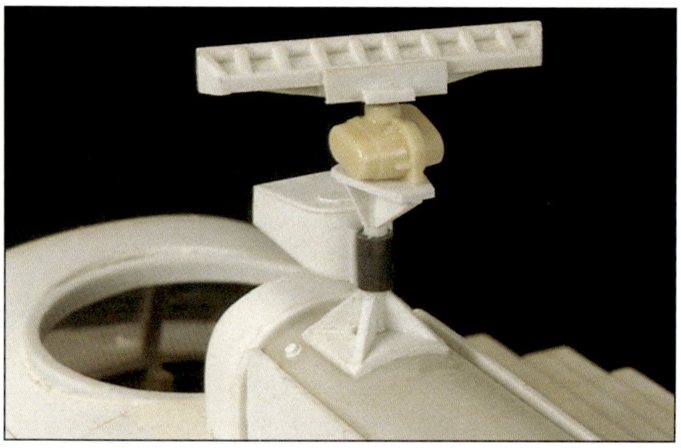

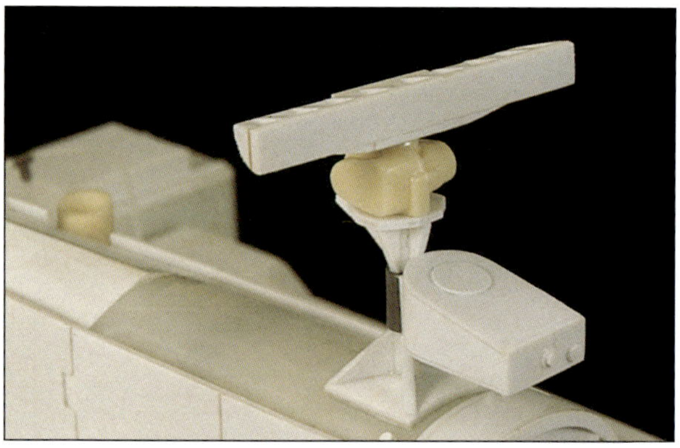

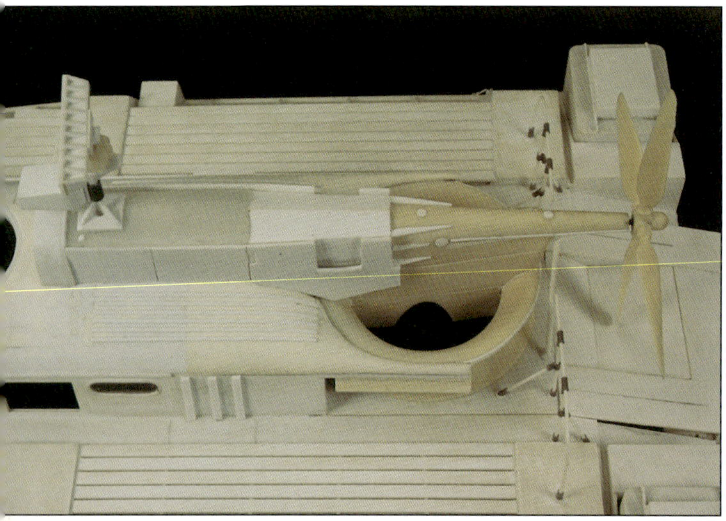

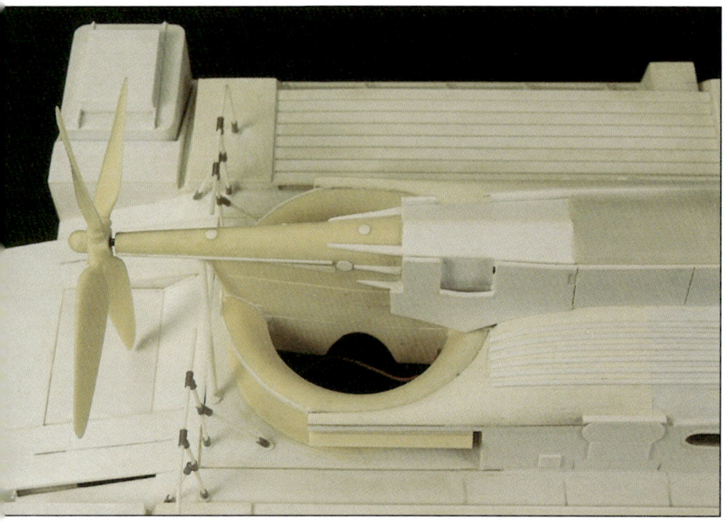

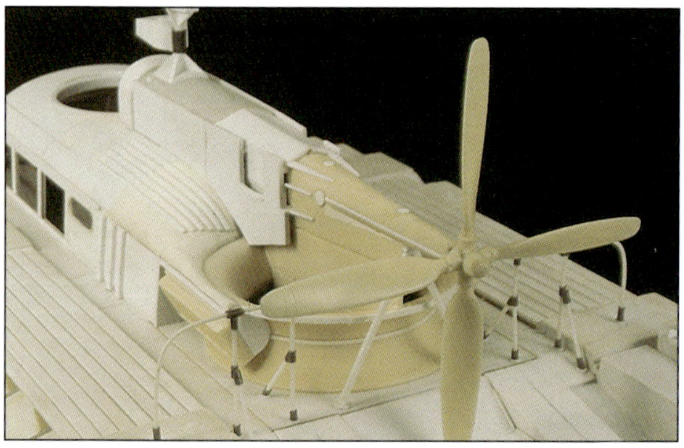

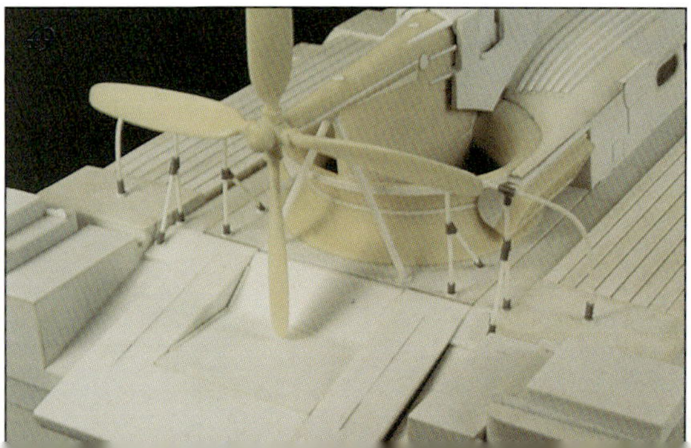

41. Details of the propeller's shaft and all surrounding areas.

42.The radar antenna's drive motor. It was obtained from an old Monogram PCE boat kit.

43. Once the part has been copied, remove it from its plastic sprue.

44-45. The rudder details, with all its different components. They are all made of plastic and follow the blueprint guidelines.

46-47. Propeller and turbo fan area complete with all their details.

48-49. On the lower area of the propeller can be seen the platform for the steering rudder.

50. The front of the windows and the point where they join the roof is made from epoxy putty. The putty is first modeled, and then sanded.

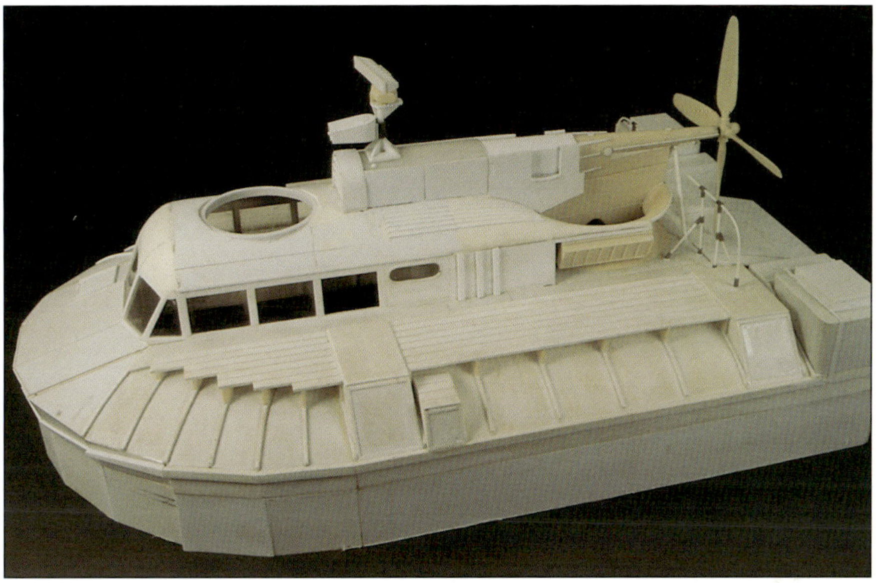

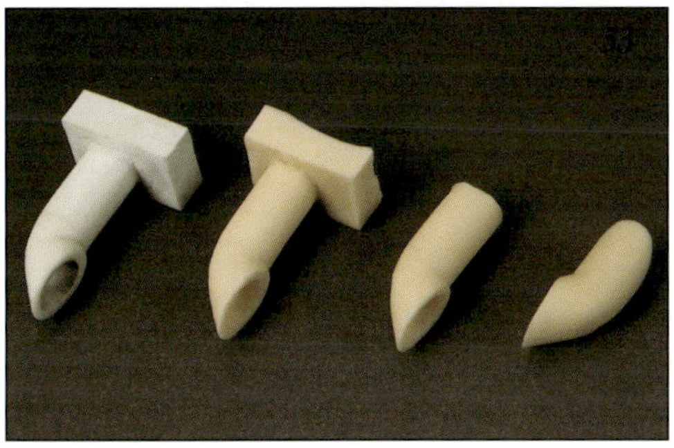

51. When making the air cushion, first make a 'wall' as tall as the cushion part.

52. The parts on the craft's bow are mounted on top of each other to obtain the necessary curve.

53. Engine exhausts made from plastic tubes cut into three sections (to make the curved shape). It is advisable to make a mold of this part.

54. 'Decorative' Plasticard parts cut at a precise angle and correctly positioned.

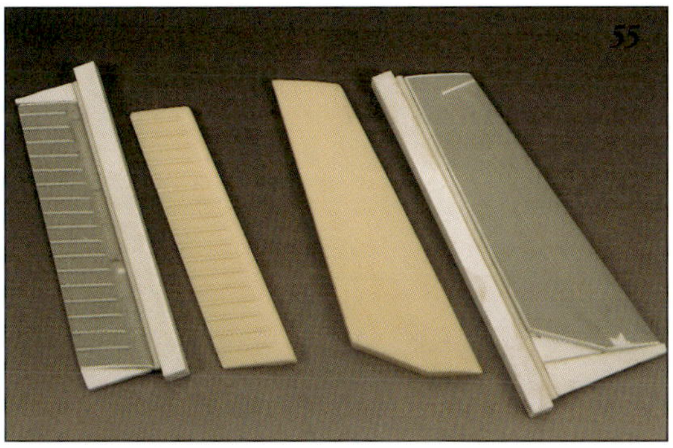

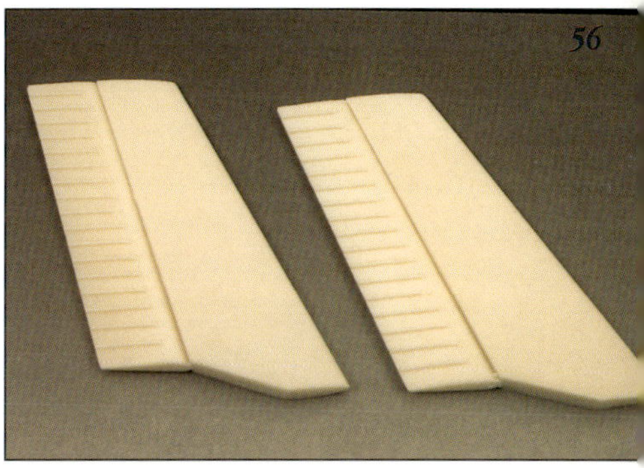

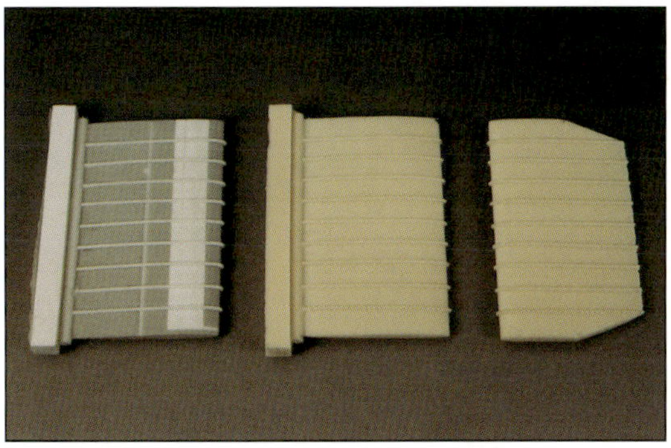

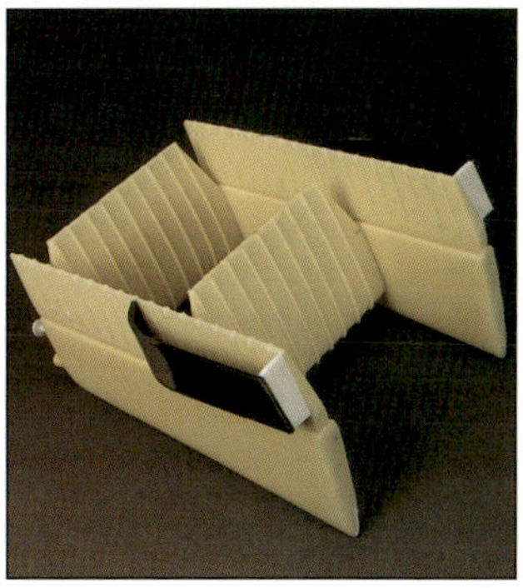

55. Working on the original parts from an old 1/32 Sabre kit, gives us the required rudder parts.

56. Once we've molded the necessary copies, glue them together using super glue.

57. For the horizontal parts of the rudder, carry on using parts from the aircraft kit. If they can't be used, make them from Plasticard instead.

58-60. Final rudder assembly and all other essential parts.

61-62. *Final positioning of the rudder and other parts of the structure.*

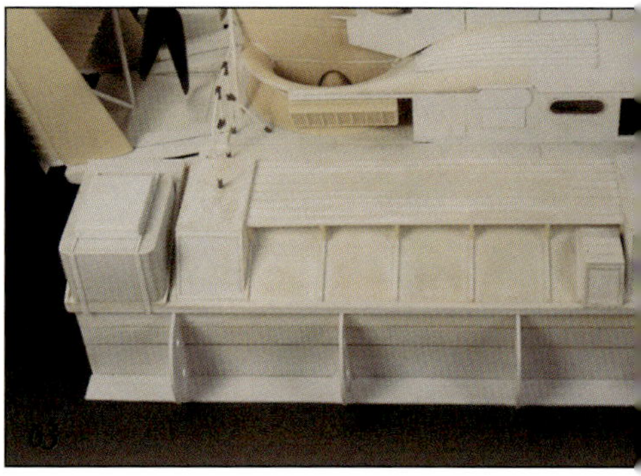

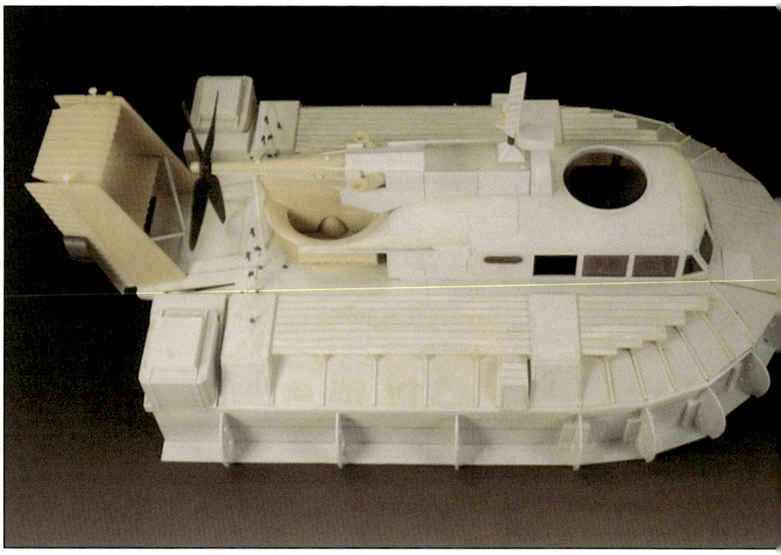

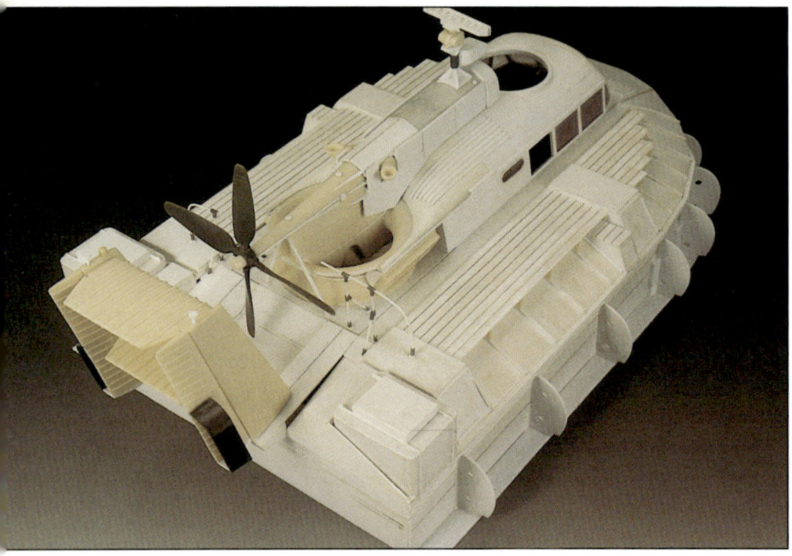

63. The round-shaped guides will assist in the making of the air cushion.

64-67. The air cushion is difficult to construct, and required several attempts, until the assembly came up to our exacting standards.

68. Paper cutouts were made to ascertain the exact measurements of the final plastic parts.

69-70. The sharp curves on the craft's corners needed some filler.

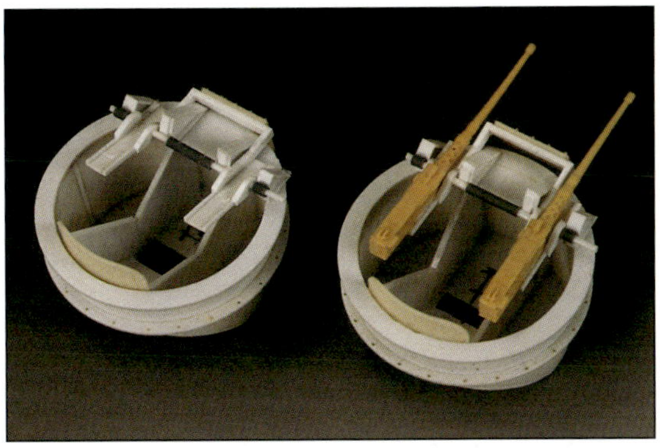

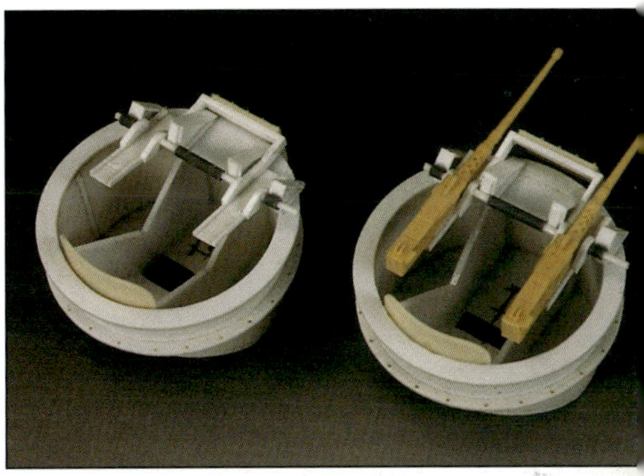

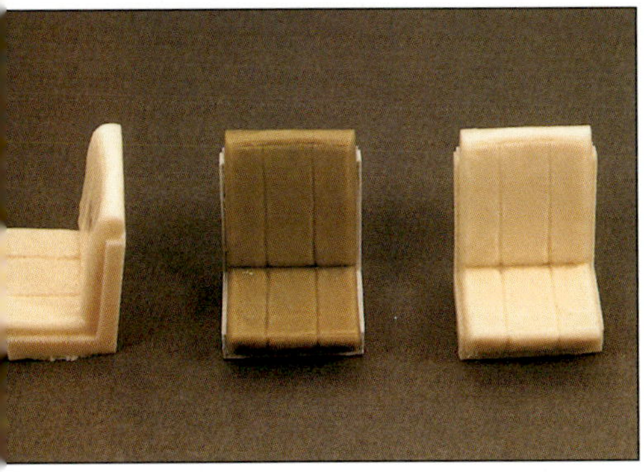

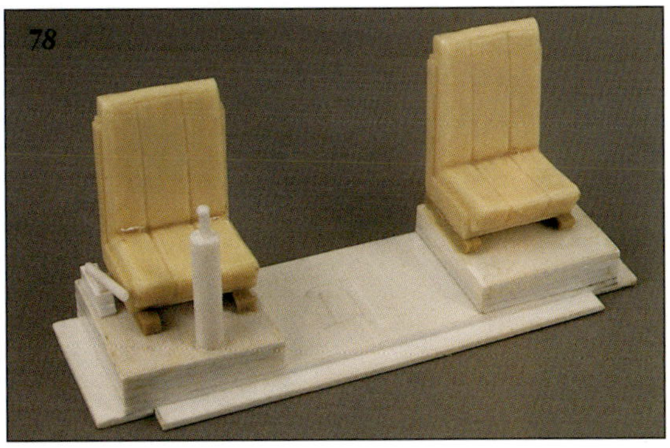

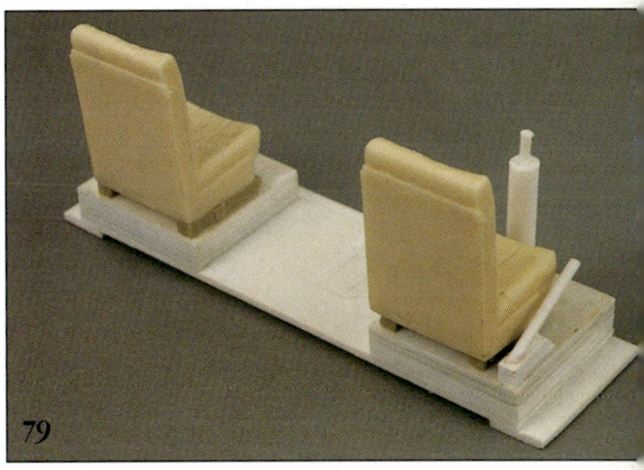

71. The machine gun pit is very similar to the one's on the Pibber patrol boats used on the Vietnamese rivers.

72. The pit is made with the cutting compass. Afterwards, assembling the resulting Plasticard circles and rings

73. One plastic ring has small holes for the rivets.

74. Lateral view, showing the strengthened areas.

75. Machine gun mounts, copying the same part on Tamiya's Pibber boat kit.

76. The twin machine guns are available from the Verlinden range.

77. The seat made from epoxy resin, and molded copies.

78-79. The platform for the seats.

80-81. Crew seats are based on contemporary helicopter seat arrangements.

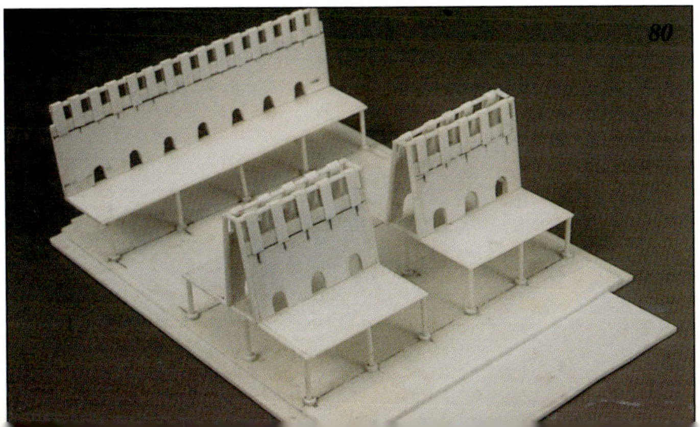

82. View of the cockpit interior.

83. Cockpit. Left side.

84. Cockpit. Right side.

85. The windows are acetate sheet. The forward windows have a wire frame.

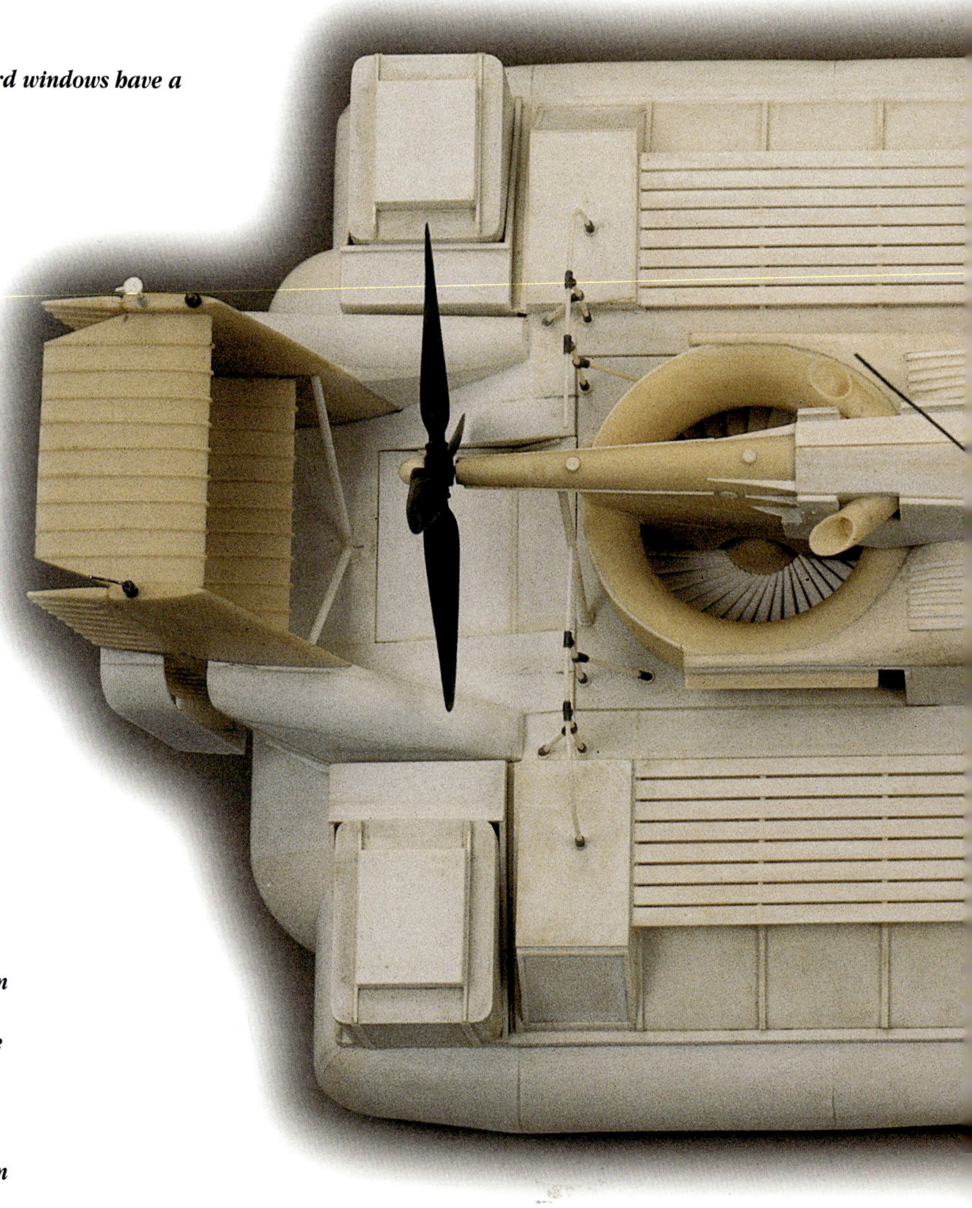

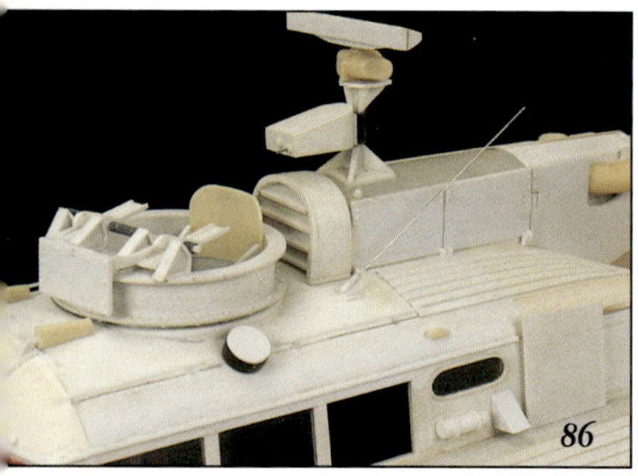

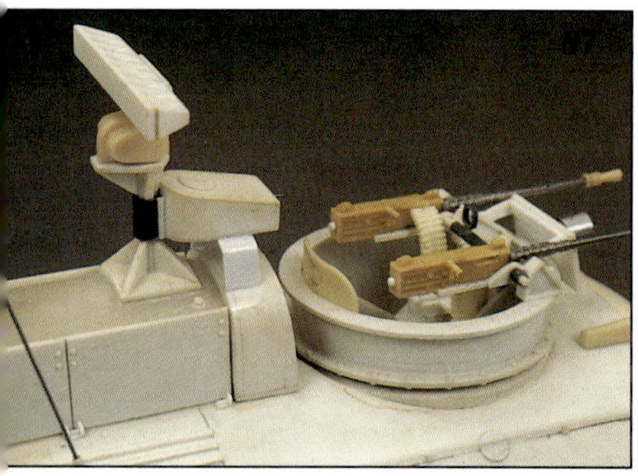

86. The machine gun pit has not been glued, as we want to be able to move it.

87. Improved machine guns, using both resin and metal parts. The ammo strips are resin copies of those from the Pibber kit.

88. There's also a machine gun in both rear windows.

89

90

91

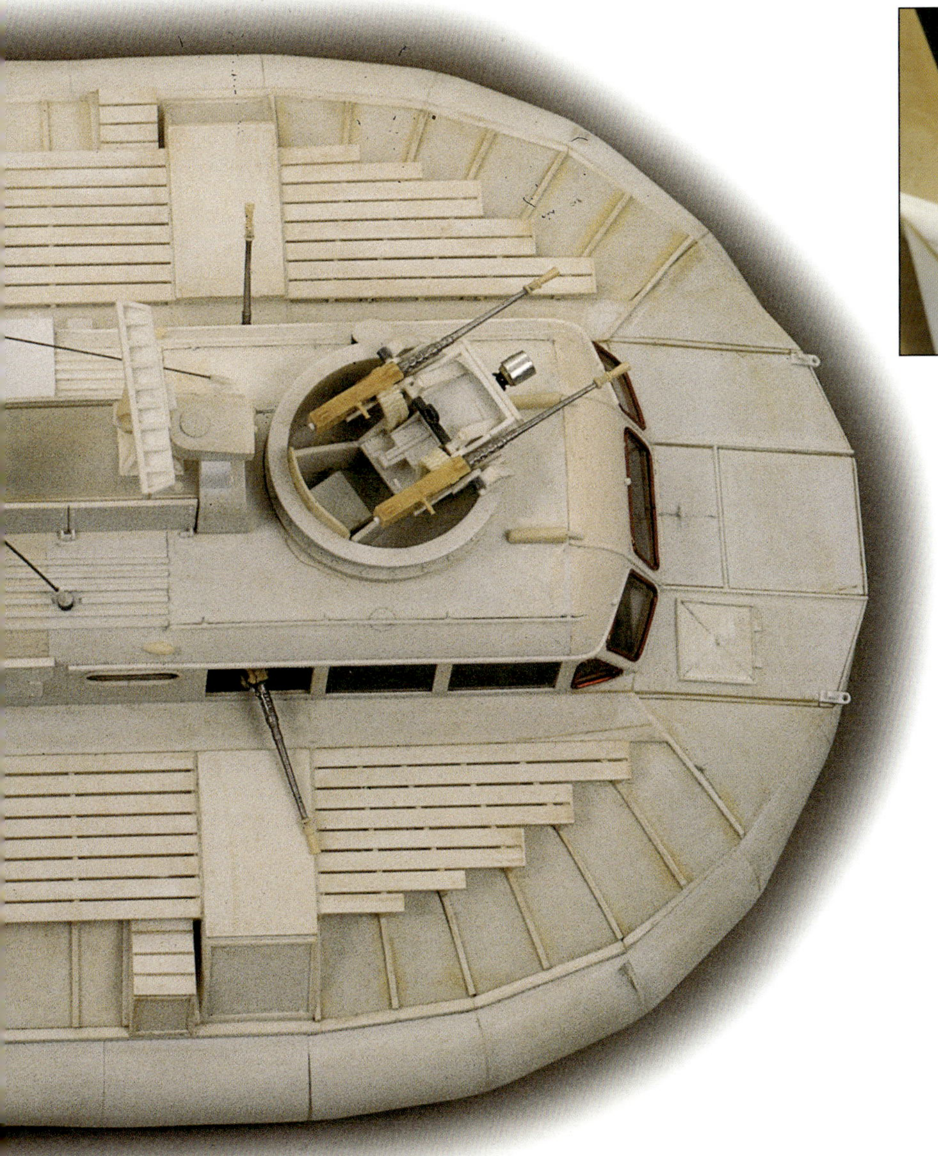

92

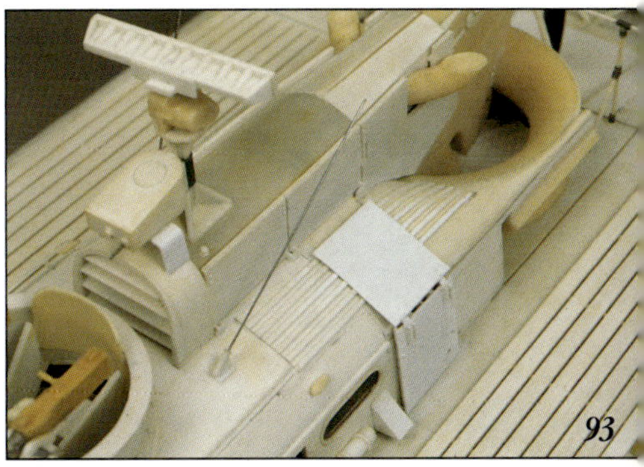
93

89. Positioning the parts around the rudder assembly.

90-91. All completed parts as in their final positions.

92. Railing (made from Evergreen rods and Plastruc pieces) separating the propeller area from the forward section.

93. Small Plasticard parts placed along the hull.

94. Front view. The wipers will be added later.

95. Fine details placed on the forward area. They are fitted with the necessary locks and hinges.

94

95

Painting the PACV

While numerous pictures of the craft during the Vietnam War were made available to the public, in fact, just three machines took part in the conflict. All three units underwent minor upgrades to equipment, weapons, and other structures on the vehicle. These changes altered little the general appearance of the olive-green craft, (with a slight touch of brown) which was similar in color to helicopters of the period. All three vehicles were numbered, with the numbers were prominent on the rudder area and on the front of the craft, in line with the 'U.S. NAVY' inscription. The vehicle had a large flag on the upper part of the rudder, with a smaller one over the number on both sides of the rudder. The air cushion was the color of natural black rubber, and had a mouth-like painting on the front to give the craft a menacing appearance. Small yellow eyes were also painted on the hull to complete the illusion of a dangerous sea animal. The safety railings between the propeller area and the rest of the craft were painted with either red, orange or yellow. That's pretty much all there is paint wise on the craft, although some added dirt can change this color scheme a little.

As there are no decals to complete the job, the eyes and mouth will have to be drawn directly onto the craft. A pencil drawing on transparent paper will help us to get the design onto the model.

Masking the glass, it should be applied on the interior and exterior. The vehicle's interior is painted in Tamiya's XF-2.

Apply the base color over the craft's entire structure (40% XF-54 and 60% XF-51). Weathering on the paint is first done with XF-58, then XF-49, followed by XF-60. All three colors give the very necessary highlights to the hull. The hull is quite large, and really needs these highlights. Shadows are added using a mixture of 70% XF-51, and

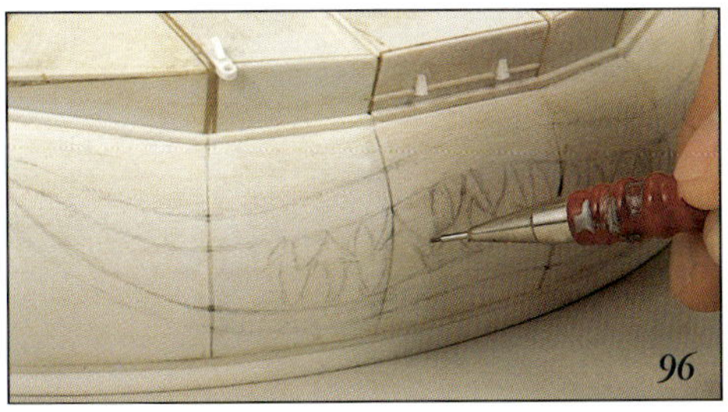

96

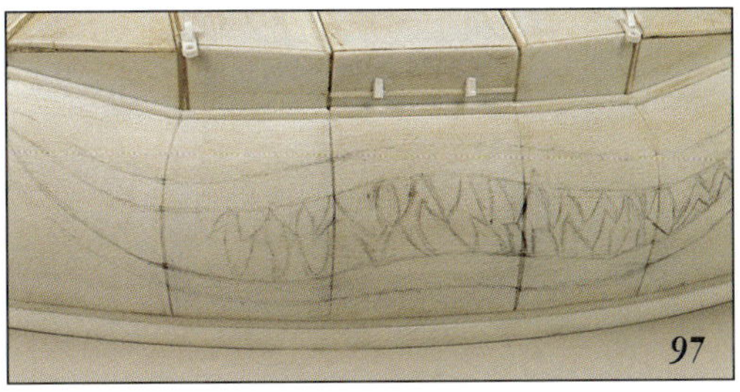

97

98

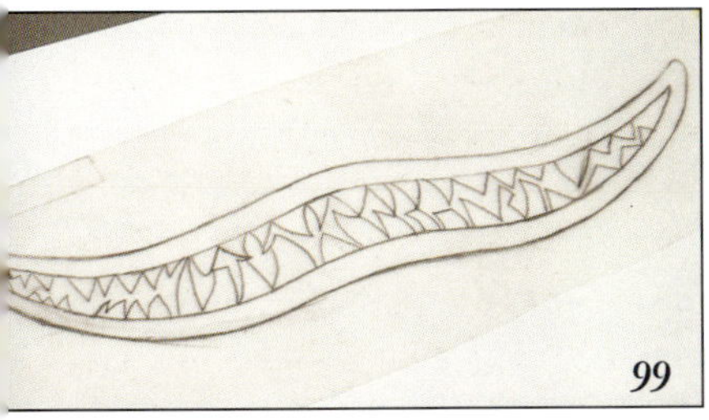

99

100

101

96-97. The shape of the mouth is traced in pencil, directly onto the model.

98-99. Trace this preliminary drawing onto the model, and then, after looking at photos of the real thing, adjust the tracing to suit.

100-101. Once the olive green base paint has been applied, add some highlights using XF-58, then XF-49, and, finally, XF-60.

102

103

102. The air cushion receives an overall coat of Tamiya's XF-1.

103. XF-53 is applied on the upper part of the cushion.

104. The mouth shape is traced and cut.

105-106. The curved shape of the model will pose stability problems for the adhesive masking, so it is important to apply it carefully.

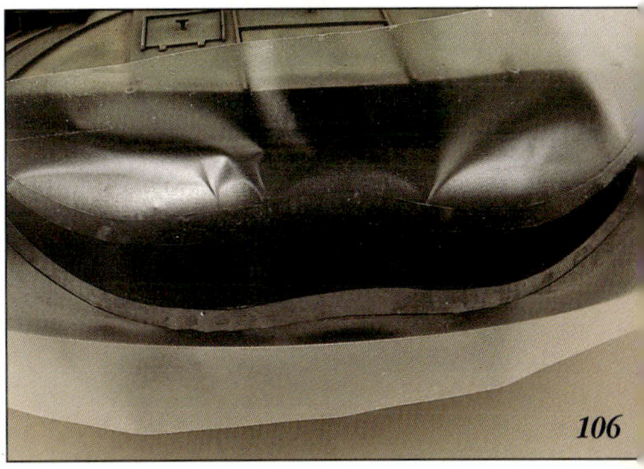

106

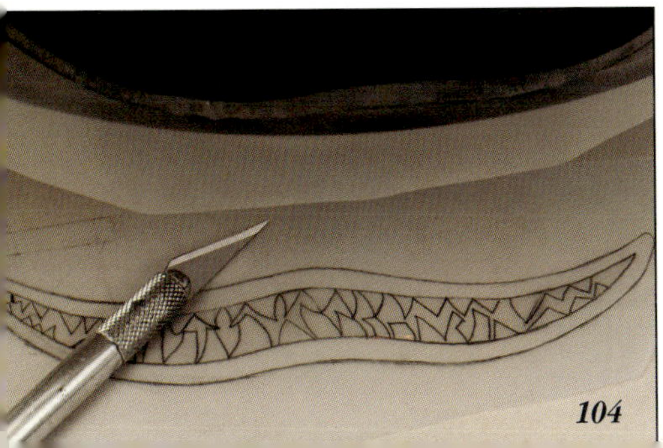

104

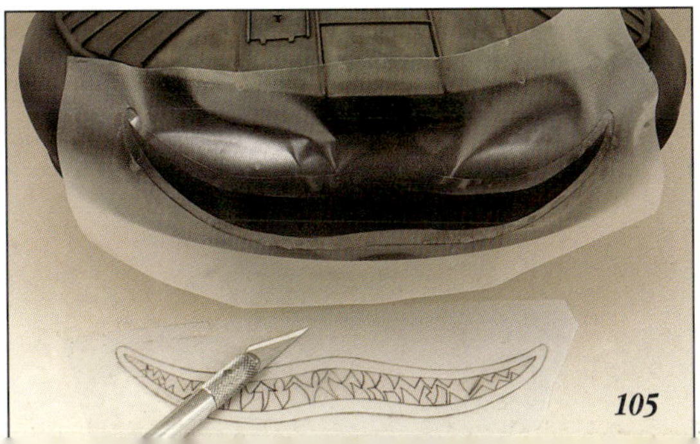

105

30% XF-1. Then, use XF-10, and, finally, some H-344 (Gunze Sangyo). The last color is used to put some mud on specific areas.

The wooden planks were 'bedded' down with XF-52, and XF-57. This will make the planks look like worn wooden surfaces, as a result of the crew continuously walking on them. The air cushion is airbrushed with XF-1, adding a little XF-53 for the upper part. We are now ready to work on the most difficult part of the paintjob...the mouth. First, place transparent adhesive masking on our mouth drawing then and cut the mask into sections, one for each color. The first color will be the white teeth (XF-2). Then replace the teeth mask and remove the lip mask and apply red paint (XF-7). Wait until it's dry, replace the lip and remove the inside of the mouth and apply the yellow mixture (90% XF-3 and 10% XF-7). The mouth's black outline was hand painted using Vallejo 950.

The rear safety railings were first painted with Vallejo's Film Color ref. C-32, and than, over it, yellow, with some 958 for the paint peels. Dry brush some 922 and 882 (both Vallejo references.) over the whole of the hull.

Finally, the whole model was given a coat of satin Marabo varnish.

107. Tamiya's matt white XF-2 is the first color.

108. All the tooth masking is replaced.

109. Now remove the lip masking, and apply Tamiya's XF-7.

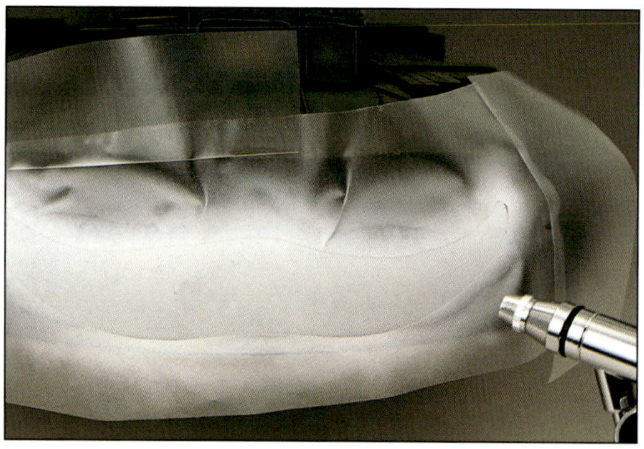

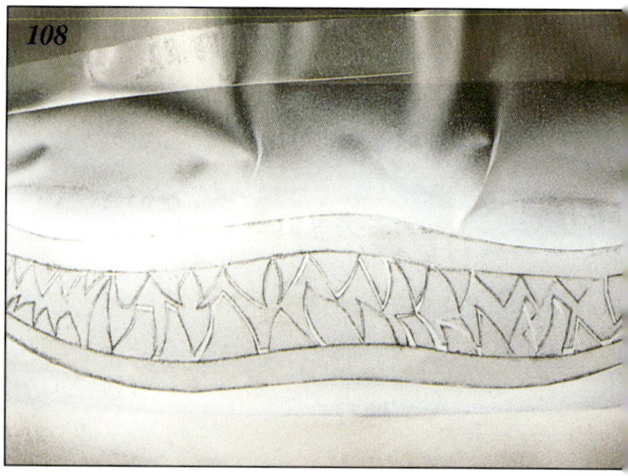

110. Paint the inside of the mouth with a mixture of 90% XF-3 and 10% XF-7.

111. Before doing the eyes, mask off the surrounding areas first.

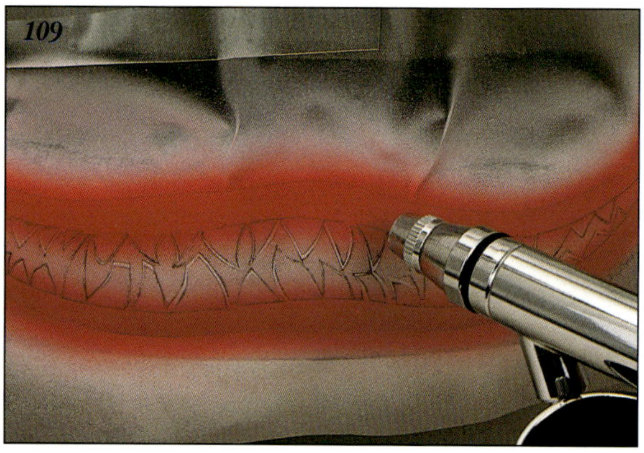

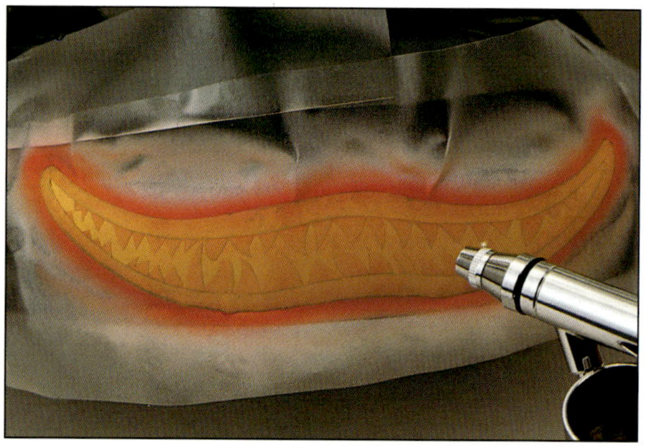

112-113. The outlines of both eyes and mouth are hand painted with Vallejo's 950.

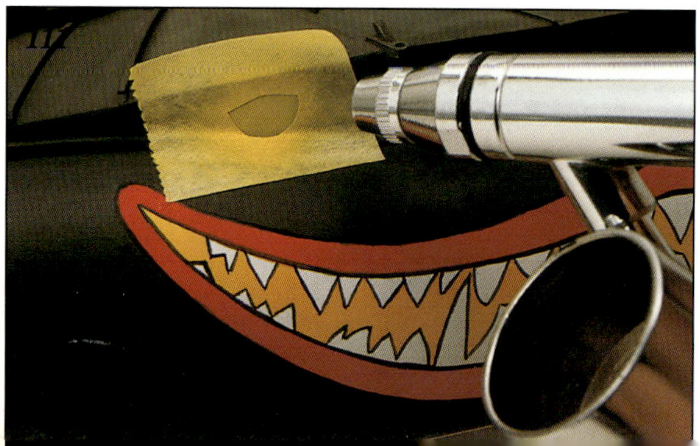

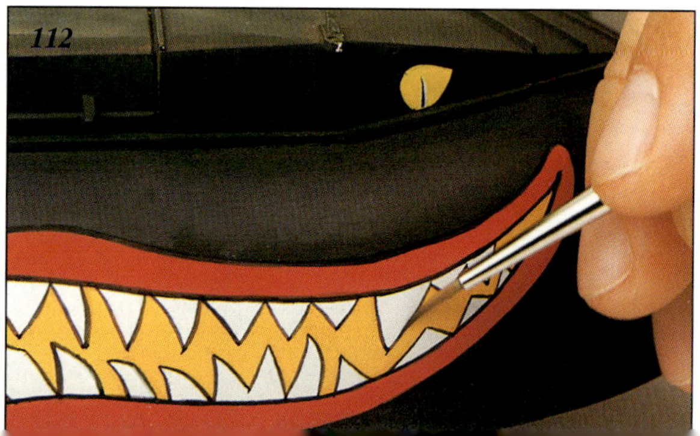

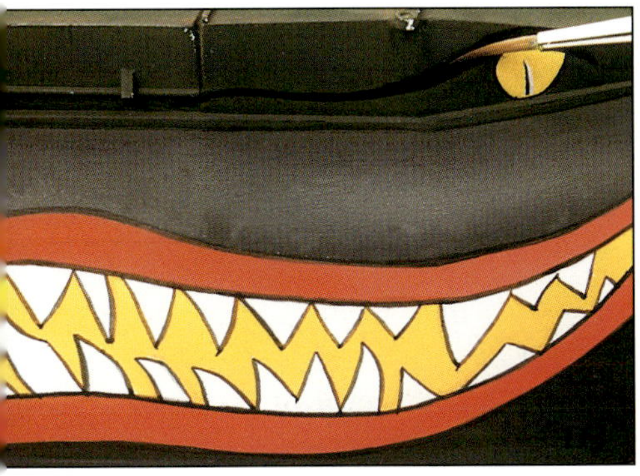

114. View of the completed job.

115. XF-10 and XF-1 is used to give a certain amount of wear to both eyes and mouth.

116. The rear safety railings were first painted with Vallejo's Film Color ref. C-32, and then they were redone with 953.

117. The lateral wood planking on both sides has been given a worn appearance with some XF-51 and XF-59.

118. The mud was made by airbrushing Gunze Sangyo's Rust H-344.

119. Dry brushing was done first with 922, followed by 882.

120. The numbers were hand painted. They were copied from the Verlinden transfer: 251 U.S.A.F. Lettering, 1/48.

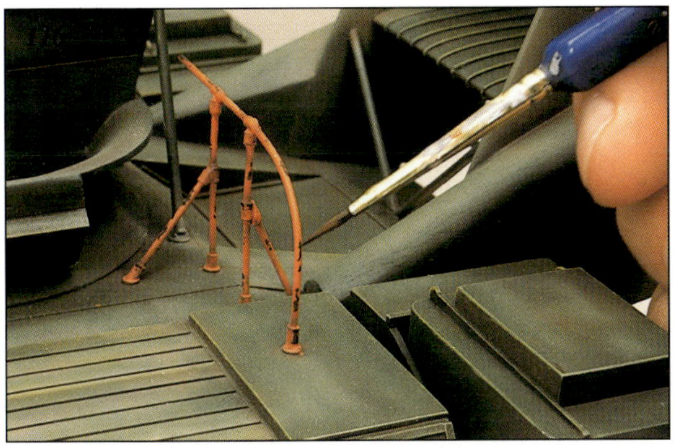

U.S. NAVY
3
3

3

U.S. NAVY

U.S. NAVY
3
3